DATE			

© THE BAKER & TAYLOR CO.

Economic INEQUALITY and Poverty

Economic INEQUALITY and Poverty

International Perspectives

Editor

LARS OSBERG

M. E. Sharpe, Inc.
Armonk, New York
London, England

Library of Congress Cataloging-in-Publication Data

Economic inequality and poverty: international perspectives
/ edited by Lars Osberg.
    p. cm.
  ISBN 0-87332-528-1   ISBN 0-87332-540-0 (pbk.)
  1. Income distribution—United States. I. Osberg, Lars, 1946–

HC110.I5R36   1991
339.2′0973—dc20   90-31795
                                                           CIP

Printed in the United States of America

MV   10 9 8 7 6 5 4 3 2 1

Contents

Figures   vi
Tables   vii
Introduction
    Lars Osberg   xi

1.   The Measurement of Income Inequality
    Stephen Jenkins   3

2.   Cross-National Comparisons of Inequality and Poverty
Position
    Timothy M. Smeeding   39

3.   Global Economic Inequality and Its Trends Since 1950
    Albert Berry, François Bourguignon, and
    Christian Morrisson   60

4.   The Distribution of Household Wealth:
Methodological Issues, Time Trends, and Cross-Sectional
Comparisons
    Edward N. Wolff   92

5.   The Definition and Measurement of Poverty
    Aldi J. M. Hagenaars   134

6.   Short- and Long-Term Poverty in the United States:
Measuring the American "Underclass"
    Patricia Ruggles   157

7.   Social Security and Income Redistribution
    Paul R. Cullinan   193

8.   The Impact of Government Tax and Expenditure Programs
on the Distribution of Income in the United States
    Patricia Ruggles   220

Conclusion
    Lars Osberg   246
Index   251
Contributors   258

Figures

1.1	Headings in Annual Economic Statement for Arthur Dent	5
1.2	Histogram	11
1.3	Pen's Parade and the Cumulative Distribution Function	12
1.4	Histogram for Log	13
1.5	The Lorenz Curve	15
1.6	Graphic Representation of SWF for $n = 2$	22
1.7	The Welfare Weight Function and Transfer Sensitivity	23
1.8	Alternative Distance Functions, $h(s)$	31
3.1	The Evolution of Economic Inequality	71
4.1	Share of Total Wealth Held by the Top 1 Percent 1920–81 (based on traditional wealth measures)	104
4.2	Share of Total Wealth Held by the Top 1 Percent, 1920–81 (including government and private pension wealth)	105
5.1	The Definition of Aggregate Poverty Indices: Head-count Ratio	138
5.2	The Definition of a Poverty Line	147
5.3	The Definition of Aggregate Poverty Indices: Average Poverty Gap	148
5.4	Poverty Index, Defined as Welfare Gap	150
7.1	Income and Consumption over the Life Cycle	195
7.2	Social Security Benefit Formula for Those Becoming Eligible for Benefits in 1990	200
7.3	Earnings Patterns of Four Birth Cohorts, 1957–69	213

Tables

1.1   Frequency Distribution Example   10

1.2   Lorenz Curve Data   14

2.1   Inequality Measures (x 1000) for Disposable Income (DPI) and Adjusted Disposable Income (ADPI) and Rank Order (RO) for Each Measure   45

2.2   Relative Economic Position of Persons Living in Various Demographic Groups   48

2.A-1   An Overview of LIS Datasets   56

3.1   Average Per-Capita Income and Distribution of Income, Selected Major Countries   62

3.2   Relative Per-Capita Expenditures of Selected Countries vis-à-vis the United States Including and Excluding Services, for Various Weighting Systems, 1970   66

3.3   Estimates of World Personal Income and Consumption Distribution in 1970   68

3.4   World Distribution of GNP and Consumption Including Socialist Countries: Selected Years   72

3.5   World Distribution of GNP and Consumption Excluding Socialist Countries: Selected Years   76

3.6   Average Annual GDP Growth during 1965–80 and 1980–85, by Regions   78

3.7   Country Composition of Selected Quantiles of the World Distribution of GNP, 1950 and 1977   80

3.A-1   Countries Included in the Analysis   84

4.1   Shares of Total Household Net Worth Held by Richest Individual Wealthholders in the United Kingdom, 1923–80   102

4.2   Shares of Total Household Taxable Net Worth Held by
        Richest Households in Sweden, 1920–83   107

4.3   Shares of Total Household Net Worth or Total Assets Held by
        Richest Individual Wealthholders in the United States,
        1922–81   109

4.4   Inequality Measures for Different Concepts of Household
        Wealth, Based on Both Unadjusted and Adjusted U.S. Data,
        1962 and 1983   113

4.5   Share of Total Net Worth of Richest Households in the United
        States: Estimates from Survey Data, 1962–84   115

4.6   A Comparision of Shares of Top Wealthholders Based
        on 1962 Estate Tax and Household Survey Data for the
        United States   118

4.7   The Concentration of Wealth in France: Estimates from
        Alternative Sources   119

4.8   Raw Age-Wealth (HDW) Profiles from Various Sources,
        1962–83   122

4.9   Percentage Composition of Household Wealth by Income and
        Wealth Class, 1969   126

6.1   Composition of the Poverty Population: 1967, 1976, and 1985 163

6.2   Percentage Distribution of Poor Households by Work Status
        of Head, Selected Years, 1967–84   166

6.3   Percentage of Entrants into Poverty Remaining at Selected
        Months, by Characteristics of Entrant   168

6.4   Civilian Employment/Population Ratio, 1979–84   171

6.5   Estimated Size of the Underclass: Review of Several Studies 174

6.6   Estimates of the Demographic Composition of the Persistently
        Poor Population, from Various Studies   183

7.1   Percentage of Work Force Covered, Average Retired Worker
        Benefit, Average Wages, Selected Years 1940–87   199

7.2   Social Security Taxes   201

7.3   Major Characteristics of Social Security Financing, Selected
        Years 1940–2060   202

7.4   Labor Force Participation Rates by Age, 1950–86   206

7.5   Average Monthly Benefits for Retirees Age 65 in 1988 with
        Different Earnings   208

7.6   Comparisons of Total Benefits for Couples with Different
        Shares of Total Earnings   210

7.7   Average Household Income by Age of Head, 1975 and 1985   211

7.8   Average Earnings for Those with Earnings in 1985, by Sex
        and Age   212

7.9   Antipoverty Effectiveness of Cash and Noncash Transfers
        for Individuals in Units with All Members 65 or Older,
        Selected Years   215

7.10   Social Security as a Proportion of Total Income for Age Units
        65 or Older, 1986   216

8.1   Sources of Revenue for the Federal Government, Fiscal Year
        1987   229

8.2   Sources of State and Local Revenues, Fiscal Year 1985–86   229

8.3   Distribution of Family Income and of Federal Tax Payments
        by Population Decile, 1988   230

8.4   Federal Outlays by Function, Fiscal Year 1987   232

8.5   State and Local Outlays by Function, Fiscal Year 1984–85   233

8.6   Distribution of Transfer Income by Population Decile, 1977,
        1984, and 1988   234

8.7   1987 Family Incomes as Percentage of the Median for Family
        Type, by Selected Income Sources   236

8.8   Median 1987 Family Incomes as Proportion of the Poverty
        Line by Family Type and Income Source   240

8.9   Antipoverty Effectiveness of Tax and Transfer Programs, 1986   242

Introduction

Lars Osberg

Economic inequality has always been one of the central issues of any social system. From the very earliest times, philosophers have debated the ethics of the coexistence of great wealth and abject poverty, while political analysts have emphasized the linkages between economic affluence and political influence. The central question of the modern discipline of sociology is the analysis of structured social inequality, which is largely derived from differences in command over economic resources. And economists have always claimed that the criteria for economic policy are efficiency *and* equity. But despite the importance of the issue, vast gaps in our knowledge about economic inequality remain.

In part, these gaps are due to the fact that economists cannot all agree on what the crucial questions about economic inequality really are. For some, the important issue is the differences among all individuals in potential command over goods and services—if society as a whole produces a certain amount of output, how is the total pie sliced up? For some, the situation of the poor is a particularly important dimension of inequality, since there is a long tradition of ethical concern with inequality which stresses the relative well-being of the most disadvantaged members of society. For others, the crucial questions are those which surround the concentration of ownership, wealth and power in capitalist societies. And for still others the social policies which affect inequality command the most interest.

This book of readings touches on all these dimensions of economic inequality. One of the themes running through the chapters is the crucial importance of conceptual and measurement issues to our perception of the nature of aggregate economic inequality, poverty, and the concentration of wealth and social policy. Another theme which pervades these readings is the value of international comparisons of the evidence on economic inequality. If we are to evaluate carefully the theories which seek to explain inequality and poverty or the policies which attempt to affect it, we should have a clear idea of what exactly it is that we are seeking to explain or to influence. Our evaluation of reasonable theories or practicable policies will also depend on the range of variation which can and does exist in human societies.

At the most general level, "economic inequality" means in this book "differences among people in their command over economic resources." By this definition we mean to distinguish between the study of *actual* differences among people (a factual exercise) and the study of *unjustifiable* differences among people (an ethical exercise). We therefore draw a distinction between the study of economic *inequality* and of economic *inequity*, while recognizing that much of the motivation for studying inequality comes from a concern with inequity. The readings in this book are mostly concerned with *actual* differences among people, not *potential* differences, and in that sense the subject of this volume is inequality of economic outcomes, rather than inequality of economic opportunity.

If we are to make comparisons, either across societies or over time, of the extent of economic inequality, we must summarize in some statistical measure (or measures) of aggregate economic inequality the differences among a large number of people in command over economic resources. Such summarization will implicitly provide a weighting of the many differences between actual individuals in society. Stephen Jenkins, in chapter 1, discusses the minimal properties which an ethically defensible measure of income inequality should possess and investigates the properties of different measures of inequality used in the economics literature. Jenkins asks: "Under what conditions can one say that inequality in one income distribution is greater (or less) than that in another income distribution? What social values are implicit in a particular measure of inequality?"

In chapter 2, Timothy M. Smeeding compares the inequality of income distribution and the incidence and distribution of poverty within ten of the world's developed economies. As he emphasizes, some broad generalizations emerge from the data—notably the relatively high level of inequality and poverty in the United States and the low levels of both in Scandinavian countries—but for many of the most interesting policy issues we must look beneath the surface of the aggregative statistics.

Although the way in which humanity is divided into nation states is politically important, it is essentially arbitrary, the end result of a large number of historical accidents. If we have an ethical concern with economic inequality, there is no ethically defensible reason why such concern should stop at national frontiers. As Albert Berry and his collaborators demonstrate in chapter 3, differences among nations, rather than economic differences within nations, dominate global inequality. Since countries vary in their rate of economic development, the pattern of world inequality changes over time, in response to economic policies and world events. These differences between and within countries can be seen as "natural experiments," which illustrate the fact that aggregate economic in-equality, at both the national and the global level, is something which is amena-ble to change.

Although most discussion of economic inequality is framed in terms of in-equality of incomes, the terms "rich" and "poor" taken literally, refer to wealth, not income. In chapter 4, Edward N. Wolff asks, "What is the proper definition of 'wealth'? What difference does our definition of wealth make to our perception of inequality in wealth? What trends in wealth inequality do we observe in advanced economies?" These issues are particularly important if one believes that the possession of some forms of wealth (e.g., equity capital) entails economic power or political and social influence.

However, although a political concern with potential concentrations of wealth and power motivàtes some of the interest in inequality, much of it also is derived from an ethically based concern for the poor. In chapter 5, Aldi Hagenaars emphasizes that the measure of poverty which we should adopt will depend on just what we understand as the meaning of being "poor." Those who think being poor means being unable to purchase a specific bundle of necessities will argue for one definition of poverty, while those who think that poverty consists in being unable to afford a decent standard of life will have a very different perception of the nature and extent of poverty.

Even those who agree on the extent of poverty at a point in time might still disagree on the significance of poverty. Those who study poverty because of a Rawlsian concern for the well-being of the least-advantaged members of society will feel that the primary focus of poverty policy should be on those who will be poor over their lifetimes. Those whose concern with poverty stems from a com-mitment to equality of opportunity will want to know how much of the poverty population is part of a "culture of poverty" which blights the lives of the children it touches. And those who emphasize the social insurance role of the state in an uncertain world will want to know how many of the poor are there temporarily, and why. In chapter 6, Patricia Ruggles uses a particular definition of poverty—that of the Social Security administration of the United States—to examine the issue of the permanence of poverty, and the reasons why some of the poor can expect to be poor for most of their lives.

This distinction between poverty in one year and poverty over a lifetime is really a special case of the distinction between annual income and lifetime in-come which is crucial to much of the discussion of economic inequality. In chapter 7, Paul Cullinan examines a particular government program, Social Se-curity in the United States, which redistributes income between different years of an individual's lifetime, as well as between individuals of the same generation and between different generations of individuals. As he makes clear, a whole series of distributional issues are raised by this one government program.

Finally, in chapter 8, Patricia Ruggles considers the impact of the full spec-trum of government tax and expenditure activities on the distribution of income in the United States. As Cullinan's chapter indicates, it is not easy to assess the impact on inequality of one program, and it is obviously much more difficult to assess the impacts of all programs considered jointly. It is especially difficult to come to a firm conclusion about the incidence of taxes such as the corporate income tax or the benefits of some types of expenditures (e.g., on defense). However, one can evaluate the impacts of personal income taxation, cash transfers and in-kind benefits to households on the rate of poverty and on the distribution of income in the United States. Transfer programs do have a significant impact on the overall poverty gap and on the poverty rate, but the net impact of government on the degree of aggregate inequality in the United States is relatively small.

In drawing these readings together, we are all very conscious that much more could be written, and should be written, on economic inequality. Nevertheless, all the readings in this volume are original articles which seek to present some examples of the state of the art of the theory and measurement of economic inequality and poverty. We hope that they will prove useful to analysts of economic inequality and that they will help to stimulate further research on this important subject.

Dalhousie University
Halifax, Nova Scotia

Economic INEQUALITY and Poverty

The Measurement of Income Inequality

Stephen Jenkins

1. Introduction

In Douglas Adams' science fiction comedy classic *The Hitchhiker's Guide to the Galaxy,* supercomputer Deep Thought revealed that the Answer to the Ultimate Question of Life, the Universe, and Everything was "42." But unfortunately no one knew what the Question was! Newcomers to the economic inequality literature might justifiably claim to have the opposite problem. There are well-defined important questions—for example, is inequality increasing or decreasing, and by how much?—but what on earth does it mean (if anything) when the Gini coefficient is 42 percent? The aim of this chapter is to help resolve such problems and thereby provide a theoretical framework for the empirical chapters following.

An essential preliminary to any inequality (or poverty) study is clarification of the nature of the distribution to be analyzed to ensure that it represents the appropriate concept of economic power and does so for each constituent unit. Important questions are: What is the economic variable of interest? What is the demographic unit to which this pertains, and how does one ensure variables are comparable across households? These issues are the subject of section 2.

The subsequent sections consider inequality measurement per se, focusing on two sorts of Ultimate Question. The first is: under what conditions can one say unambiguously that one distribution is more or less unequal than another? This covers issues such as whether or not inequality has increased over the last decade, is larger in the United States than in the United Kingdom, or whether the post-tax income distribution is more equal than the pretax one. A more demanding requirement is not only the

This paper was revised while I enjoyed the hospitality of the Economics Department, Research School of Social Sciences, Australian National University. Thanks are due to the editor and especially James Foster for their helpful comments.

ability to rank the distributions in terms of their inequality, but also to know how much more or less unequal one is relative to the other. On this basis a distinction can be made between ordinal inequality measures (the first case), and cardinal ones (the second). The advantage of the first sort of measures is that the set of basic assumptions underpinning them is smaller than for the second sort—which increases the possibility of having society-wide agreement about their use—but the penalty is that there are situations where unambiguous rankings cannot be made. However, using measures incorporating extra assumptions (the second class) extends the range of potential conclusions that can be drawn. Note that two summary measures may rank a set of distributions in exactly the same way, but represent this using different numerical scales; in this situation the measures are said to be ordinally, but not cardinally, equivalent.

At the heart of the survey is an investigation of the properties of different measures used in the literature and their implications. Section 3 discusses the information provided by several alternative graphical summaries of distributions such as histograms, Pen's Parade, and Lorenz curves, plus the properties of some related and commonly-used measures of a distribution's dispersion, including the Gini coefficient. Inequality measures for ranking distributions are considered in section 4, where attention is drawn to the links between inequality orderings, nonintersecting Lorenz curves, and certain underlying axiomatic properties, and to analogous results in the literature on decision making under uncertainty. Section 5 focuses on two important classes of cardinal measures. The first is the Atkinson family derived from sets of assumptions about society's Social Welfare Function. The Generalized Entropy family of indices considered second has a rather different pedigree but is shown to be closely related to the Atkinson one and to have an additional property very useful for empirical work, namely, additive decomposability by population subgroup. This property can be used to answer important questions such as: how much of overall inequality can be attributed to differences in household composition, or age differences? Section 6 provides concluding comments. It reiterates the main themes of the chapter and draws attention to some other topics not covered.

It needs to be stressed that this chapter provides only an introduction to the topic of inequality measurement, and concentrates on theoretical aspects. As a survey it relies heavily on previous work. For these reasons a brief Further Reading section has been included, providing a selective annotated guide to the literature.

2. Essential Preliminaries

The Variable of Interest

The study of economic inequality is the analysis of differences across the population in *access to, and control over, economic resources*. Consider how the concept italicized might be measured, taking first the situation of a single work-

Figure 1.1. **Headings in Annual Economic Statement for Arthur Dent**

Income   (a)   earnings
in year t (b)   income from savings (including occupational pensions)
                 (c)   capital receipts (gifts, inheritances, etc.)
                 (d)   transfers from the government

Minus

Outgoings   (e)   expenditures
in year t (f)   capital transfers (gifts made, etc.)
                 (g)   taxes

Equals

Savings in year t.

Net wealth at end of year t = net wealth at end of year $t-1$, plus savings in year t.

ing man, Arthur Dent (complications arising from having other types of demographic unit are considered below). In any given year one could draw up a
personal economic statement for Dent, just as the Treasury Department does for
the country, summarizing his income and expenditures during the year plus his
assets and liabilities at the year's end. See Figure 1.1.

The most commonly used variable in inequality analyses is *income*, but this may
be defined in many ways. An emphasis on the potential economic power under Dent's
own direct control suggests the use of (i) *pre-tax-and-transfer income* = (a) + (b) +
(c). This may be contrasted with a measure based on (e) *expenditure* which reflects
the exercise of power. This is rarely used—miserly millionaires are not usually
considered poor—but on the other hand consumption of specific resources may
sometimes be of special importance. A good example is food in underdeveloped
countries. Dent's overall economic power also depends on the effects of government.
This might be summarized by incorporating (d) and (g) into (i) to give (ii) *post-tax-
and-transfer income*, but there remain ambiguities.

A case could be made for excluding indirect taxes paid (for example local
sales taxes), since otherwise (ii) may simply reflect differences in consumption
preferences, not in the resources at Dent's disposal. Noncash income such as the
value of government-provided health insurance or housing subsidies, employ-
ment-related fringe benefits, or the value of home-produced activities could also
be included. Although difficult to value, these increase Dent's total purchasing
power, and should be included in a comprehensive definition of income. More
controversially, there have also been proposals to incorporate the value of an
individual's leisure time as well. If everyone is freely able to vary their hours of
work, then hours spent in leisure represent foregone wages and hence potential
economic power, but this amounts to assuming away the existence of involuntary
unemployment and is obviously controversial.

Valuation problems are also particularly relevant to the measurement of capital receipts. A gift of $1,000 to Dent from his uncle can be handled relatively straightforwardly, but what if instead he was given an Andrew Wyeth original or a block of IBM shares. And if either of these were to appreciate in value, the resultant capital gain is an increase in potential income, realizable if the assets were to be sold. On the other hand the actual purchasing power clearly depends on the marketability of the assets.

Of course asset holdings are relevant to power over economic resources in their own right, not just for the income they yield. There is an ongoing debate about the nature of the relationship between wealth and power, and whether certain assets deserve special emphasis—historically, land ownership has been associated with influence and status in society. And the principal shareholder in a large, private company clearly has a different type of control over society's resources than someone with the same amount of savings held in a savings account, or tied up in a pension scheme.

In summary, there is a large range of potential variables corresponding to alternative definitions of economic power and one's choice will depend on the particular purpose at hand. In practice one is often also constrained by what is included in the statistics available. This must be taken account of when drawing conclusions.

The Time Period

The cautionary remarks just made apply with equal force to the question of the appropriate time period over which income should be measured. Should it be a month, a year (as above), or perhaps a lifetime? Each gives different answers: lengthening the time period will tend to reduce the degree of dispersion observed across the population, because averaging over time tends to iron out fluctuations, producing income differences between people which are smaller than in any given time period.

Which interval length is of most social relevance will depend on how much Dent's income actually fluctuates over time, and on his ability to transfer income between time periods if desired by borrowing or lending. For workers with substantial commission or piece-rate elements to their earnings, incomes may fluctuate dramatically from month to month. This may be of no social concern if rich brokers and poor bricklayers can borrow and lend on equal terms, but generally they cannot. The rich are more likely to have assets that may be liquidated to tide over pressing emergencies or, as collateral, help secure cheaper borrowing. Nevertheless with incomes tending to even themselves out over several pay periods the primary social interest is probably whether the fluctuations lead to incomes falling below certain minima, which would reflect a concern with poverty rather than inequality.

Systematic variations in income over individuals' lifetimes are of greater significance. As a young medical intern Arthur Dent may this year earn less than a similarly aged car assembly worker, but the knowledge that Dent's subsequent career earnings are likely to be much greater substantially moderates any assessment of the current situation as representing "genuine" inequality. Two main strategies are open to researchers. First, "lifetime income"—the total net present value of the incomes in different periods—may be calculated, but this is rarely done because of a lack of appropriate longitudinal data sets. The remarks above about access to capital markets apply here too. An alternative approach is to isolate the contribution of age differences to overall inequality using decomposition methods; see section 1.5.

The Income Unit

The next set of issues concerns the demographic unit used in the analysis. Arthur Dent may have two-thirds the income of Patricia McMillan, but perceptions of the inequity of this depend on whether each is single, or has a spouse and children to support and hence greater needs. The most important distinctions to be made are between individuals, families, and households, where the last also includes individuals at the same address who are not part of the nuclear family (such as grandparents or unrelated lodgers).

Although it is the well-being of individuals that is of ultimate interest, using the observed incomes of each family member is likely to be a poor proxy. Although some people, notably children, have no income in their own name, they benefit from income sharing within the household or family in which they live. The terms "family" and "household" are used interchangeably in the rest of this chapter, but it should be remembered that they are not substitutes in practice. With secular changes in demographic structure in the United States, trends in measured inequality are sensitive to the definition chosen.

The simplest adjustment to observed incomes that we could make would be to assume equal sharing of income among all members and to calculate incomes per capita, but this is unsatisfactory; equal per capita incomes do not necessarily reflect equal commands over economic resources. Unfortunately there is little information available about patterns of income redistribution within families and in particular on the extent to which breadwinners (typically men) transfer resources to those with the major domestic responsibilities (typically women).

One adjustment to the data is based on the view that the appropriate income deflator is not the actual numbers of individuals per family but the numbers of "equivalent adults." All households require items such as light and heating but since additional members can also benefit at little extra cost from their provision, there are economies of scale in larger units. However, children and adults do not have equal needs; $100 is likely to go further in a two-adult one-child family than in a three-adult one.

Equivalence Scales

An index which deflates family incomes by a score that may be less than one for each extra member is what is known as an "equivalence scale." "Equivalent income" for a household equals observed income divided by the equivalence scale value for households of its type. Not surprisingly there is considerable and continuing debate about the derivation of such scales. If there were a social consensus about the minimum necessary consumption requirements (food, clothing, housing standards, etc.) for families of different types, then one could straightforwardly specify these, cost them using assumptions about prices, and hence derive the income levels just sufficient to meet total expenditure needs. The problem is that no such agreement exists, about even dietary requirements let alone other items and, typically, not everyone can buy the items at the same set of prices.

An alternative approach is to derive the scales from data sets with information on actual household incomes and expenditure patterns. As the share of a family's budget spent on necessities such as food tends to decline with income for all household types, this budget share may be used as an indicator of household well-being. Having estimated the relationship between food share and income from the data, the differences in total income across households at a particular food share level can provide measures of the differences in income required to reach the same level of welfare; the equivalence scales required. The approach can be further developed to incorporate more sophisticated relationships between household utility and expenditure patterns (not just food shares), drawing on advanced econometric methods.

However the use of advanced techniques like these should not blind one to the essentially normative aspects of the problem—for example, the prior choice of the characteristics used to distinguish family types. The number of adults and children (and sometimes their age) are the most commonly used, but a case can be made for also distinguishing differences in expenditures between the disabled (or the elderly) and others, or allowing for differences in labor force participation.

The equivalence scale implicit in the United States official poverty line incorporates elements of both the minimum consumption and expenditure approaches. For families of different sizes a Department of Agriculture dietary plan is used to specify the minimum necessary food requirements and the overall poverty line is taken as a multiple of this—chosen to ensure that the budget share for food is not atypically large—a judgment made on the basis of expenditure survey data. (The measurement of poverty is discussed in more detail in the chapter by Aldi Hagenaars.)

The Weighting of Income Units

The final task in constructing a distribution for analysis is to indicate the number of income units with a given income. Suppose household i has income y_i, number of members n_i, and number of equivalent adults r_i. Even if it is agreed that i's equivalent income y_i/r_i is the best estimate of resources received per member, there remains the choice of whether the family should count as one, n_i, or r_i units. As incomes are measured per head then the most consistent position is to use either of the last two as the weights. Which of these should be preferred is related to the philosophical issue of whether one should regard all individuals as counting equally within the population in question, or whether children for example should not be rated as much. Note that both strategies may provide a distribution with a shape, and hence measured inequality, which is different from that produced using data on incomes weighted *per household*.

3. Graphical Representations and Some Common Inequality Measures

From now on it will be assumed that all the essential preliminaries have received their due attention, and there is now a set of comparable distributions. For convenience the variable of interest will be referred to as "income" and the demographic unit as the "individual." Much inequality analysis builds on foundations provided by statisticians, who are long accustomed to summarizing distributions. This section discusses several graphical representations of the basic data, and then some commonly-used inequality measures related to these. An analysis of their properties provides the motivation for the measures considered in later sections.

Graphical Representations

The most common graphical device is probably the histogram, which is based on the frequency distribution and shows the numbers of individuals with income in specified ranges. Example data are given in Table 1.1 and Figure 1.2 is based on this, with the diagram drawn so that equal areas on the chart represent equal relative frequencies. The general shape—skewed to the right, with the mean above the median—is typical. One problem immediately apparent is that the figure does not include all the information in the table: in order to picture the lower middle and bottom of the distribution, very large incomes have had to be omitted.

An alternative method and one that highlights the presence of very large incomes is the so-called Pen's Parade. Suppose everyone in the population is represented by a person who has a height proportional to his income. Now line these agents up in order of height with the tallest at the front and have them all march past a certain spot in an hour. At a distance the silhouette of the parade would be as in Figure 1.3(a). (The horizontal axis has been scaled by expressing people's positions as cumulative population shares. Allocating each individual in order a number from 1 to n—n is the population size and is the number given to the tallest person—these shares equal i/n for each $i = 1, \ldots, n$.) Heights increase

Table 1.1

Frequency Distribution Example

Income (£ 000s)	Frequency	Percentage	Cumulative percentage
0.0–0.5	6	0.1	0.1
0.5–1.0	13	0.2	0.3
1.0–1.5	58	0.8	1.0
1.5–2.0	375	5.0	6.0
2.0–2.5	507	6.7	12.8
2.5–3.0	433	5.8	18.5
3.0–3.5	433	5.8	24.3
3.5–4.0	396	5.3	29.5
4.0–4.5	379	5.0	34.6
4.5–5.0	390	5.2	39.8
5.0–5.5	389	5.2	44.9
5.5–6.0	394	5.2	50.2
6.0–6.5	425	5.7	55.8
6.5–7.0	369	4.9	60.7
7.0–7.5	367	4.9	65.6
7.5–8.0	301	4.9	69.6
8.0–9.0	525	7.0	76.6
9.0–10.0	466	6.2	82.8
10.0–11.0	353	4.7	87.5
11.0–12.0	237	3.2	90.6
12.0–13.0	189	2.5	93.2
13.0–14.0	130	1.7	94.9
14.0–15.0	86	1.1	96.0
15.0–16.0	72	1.0	97.0
16.0–17.0	51	0.7	97.7
17.0–18.0	35	0.5	98.1
18.0–19.0	28	0.4	98.5
19.0–20.0	26	0.3	98.8
20.0–25.0	54	0.7	99.6
25.0–30.0	20	0.3	99.9
30.0–	13	0.2	100.0
Total	7520	100.0	

Source: Author's calculations from the microdata tape for the 1981 UK Family Expenditure Survey. Income is *net household disposable income per annum* = total household money income including cash transfers, less direct taxes. The variable is unadjusted for differences in family size, etc., and each household receives a weight of one. (Five households, with zero or negative incomes, are excluded from the analyses.) Mean income is £6729 and median is £5981.

Figure 1.2. **Histogram**

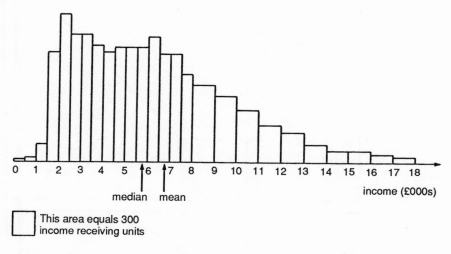

median   mean

This area equals 300
income receiving units

income (£000s)

Source: Table 1.1.

slowly for a very long time and it is over half an hour before the representative
with mean income ($\mu = (1/n)\Sigma_i\ y_i$) passes the finishing post, and the one with
twice mean income only arrives in the last five minutes. But there is then a
dramatic change in heights; indeed to include the largest income in the sample
used, the page would have to be extended vertically by over two yards. And if
the late Paul Getty had sent a representative, his height would be several miles
high! There is a close relationship between this parade and the frequency distribution; using the latter, calculate for each possible income level the total number
of individuals having incomes below this (see Table 1.1, column 2). Dividing
these cumulative frequencies by n and plotting the results against income yields
Figure 1.3(b), a graph with exactly the same shape as Figure 1.3(a).

By taking a logarithmic transformation of income it is possible to include
very rich people on the graph as well. In this case, shown in Figure 1.4, equal
distances along the horizontal axis now correspond to equal proportionate, not
absolute, differences in income so high incomes are now compressed.

The final graphical device to be considered, and one which turns out to have
particular relevance for subsequent sections, is the Lorenz Curve (LC). Call
again upon the representatives used in Pen's Parade, ensuring they are still
ranked the same, but this time make each agent's height equal to the sum of the
individual shares in total income held by him and all the people behind (i.e., the
same height or shorter). The new parade's silhouette is that pictured in Figure
1.5; more formally it is the graph of cumulative income shares

Figure 1.3. **Pen's Parade and the Cumulative Distribution Function**

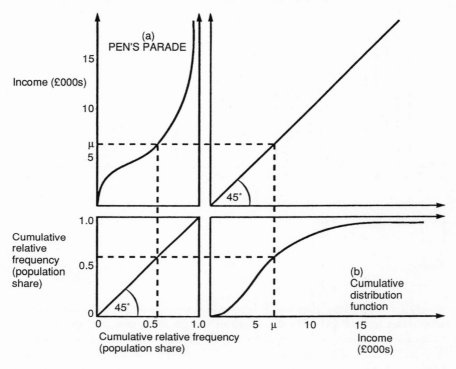

Source: Table 1.1.

$$(1/n\mu)\sum_{i=1}^{k} y_i, \text{ for each value of } k=1, \ldots, n$$

against cumulative population shares, defined above. Example data are given in Table 1.2. Because of the way people are ranked, heights must range from zero to one and the graph be convex towards the bottom right hand corner. Note that if everyone had the same income the Lorenz Curve would lie along the diagonal line, and if all income were held by just one person the curve would lie along the axes. The two parades are closely related since the slope of the Lorenz Curve at any given cumulative population share is in fact equal to y_i/μ, which is directly proportional to the height of Pen's Parade (y_i).

It should now be apparent that there is no obvious best way of representing income distributions graphically; each uses the same basic data but gives a different perspective. However, as far as inequality measurement is concerned, it will be seen below that the Lorenz Curve has some very important properties.

Figure 1.4. **Histogram for Log** (income)

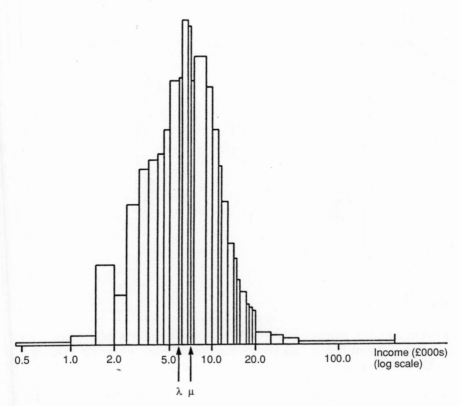

Source: Table 1.1.

Some Commonly-used Inequality Measures

A first measure of inequality, suggested by Figures 1.1 and 1.2, is the *range*, the difference between the largest and smallest incomes. An immediate difficulty with this is that if every income is increased by the same proportion inequality would rise, even though the distribution retains the same fundamental shape. This may be dealt with by deflating all incomes by the mean, thence giving a mean-independent (alternatively, scale invariant, or relative) measure. Nevertheless even if adjusted, the range would still completely ignore information about income differences between the extreme values, and a distribution which had an even spread of people between these points would be given exactly the same inequality score as one within which everyone was concentrated at either one

Table 1.2

Lorenz Curve Data

Cumulative share of population (%)	Cumulative share of total income (%)
0	0.0
5	1.2
10	2.8
15	4.6
20	6.8
25	9.3
30	12.1
35	15.3
40	18.9
45	22.8
50	27.0
55	31.6
60	36.6
65	41.9
70	47.7
75	53.9
80	60.7
85	68.1
90	76.3
95	85.8
100	100.0

Source: See Table 1.1.

point or the other. Indeed any measure based on distributional information at just one or two cut-off points (for example the "income share of the top 5 percent," or the "ratio of mean income among the richest 10 percent to that among the poorest 10 percent") will have the undesirable property of being completely insensitive to transfers of income over large sections of the distribution. Turn then to measures using data on all incomes.

The most commonly used measure in statistics of dispersion within distributions is the *variance* V (or its square root, the standard deviation):

(1) $$V = (1/n) \sum_{i=1}^{n} (y_i - \mu)^2$$

This is not mean-independent, but standardizing using the mean, μ, yields the *coefficient of variation*,

(2) $$C = \sqrt{V}/\mu,$$

or its square, $C^2 = V/\mu^2$ (which is ordinally, though not cardinally, equivalent). Using log income analogous measures can be based on the formula

Figure 1.5. **The Lorenz Curve**

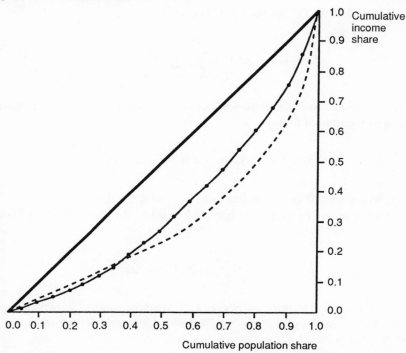

Source: Table 1.2.

(3) $$L = (1/n) \sum_{i=1}^{n} [\log(y_i) - \log(\theta)]^2 = (1/n) \sum_{i=1}^{n} [\log(y_i/\theta)]^2.$$

When $\theta = \mu$, $L = L_1$ the *logarithmic variance*, and if $\theta = \lambda$ where $\log(\lambda) = (1/n) \Sigma_i \log(y_i)$, i.e., λ is the geometric mean, then $L = L_2$ the *variance of the logs*. Both are mean-independent.

One of the most commonly calculated inequality statistics is the *Gini coefficient G*, which is closely related to Figure 1.5. It is equal to the ratio of the area enclosed by the Lorenz Curve and the diagonal line of perfect equality to the total area below the diagonal, or since the latter equals 0.5 (by construction), G equals twice the latter area. It ranges from a maximum of 1.0 (perfect inequality) to zero (perfect equality). Statisticians know G as one half of the relative mean difference—the average of the absolute values of the differences between all pairs of incomes, relative to the mean. Alternatively, think of it as the expected difference (in a relative sense) between two incomes drawn at random from the income distribution. The formula for G is given by

$$(4) \qquad G = [1/(2n^2\mu)] \sum_{i=1}^{n} \sum_{j=1}^{n} | y_i - y_j |$$

where $| . |$ represents "the absolute value of," but it can also be written as, and more easily estimated from,

$$(5) \qquad G = 1 + (1/n) - [2/(n^2\mu)] \sum_{i=1}^{n} (n - i + 1)y_i,$$

remembering individuals are ranked by income so that y_i is the lowest.

An index originally motivated from rather different considerations is *Theil's "entropy" index, T*, where

$$(6) \qquad T = (1/n) \sum_{i=1}^{n} (y_i /\mu) \log (y_i /\mu).$$

The motivation for this requires a brief excursion into information theory which is concerned with valuing knowledge that an outcome, one of the many possible, has occurred. (This detour is also relevant to section 5.) Suppose there are n mutually exclusive events which may each occur with probability p_i, $i = 1, \ldots, n$, with $0 \le p_i \le 1$ and $\Sigma_i p_i = 1$. If a particular event is very rare, then the information value of a message saying it has occurred is valuable, but the information value of very common events is relatively low. Hence if $h(p_i)$ is the function summarizing value, it will be decreasing in p_i. It is also sensible in this context to require that the information content of knowing that two statistically independent events i and j have taken place should be the sum of the values of the separate messages. But since the probability of i and j both occurring is $p_i \cdot p_j$, then it must be that

$$(7) \qquad h (p_i \cdot p_j) = h (p_i) + h (p_j)$$

and the decreasing function having this property is $h(p_i) = -\log(p_i)$. The expected information content ("entropy" or "disorder") of the whole system is given by the sum of the $h(.)$ weighted by the respective probabilities:

$$(8) \qquad \sum_{i=1}^{n} p_i h (p_i) = -\sum_{i=1}^{n} p_i \log (p_i) .$$

This expression is in effect a measure of the degree to which the probabilities of the various events are equal. The maximum possible value $\Sigma_i (1/n)h(1/n)$ occurs when the events are equally likely, and the more disorder—differing probabilities—there is, the more it falls below this. The index subtracting actual from maximum entropy

$$(9) \qquad \sum_{i=1}^{n} (1/n) \, h \, (1/n) - \sum_{i=1}^{n} p_i \, h \, (p_i) = \sum_{i=1}^{n} p_i \, [\log(p_i) - \log(1/n)]$$

will record higher values the more disorder there is.

The analogy between disorder and income inequality provides the rationale for using such an index in the current context, and if income shares $s_t = y_t /(n\mu)$, $t = 1, \ldots, n$ are substituted for the probabilities, T is the result.

Properties of Inequality Measures

Although C, L_1, L_2, G, and T each take account of all (changes in) income differences in a distribution, the various formulae indicate that the same information is being weighted differently in the aggregation process. To explore this further, consider some distribution A from which a person (labelled i) is arbitrarily chosen. Now form a new distribution B by transferring a small amount of income to a poorer person j, though keeping i richer overall. Faced with this situation virtually everyone would agree that the inequality falls in going from B to A (though they may disagree about how much), and an inequality measure I satisfying this property is said to satisfy the *Principle of Transfers*. For infinitesimal progressive transfers of the type described, this reduces to the condition $dI < 0$, where

$$(10) \qquad \begin{aligned} dI &= (\, \partial I \, /\partial y_j) \, dy_j + (\partial I \, /\partial y_i) \, dy_i \\ &= dy \, [(\partial I \, /\partial y_j) - (\partial I \, /\partial y_i)], \end{aligned}$$

and the change in inequality, dI, is the total differential of I, and note that by construction the transfer $dy_i = -dy_j$.

Views about the precise size of the inequality reduction from the transfer dy are likely to depend on the income level of the recipient. Taking two pairs of individuals the same income distance apart, where one pair is relatively rich and the other relatively poor, many would argue that a given transfer from richer to poorer should reduce inequality more for the second pair than the first. (Or in other words, a progressive transfer between the poor pair combined with a regressive transfer of the same size between the rich pair would reduce overall inequality.) Inequality measures satisfying this property are known as *transfer sensitive*. For transfer sensitivity to hold the fall in inequality from a progressive transfer must be greater (dI more negative) the lower the income of the recipient is.

Do the measures cited satisfy the principle of transfers? From equations (2)–

(6) one may calculate that the changes in inequality arising from an infinitesimal mean-preserving progressive transfer are given by

(11a) dC $= [dy / (n\mu^2 C)]\{y_j - y_i\} < 0$

(11b) $d(C^2 / 2)$ $= [dy /(n\mu^2)]\{y_j - y_i\} < 0$

(11c) dL

$= (2\theta dy / n)\{(\theta/ y_j)\log(y_j / \theta) - (\theta / y_i)\log(y_i / \theta)\} \lessgtr 0$

(11d) dG $= [2dy / (n^2\mu)]\{j - i\} < 0$

(11e) dT $= [dy / (n\mu)]\{\log(y_j) - \log(y_i)\} < 0.$

These equations show that the Principle of Transfers is satisfied for every possible income pair by all measures, *except* the logarithmic variance and the variance of the logs, with the effects in different parts of the distribution summarized by the terms in curly brackets.

The coefficient of variation (C), and the ordinally equivalent $C^2/2$ (relevant to section 5), would record exactly the same change if $100 were transferred from someone with $500 to another with $400 (20 percent lower in relative terms), or from someone with $50,000 to someone with $49,900 (0.2 percent lower). The measure is therefore much more strongly affected by relative income differences amongst those with high incomes, than amongst low incomes. It is also not transfer sensitive.

In contrast the Theil index depends on relative rather than absolute income differences and is transfer sensitive. A $100 transfer from someone with $50,000 to someone with $40,000 would change T by as one from someone with $500 to someone with $400.

The Gini coefficient is rather different, for here the response to transfers depends on the rank orderings of the two persons. The change will be the larger the closer the pair is to the more crowded middle of the distribution (more precisely, the mode) rather than the sparser upper and lower tails. Although the Principle of Transfers is satisfied, the measure is not transfer sensitive because of the dependence on ranks rather than income.

Figure 1.4 showed how a log transformation radically compressed absolute income differences at the top of the distribution, and so one might expect the log-income-based measures (L_1 and L_2) to be relatively sensitive to transfers amongst those with low incomes, like Theil's T. This is indeed true but the problem is that the log income measures satisfy the Principle of Transfers only as long as the poorer person has an income less than e times the mean θ (where e is the exponential constant 2.718 . . .). If it is higher than this then $dL > 0$, which may be checked by examining the properties of the function $(1/z)\log(z)$. The intuition is that at very high incomes the transfer reduces absolute income differences but the compression effect from taking logs overdoes things, to give a perverse effect overall. It is this failure of the L measures to satisfy the Principle of Transfers that has led to frequent criticism of it as an inequality measure.

The conclusion to be drawn from this analysis is that all inequality measures, even ones related to apparently objective diagrams, inevitably involve value judgments of various kinds, and that some of these implicit assumptions are not necessarily desirable. Subsequent theoretical work has therefore largely followed the strategy of incorporating at the very outset properties seen as desirable.

The first axiom usually used is *Symmetry*, sometimes known as anonymity, which means that the inequality measure is based only upon the information provided by the incomes in a distribution, and not for example, by who the people are that have particular incomes. This may appear a strong assumption, but it is hardly objectionable as long as appropriate adjustments, such as for differing family sizes, have been made beforehand. This emphasizes the importance of getting the "essential preliminaries" right. All the indices considered so far satisfy Symmetry.

A second axiom, *Mean-Independence* has already been discussed. The desirability of having inequality measures invariant to proportionate changes in all incomes has been assumed by most writers in the literature and, as will be seen below, plays an important role in characterizing further measures.

A third property is *Population Homogeneity* which requires that measures be invariant to replications of the distribution; a population formed by merging q identical populations would be q times as large but have the same degree of inequality. (The desirability of the axiom is often taken for granted, but it is not absolutely persuasive: is a distribution where one person has $1 million and another $100 as unequal as one where five have $1 million each and five, $100 each?)

The fourth and most fundamental axiom used is the *Principle of Transfers*, defined above, which encapsulates the link between a reduction in inequality and (mean-preserving) progressive transfers. The fifth property, *Transfer Sensitivity*, is sometimes used in tandem with this.

Suppose now that a whole series of transfers from richer people to poorer people are carried out. At each step pair-wise comparisons of distributions using the *Principle of Transfers* imply that each new distribution is more equal than any older one. It means that if a distribution can be reached from another by a sequence of mean-preserving transfers then it is unambiguously more equal, and this provides a method for ranking distributions. However verifying that such sequences exist is tedious and impractical in reality, and so analysts have searched for conditions that are much more easily checked.

4. Measures for Inequality Rankings

To motivate the results following, consider two distributions of income $y = (5, 10, 20, 25, 40)$ and $x = (5, 10, 21, 24, 40)$, where y has been derived from x by a single mean-preserving transfer taking $1 from the person with $25 and giving it to the one with $20. Drawing the Lorenz Curves for the two distributions will reveal that they exactly coincide except between cumulative population shares 40 percent and 80 percent where the curve for x lies above that for y. Given the Principle of Transfers it follows that $I(x) < I(y)$, a result consistent with the area-based interpretation of the Gini coefficient above. One can check that also transferring \$1 from the person with \$10 to the one with \$5 has a similar consequence. This suggests that where x and y are now any two distributions, the statement that ''x is obtained from y by a series of mean-preserving progressive transfers,'' (and hence ''more equal'' than y) directly corresponds to ''x has a Lorenz Curve never lying below that for y and somewhere lying above'' (i.e., x Lorenz-dominates y). And this has been formally proven:

(T1) *For any two arbitrary distributions x, y, with the same number of members and $\mu_x = \mu_y$, whose members are ranked by income to give ordered distributions x' and y' respectively, then x' is obtained from y' by a finite sequence of progressive transfers if and only if x Lorenz-dominates y.*

The result is particularly useful because the condition on Lorenz Curves is so easily checked. The problem is, of course, that inequality comparisons will be indecisive wherever Lorenz Curves cross (see the dotted line in Figure 1.5), and the result cannot be applied where the distributions have different means. Before considering some of the strategies adopted as a consequence of this, it will be fruitful to redevelop the results within a different framework.

Social Welfare, Inequality Rankings, and Lorenz Curves

Those familiar with welfare economics will know that it is standard practice to evaluate the desirability of policy outcomes in terms of their effects on social welfare. This in turn is measured by using some form of social welfare function (SWF) to aggregate outcomes across all persons in the population. It has been seen in the preceding sections that different inequality measures incorporate different systems for weighting individual incomes, and so in this sense are just like some form of SWF. This suggests that an alternative approach could be to start with a SWF, specified to incorporate certain social values, and then to derive an inequality measure from this, knowing that it must reflect these same properties.

A typical specification of the SWF is

(12) $$W = \sum_{j=1}^{J} p_j U(y_j),$$

where p_i is the proportion of the population with income y_j, and $U(.)$, the social income valuation function is nondecreasing in each y_i and strictly concave. Where everyone has a different income this reduces to

(13)
$$W = (1/n) \sum_{i=1}^{n} U(y_i),$$

which, for expositional reasons, is the form used below. It follows that the change in social welfare arising from moving from one distribution to another is given by

(14)
$$dW = (1/n) \sum_{i=1}^{n} (\partial U / \partial y_i) \, dy_i,$$

the sum of the changes in each individual's income dy_i weighted by a factor $\partial U / \partial y_i$, the marginal social evaluation.

The assumptions incorporated are, first, that an increase in someone's income must improve social welfare or at worst, leave it unchanged; it cannot fall. Second, everyone's incomes are evaluated using the same $U(.)$ function, so that W is symmetric (for the same reasons as discussed previously, and with the same caveat). Third, W is an additively separable function of the individual incomes. This means that changes in social welfare arising from changing one individual's income are entirely unaffected by those of others. Social recognition of, say, envy ($\partial U(y_j)/\partial y_i < 0$) is thus ruled out.

The fourth assumption, strict concavity, is the key axiom encapsulating the way in which individuals' incomes, and differences between them, are evaluated by society. It says that the welfare weights used in the assessment process are non-negative for each individual ($\partial U/\partial y_i \geq 0$, all i), but the higher a person's income is, the lower the weight received ($\partial^2 U / \partial y_i^2 < 0$, all i), and implies a social preference for equality.

This is shown by Figure 1.6, which illustrates equation (13) for the case where $n = 2$. Higher levels of W correspond to higher contour lines (social indifference curves), and the symmetry assumption ensures these are symmetric about the 45° ray from the origin. Strict concavity ensures the curves are bowed towards the origin (they are straight lines like AD when only concavity is assumed). The point B represents the distribution (y_i, y_j). If some income is transferred from the richer person i to the poorer j, the new distribution must lie at a point somewhere along the line BC (in the limit at point C, where they are equal), and corresponds to a higher level of social welfare.

Assumptions about the degree of concavity of the SWF, or equivalently about the individual welfare weights, see (14), thus correspond to assumptions about the Principle of Transfers. The more averse to inequality society is, the more bowed the contours will be, with the limiting case being where they are the dotted right-angle shape. In this situation progressive transfers reduce inequality only if the income of the very worst-off person is improved.

Figure 1.6. **Graphic Representation of SWF for n = 2**

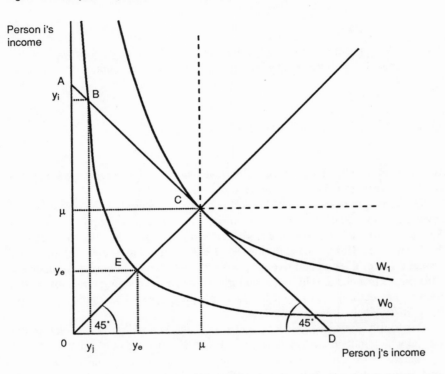

The assumption corresponding to transfer sensitivity is that the third partial derivative of $U(.)$ be positive. To see this, suppose there is a transfer from i to j of amount dy, and this changes social welfare by (from (14))

(15) $dW = (\, dy \, / \, n \,) \, [(\, \partial U \, / \, \partial y_j \,) - (\, \partial U \, / \, \partial y_i \,)] > 0.$

Transfer sensitivity requires the term in square brackets to be larger when i and j are both relatively poor than when they are both relatively rich. As Figure 1.7 illustrates, a sufficient condition for this is that the slope of the welfare weighting function $(\partial^2 U/\partial y^2)$ becomes less negative as y increases, i.e., $\partial^3 U/\partial y^3 > 0$.

Note, finally, that W is invariant to replications of the population.

An important result regarding SWFs can now be stated:

(T2) *For distributions x, y with associated levels of social welfare W_x and W_y respectively, where W is any additively separable strictly concave non-decreasing social welfare function, and $\mu_x = \mu_y$, then $W_x > W_y$ if and only if x Lorenz-dominates y.*

This summarizes the intimate relationship between inequality measurement

Figure 1.7. **The Welfare Weight Function and Transfer Sensitivity**

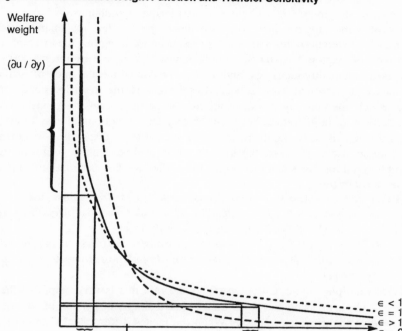

and social judgments, and can be linked up with T1. Different specific forms might be chosen for $U(.)$, but as long as they are nondecreasing and strictly concave, they will each rank distributions identically. As an illustration, suppose $U(y_i) = (y_i - \mu)^2/2\mu^2$ or $(y_i/\mu)\log(y_i/\mu)$, and substitute these into equation (13). The theorem implies that $C^2/2$ and T are ordinally equivalent measures.

Extensions to the Results

The result summarized in T2 is restricted to comparisons of distributions with equal means, and even then there may be situations where Lorenz Curves intersect so that unambiguous conclusions cannot be drawn.

When means differ, one approach is to persist in ranking the distributions by the Lorenz criterion which is equivalent to assuming that the inequality measure implicit in the analysis is mean-independent. In fact it can be shown that:

(T3) *The class of inequality measures satisfying Symmetry, Mean-Independence, Population Homogeneity, and the Principle of Transfers simultaneously is exactly equivalent to the class satisfying the property that a higher (the same) Lorenz Curve implies less (the same) inequality.*

This is the key theorem, for it gives the conditions under which all standard relative inequality measures will agree in their inequality rankings.

Recent work has attempted to widen the scope for deriving unambiguous rankings by different routes. One strategy has been to strengthen the Principle of Transfers and require Transfer Sensitivity as well. Stronger assumptions narrow the class of inequality measures (and SWFs) considered but the trade-off is that dominance requirements are reduced. Results giving the modified conditions under which one may say two distributions can be ranked unambiguously have been derived in the literature, but unfortunately they are not at all easy to interpret, and there is no straightforward check available corresponding to Lorenz Curve comparisons. However the analysis has proved particularly useful in providing a condition for situations where the earlier weaker assumptions lead to inconclusive results:

(T4) *If the Lorenz Curve for x intersects that for y once from above, then*

(a) where $\mu_x = \mu_y$, $I(y) > I(x)$ for all transfer-sensitive inequality measures $I(.)$, i.e., $W(x) > W(y)$, if and only if $V(y) \geq V(x)$, or

(b) where $\mu_x \neq \mu_y$, $I(y) > I(x)$ for all transfer sensitive inequality measures that also satisfy Mean-Independence and Population Homogeneity if and only if $C(y) \geq C(x)$.

Since multiple Lorenz Curve crossings are rare this is very helpful. Where there is a single crossing and equal means, just a simple inspection of variances may resolve the previous impasse. When the means differ, checks can still be done as long as two additional but not implausible assumptions are invoked. Then the comparison is of the coefficients of variation.

An alternative approach is to rank distributions in terms of *social welfare* rather than just inequality per se, by incorporating information about average living standards into the analysis as well.

Take the distributions x and y again and suppose now that $\mu_x > \mu_y$. Raising all incomes in y proportionately up to the point where the new mean equalled μ_x would raise social welfare since W is nondecreasing in each income. But, by definition, the Lorenz Curve for y would be unchanged, and so by T2 the scaled-up y distribution would still not be socially preferred to x. Thus the "$\mu_x = \mu_y$" phrase in T2 can be replaced by "$\mu_x \geq \mu_y$"—clearly, social welfare increases if there is less inequality and average income is higher.

If average income is lower ($\mu_x < \mu_y$), unambiguous rankings are more difficult to derive because society's equality preference (built into W by the concavity assumption) conflicts with efficiency preference (the desire for higher incomes, ceteris paribus, built in by making W nondecreasing). On the other hand it is also intuitively plausible that there could be circumstances where if μ_y were sufficiently high then this could offset having a lower Lorenz Curve over parts of (or all) the population. Making some of the poor poorer might be tolerated if average living standards amongst *all* poor people were raised by enough. Deriving ranking criteria taking account of this idea is all the more important given that in practice differences between Lorenz Curves are relatively small compared to differences in means.

Before stating the required result it will be necessary to revise the definition of a Lorenz Curve: instead of plotting cumulative income shares against cumulative population shares, now plot *cumulative mean incomes,*

$$(1/n) \sum_{i=1}^{k} y_i, \text{ for each value of } k = 1, \ldots, n.$$

This gives the *Generalized Lorenz Curve,* which is the ordinary Lorenz Curve with each point scaled vertically by mean income. The theorem may now be stated.

(T5) *For all additively separable nondecreasing strictly concave SWFs, x yields a higher (the same) level of social welfare than y if and only if the Generalized Lorenz Curve for x lies above (on) that for y.*

This represents a notable strengthening in the ability to make unambiguous comparisons of distributions. However it needs to be remembered that the underlying yardstick is overall social welfare, not inequality per se. Whether this is appropriate will depend on the particular goal of the analyst.

Analogies with Decision Making under Uncertainty

Many of the results summarized above have been inspired by the literature on decision making under uncertainty, and it is useful to draw out this link in more detail.

Ranking income distributions in terms of social welfare is a problem with exactly the same structure as ranking probability distributions in terms of their expected utility. It is as if an individual is to be given an income drawn at random from one of two distributions, where the probability p_j of getting any particular value is known (but not, in advance, which specific income would be received ex post), and the individual has to choose which distribution the draw will be from. If the means of the distributions are the same, the decision will depend both on the relative risks involved (related to the differences in probabilities) and on attitudes to risk (which are related to the concavity of $U(.)$ if this is now interpreted as the individual's utility function). A choice based on maximizing expected utility is then exactly analogous to maximizing W as given in (12). Aversion to risk is like aversion to inequality.

But in the uncertainty literature there is a well-known result which says that for two distributions with the same mean, and all increasing concave $U(.)$, then x will be unambiguously preferred to y if and only if x second order stochastically dominates y. Second order stochastic dominance can be explained with reference to Figure 1.3(b). Let the curve shown be that for y and suppose another is added for x with the same general shape. If this new curve is everywhere on or below that for y then x is said to first order stochastically dominate y. Now suppose the curves intersect (possibly several times), and evaluate the areas between the curves, cumulatively for each income share along the horizontal axis, using the convention that where the curve for x lies below that for y the area is negative. Second order stochastic dominance is the condition requiring that the cumulative areas are never strictly positive, and are strictly negative at least one point. This condition is difficult to handle (even for decision theorists!), but fortunately it can be shown that the statement "x second order stochastically dominates y" is exactly equivalent to "x Lorenz-dominates y." T1 and T2 are thus further extended. Intuitively, the result arises from the close link between Figures 1.3(b) and 1.5. The area under the graph and to the left of a given point on the *horizontal* axis of Figure 1.3(b) corresponds to a point on the *vertical* axis of Figure 1.5. And both figures record population shares on their other axis.

Note, finally, that Transfer Sensitivity is analogous to decreasing absolute risk aversion. Making this assumption, x is preferred to y if and only if x third order stochastically dominates y. Checking this condition requires a further cumulation of areas and is not straightforward. The role for the variance summarized in T4 is therefore very useful.

5. The Atkinson and Generalized Entropy Families of Inequality Indices

The easily-implementable checks discussed above may not resolve ambiguities when applied and, anyway, one may also want to say whether a given change in inequality is larger than another, or to decompose total overall inequality into constituent components. In these situations numerical measures are required.

The Atkinson family of indices is derived by making additional assumptions about the functional form of the SWF welfare weights and hence relationships between transfers and changes in inequality. The Generalized Entropy (GE) family in contrast is developed by considering these connections directly, and can be interpreted as making assumptions about how distances between individuals' income shares are measured.

The Atkinson Family of Inequality Indices

Consider Figure 1.6 again. Remembering that point B represents a position of inequality and point C one of perfect equality consistent with redistributing the same aggregate income total, a natural way to measure inequality is to use the relative difference in social welfares possible at the two points, i.e.,

(16) $$I = (W_1 - W_0)/W_1 = 1 - (W_0/W_1).$$

The standard assumption made about $W(.)$ in addition to those discussed above is that the social income evaluation functions $U(.)$, and hence $W(.)$, have constant elasticity. Multiplying every individual's income by a certain proportion would change total social welfare by the same fraction, and this would leave the degree of inequality measured using equation (16) unchanged. This assumption therefore ensures that the measure is mean-independent. (In Figure 1.6 the slopes of the social indifference curves at each point along a ray from the origin will always be the same.)

For this to be true $U(.)$ must have the form

(17)
$$U(y) = a + by^{1-\varepsilon} / (1 - \varepsilon) , \varepsilon \neq 1, \varepsilon \geq 0$$
$$= \log_e(y), \varepsilon = 1.$$

where, by analogy with the literature on uncertainty, ε may be interpreted as the constant degree of relative inequality (rather than risk) aversion. The restriction $\varepsilon \geq 0$ ensures the W contours are concave to the origin with the higher the value of ε, the more bowed they are ($\varepsilon = 0$ is the straight line case in Figure 1.6). The welfare weights implied are

(18)
$$\partial U / \partial y = by^{-\varepsilon}, \varepsilon \neq 1, \varepsilon \geq 0$$
$$= 1 / y, \varepsilon = 1$$

which have graphs with the same shape as Figure 1.7—higher values of ε corresponding to steeper-sloped curves—which means that measures derived will be transfer sensitive.

One could now derive inequality measures by simply substituting equation (17) into (16), but a problem with this is that the number calculated would depend not just on ε, but also on a and b, as arbitrary constants. (Variations in the constants would provide a series of ordinally equivalent measures.) However this may be fixed by introducing the concept of the equally distributed equivalent level of income (y_e), which is the amount of income which if equally distributed amongst all persons would give the same level of social welfare as the original distribution, i.e., y_e such that

(19)
$$W = (1 / n) \sum_{i=1}^{n} U (y_i) = (1 / n) \sum_{i=1}^{n} U (y_e) = U(y_e)$$

and so, from (17)

(20)
$$y_e = [(1 / n) \sum_{i=1}^{n} y_i^{1-\varepsilon}]^{1/(1-\varepsilon)}$$

which does not depend on a or b. The measure of inequality is redefined as

(21)
$$I = 1 - (y_e / \mu),$$

which corresponds to the (relative) distance EC/OC in Figure 1.6, and ranges between zero (perfect equality) and one (perfect inequality). In risk analysis, $\mu - y_e$ is the maximum value a risk-averse decision maker would be willing to pay to swap a risky choice for a riskless one with equal expected value.

Substituting equation (20) into equation (21) gives the Atkinson family of indices:

(22)
$$A_\varepsilon = 1 - [(1/n) \sum_{i=1}^{n} (y_i / \mu)^{1-\varepsilon}]^{1/(1-\varepsilon)}, \varepsilon \neq 1, \varepsilon \geq 0$$

$$= 1 - \exp[(1/n) \sum_{i=1}^{n} \log_e (y_i / \mu)], \varepsilon = 1.$$

where $\exp[.] = e^{(.)}$.

Equation (21) shows that estimated values have a clear intuitive interpretation in terms of the gains from redistribution. A value of say 0.3 ($= 1 - 0.7$) indicates that if incomes were equal, then only 70 percent of current total income would be required to achieve exactly the same level of social welfare. Policies having both efficiency effects (changing total income) and redistributive ones can be explicitly compared. For example one could say that the equalizing effect of some pro-poor social security reforms were equivalent to a certain percentage increase in equally distributed income, a measure of social welfare. It is sometimes argued, rightly or wrongly, that efficiency enhancing policies have adverse distributional effects. Equation (21) implies $y_e = \mu(1-I)$, an expression which brings out the policy tradeoff between efficiency (μ) and equality $(1-I)$ explicitly.

Of course answers will depend on the particular SWF used or, equivalently, the degree of risk aversion, ε. How might this be chosen? A tax-transfer policy that paid \$1 to some poor person P via a tax of \$1 on richer person R would certainly be approved by all inequality-averse people (those with $\varepsilon \geq 0$). But many would endorse giving \$1 to P even if it meant that R was taxed by more than this and the extra was "lost" (for example in administrative costs). Suppose R has four times the income of P, then from equation (15) the maximum amount society would be willing to tax R to ensure P got \$1 is \$$4^\varepsilon$. Hence, when

$\varepsilon = 0$	the tax on R would be	$\$4^0$	$= \$1.00$
0.25	the tax on R would be	$\$4^{0.25}$	$= \$1.41$
0.5	the tax on R would be	$\$4^{0.5}$	$= \$2.00$

1.0   the tax on R would be $\$4^1 = \$4.00$
2.0   the tax on R would be $\$4^2 = \$16.00$
4.0   the tax on R would be $\$4^3 = \$256.00$.

With an infinitely large ε there is no limit to the amount; improvement of the position of the very poorest person is given absolute priority in this case.

For an alternative interpretation, suppose now that the top 5 percent of the income distribution all have incomes equal to y_R, and each of the bottom 20 percent, y_P, so that a tax of $1000 on each of the former could, if costlessly transferred, provide $250 per capita for the latter group. But in practice the "bucket" carrying the money from the rich to the poor leaks during the transfer process. The amount of leakage one would tolerate and yet still be in favor of the redistribution also gives clues about the choice of ε. With the distribution described, those with $\varepsilon = 1$ would allow up to 75 percent spillage; with $\varepsilon = 0.5$, 50 percent; with $\varepsilon = 0.25$, 33 percent; and with $\varepsilon = 0$, none at all.

Larger values of ε give greater emphasis to redistributions reducing income differences at the bottom of the distribution relative to those at the top (see Figure 1.7), with measures becoming very bottom-sensitive for values greater than one.

The Generalized Entropy Family of Inequality Indices

Rather than strengthening the discriminatory power of the theorems of section 4 indirectly, by specifying SWFs and imposing plausible restrictions on these, the main alternative approach is an axiomatic one: it specifies at the outset a set of desirable properties for the measure itself to have directly, and then uses these to characterize the index. The formulae derived are not always easy to rationalize intuitively, but here follows one quite plausible interpretation.

Focus attention on the relationship between the Principle of Transfers and changes in inequality. Equation (11) summarized this link for a range of measures and it was noted that a minimal requirement for the Principle of Transfers to be satisfied was $dI < 0$, and the size of the redistributional effect varied with the $\{.\}$ term.

Suppose now that the Principle of Transfers is modified to require not only $dI < 0$ but also that it depends only on the income shares of i and j. The transfer effect cannot then depend on their ranks (as with G), and must be independent of all other persons' income shares. The two measures T and $C^2/2$ certainly satisfy this *Strong Principle of Transfers*, since equations (11b, 11e) can be rewritten as

(23a) $d(C^2/2)$ $= (dy/\mu)\{s_j - s_i\}$, and
(23b) dT $= (dy/\mu)\{\log(s_j) - \log(s_i)\}$

where $s_t = y_t/(n\mu)$ is t's income share, $t = i, j$, and moreover there is a very close similarity in the way the transfer effect is quantified. The key element (in curly brackets) is simply the absolute difference between i's and j's income shares for $C^2/2$, while for T it is based on relative income differences. Each measure incorporates a different concept of "distance between income shares," which suggests that a family of inequality measures could be built up by developing the distance idea. What the "generalized entropy" approach does is generalize the notion of distance used in equation (9), with the rationale that there seems little reason for imposing the restriction implied by equation (7) in the income distribution context.

Taking the $\{.\}$ term to represent distance between income shares, then those used in equations (23a, 23b) are both special cases of the more general form

$$(24) \qquad \{h\,(s_i) - h\,(s_j)\} \text{ where}$$
$$h\,(s_t) = (-1\,/\,\beta)\,s_t{}^\beta\,,\,\beta \neq 0$$
$$= -\log(s_t)\,,\,\beta = 0, \text{ and } t = i, j.$$

Note that $\{.\} < 0$ whatever the β, so the Principle of Transfers is always satisfied.

Views about sensitivity to income transfers are thus incorporated directly, with smaller and more negative values of β giving increasing emphasis to income differences at the bottom of the distribution (by lengthening the distance). The parameter β appears to play an analogous role to ε, and the distance function to the welfare weights function. The relationship is brought out by Figure 1.8, which graphs $h(s)$ against s, showing figures bowed towards the origin—as in Figure 1.7—for all $\beta < 1$. It may be checked that the cases $\beta \geq 1$ are those for which the measure is not transfer sensitive $(\partial^2 h/\partial s^2 \leq 0)$.

If the specification of distance in equation (24) is used, then the inequality measure that naturally generalizes equation (9) is (for $\beta \neq 0$ or -1)

$$(25) \qquad I_\beta = [1\,/\,(1+\beta)\,]\sum_{i=1}^{n} s_i\,[h\,(1\,/\,n) - h\,(s_i)\,].$$
$$= [1\,/\,(\beta^2 + \beta)][(\sum_{i=1}^{n} s_i{}^{\beta+1}) - n^{-\beta}\,].$$

This does not satisfy "Population Homogeneity" (except when $\beta = 0$); note the $n^{-\beta}$ term. However a measure that does, and which has exactly the same $\{.\}$ terms in the transfer equation as I_β, is $n^\beta \cdot I_\beta$, and it is the latter which is referred to as the *Generalized Entropy family*. The formula, for $\beta \neq 0$ or -1, is given by

$$(26) \qquad E_\beta = [1\,/\,(\beta^2 + \beta)][(1\,/\,n)\sum_{i=1}^{n} (ns_i{}^{\beta+1}) - 1]$$

Figure 1.8. **Alternative Distance Functions, h(s)**

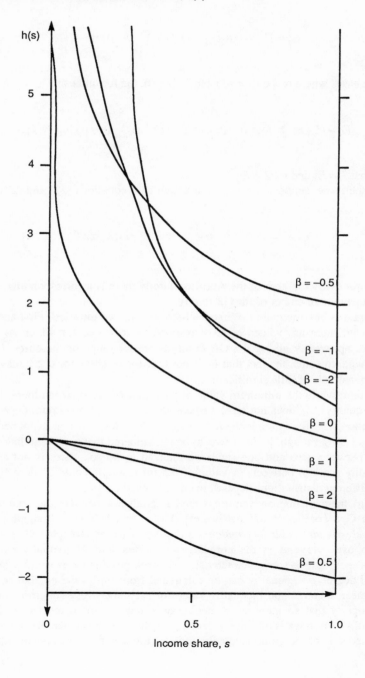

which may be rewritten, setting $\alpha = \beta + 1$, as

(27) $$E_\alpha = [1 / (\alpha^2 - \alpha)] \left\{ [(1 / n) \sum_{i=1}^{n} (y_i / \mu)^\alpha] - 1 \right\}$$

For the cases where $\alpha = 0$ ($\beta = -1$) and 1 ($\beta = 0$), the formulae are

(28) $$E_0 = (1 / n) \sum_{i=1}^{n} \log(\mu / y_i), \text{ and } E_1 = (1 / n) \sum_{i=1}^{n} (y_i / \mu) \log (y_i / \mu).$$

Note that $T = E_1$ and $C^2/2 = E_2$.

Furthermore, suppose $\alpha = 1 - \varepsilon$, in which case equations (22) and (27) show that

(29) $$A_\varepsilon = 1 - [(\alpha^2 - \alpha)E_\alpha + 1]^{1/\alpha}, \alpha < 1, \alpha \neq 0$$
$$= 1 - \exp(-E_\alpha), \alpha = 0$$

and so for every member of the Atkinson family there is a corresponding, ordinally equivalent, member of the GE family.

What then are the main differences between the two families? First and most obviously, there are values of α corresponding to $\varepsilon < 0$ for which A_ε is not defined, apparently giving the GE family a greater range of measures. On the other hand, to some, the fact that E_α is not transfer sensitive for $\alpha \geq 2$ may mean this extension is of little significance.

Second, while the minimum value of each index is zero (when there is complete equality), E_α does not have a maximum of one; the maximum depends on population size (for example the maximum for E_1 is $\log(n)$). This is not necessarily a bad thing though. It also needs to be remembered that even if an index does range between zero and one (or is normalized to do so), there is not a linear inequality scale in between. A value of 0.5 for example could be derived from very different distributions depending on the measure used.

Third, there is a major advantage of the GE family not shared by the Atkinson one (or the Gini coefficient for that matter). This is that it is very straightforwardly *additively decomposable by population subgroup*. This can be explained as follows.

Suppose everyone in the population is sorted into M mutually exclusive groups according to some characteristic. A decomposable index is one where the overall degree of inequality can be calculated from (only) the number of members, mean income, and inequality value for each and every subgroup, and has the property that an increase in inequality in one subgroup must raise overall inequality. An index is additively decomposable when it can also be written as a weighted sum of the group inequality indices (the weights are all positive), plus a between-group inequality term based on mean incomes and group size. It can be shown that:

(T6) *The GE family encompasses all possible indices simultaneously satisfying Symmetry, Mean-Independence, the Strong Principle of Transfers and Additive Decomposability. If the latter property is relaxed to Decomposability, the index must be some positive transformation of the GE family.*

Hence, for example, T and $C^2/2$ are additively decomposable and the Atkinson family members only decomposable. The Gini coefficient is neither: with this measure it is possible for inequality within one group to increase and yet overall inequality to decrease!

The disaggregated version of the formula for E_α illustrating additive decomposability is given by :

$$(30) \qquad E_\alpha = \sum_{m=1}^{M} (v_m{}^\alpha)\,(w_m{}^{1-\alpha})\,E_{\alpha m} + E_{\alpha B}$$

where the population share of a given group m is $w_m = n_m/n$; mean income within the group, μ_m; and the share of total income held by m's members is $v_m = w_m \mu_m/\mu$. The within-group inequality terms $E_{\alpha m}$ are calculated as if each group were a separate population, while the between-group inequality term is derived by assuming every person within a given group receives the group's mean income:

$$E_{\alpha B} = [1 / (\alpha^2 - \alpha)]\{[\Sigma_m\, w_m\,(\mu_m / \mu)^\alpha\,] - 1\},\ \alpha \neq 0,\ 1;$$
$$E_{0B} = \Sigma_m w_m \log (\mu / \mu_m\,);\ \text{and}\ E_{1B} = \Sigma_m\, v_m \log (\mu_m / \mu).$$

There is an obvious attraction in also requiring that the aggregating weights $(v_m{}^\alpha)(w_m{}^{1-\alpha})$ on the $E_{\alpha m}$ add up to one, which means they reduce to the group population shares for $\alpha = 0$, and group income shares for $\alpha = 1$. Amongst other things, this means that if inequality were to increase by the same proportion in every group, with everything else (including group means and income shares) staying the same, total inequality increases in the same proportion.

The additive decomposability property is very important for empirical work on the structure of inequality and changes in it. For example one may compare inequality within and between groups of individuals partitioned according to their age to draw conclusions about the relationship between age and inequality. If age had a very small association with inequality one would expect the intergroup component to be very small and the intra-group ones of a similar size. It is also straightforward to investigate the relative contributions of changes in the age structure and within-group inequality to changes in total inequality over time. Obviously the technique is also applicable to decompositions by other variables such as family composition, geographical location, or principal source of income received. It should be noted however that the appropriate method for considering the contribution of different income sources (such as primary and secondary earnings, taxes, pensions) to total inequality—decomposition by factor components—is an entirely different issue and can be shown to be independent of the choice of inequality measure.

6. Concluding Comments

The process of inequality measurement may be broken down into three main steps: (i) preparation of the distribution to be analyzed; (ii) choice of inequality measure; and (iii) calculations and assessment of results. This chapter has focused on the theoretical issues involved with the first two of these, one of the principal goals being to draw attention to the normative character of many of the assumptions involved. For example, important issues raised in section 2 are those of how to standardize incomes to take account of differences in household composition and how to weight each income unit. The underlying theme of subsequent sections is that it is better to use measures that at the outset measure (sets of) social values in a consistent way. This suggests increased utilization of indices from the Atkinson or Generalized Entropy family and relatively less emphasis on commonly used indices such as the Gini coefficient. Moreover there are also easily implementable checks available which often enable conclusions about inequality to be drawn even when there is no agreement about which particular index should be used.

Theoretical issues in the third measurement stage have not been discussed at all, and there is space here only to mention briefly the most important of these. The first arises from the fact that distributional data have often been available to researchers in grouped form, giving only the numbers of people with incomes falling within particular ranges (as in Table 1.1) plus possibly average income within each range. There has therefore been much written on "interpolation" methods, i.e., optimal ways of estimating inequality measures given the limited information. This issue is becoming of less importance as analysts increasingly have access to microdata sources with information available for each income unit. Second, in practice, individuals may sometimes have recorded incomes that are negative or zero if the accounting period is short or if pretransfer incomes are used. None of the measures discussed are designed to cope with negative incomes, and measures requiring log incomes cannot be applied to units with zero income. The standard procedures used are either to omit the troublesome units from the analysis, or to allocate each of them a very small positive income, say $1. Neither procedure is particularly satisfactory and each may give very different answers. (Note that this problem is much more serious when measuring the inequality of *wealth*, since quite a few households have liabilities in excess of assets or no net assets.) Third, virtually all data sets are based on samples rather than complete populations, and so estimates of inequality measures are subject to sampling errors. It is possible for apparent differences in equality not to be statistically significant. This is an issue that has only rarely received attention in the past, but it should receive increasing emphasis as theoretical results become more widely known and the checks implied by them more easily implemented.

7. Further Reading

This section provides a very selective annotated guide to the theoretical literature on inequality measurement. More wide-ranging and comprehensive discussions are given in the books by Atkinson (1983a), Cowell (1977), and Sen (1973). (Section 2 follows closely the structure of Atkinson's chapter 3, and sections 3–5, Cowell's chapters 2 and 3.) At a more technical level, see the books by Nygård and Sandström (1981) and Lambert (1989), and the survey article by Foster (1985). Each of these has extensive bibliographies. The distinction between inequality and poverty is discussed by Atkinson (1987), though note that the modes of analysis used to analyze each topic increasingly overlap (as this chapter and the one by Hagenaars illustrate).

Comprehensive definitions of income are much discussed in the taxation literature; two critiques of approaches adopted in the recent U.S. tax reforms are Pechman (1987) and Musgrave (1987). The relationship between income variability, length of time period, and inequality is analyzed by Shorrocks (1978). Methods for estimating lifetime earnings and thence inequality are considered by Creedy (1977) and Irvine (1981). Paglin (1975) discussed lifetime variations but his methods have been much criticized and they have now been superceded by approaches based on decomposable indices; see Cowell (1984). The unit of analysis is discussed by Morgan et al. (1962). Deaton and Muellbauer (1980) provide the best available survey of equivalence scales, but they should be read alongside the papers by Pollak and Wales (1979) and Fisher (1987) which emphasize normative aspects. The different ways of weighting units are considered by Danziger and Taussig (1979) and Cowell (1984).

All elementary statistics texts have sections on summarizing distributions, but Pen's Parade is best described in its originator's own very evocative terms; see Pen (1971). Dalton's (1920) classic article anticipates by half a century the modern approach of analyzing inequality measures in terms of desired properties. Subsequent landmarks include the papers by Kolm (1969, 1976) and Atkinson (1970). Kolm also provides the most well-known defense of translation independence (equal absolute, not proportional, changes in income leave inequality unchanged). Atkinson's article is the most cited in the inequality measurement literature. Drawing upon analogies with the uncertainty literature it demonstrated the links between sequences of progressive transfers, changes in social welfare, and the crossing of Lorenz curves, summarized in T1 and T2. Subsequent work showed that the relationships still hold if a SWF concavity assumption weaker than that cited in this chapter is used (Dasgupta, Sen and Starrett 1973). The "leaky bucket" interpretation of the inequality aversion parameter is taken from Okun (1975, chapter 4), whose book is a most eloquent discussion of the tradeoff between equality and efficiency and the role of the market vs. the state. T3 is taken from Foster (1985); see also Fields and Fei (1978). The transfer sensitivity axiom and the role of the variance in extending comparisons of previously noncomparable distributions summarized in T4 are discussed by Shorrocks and Foster (1987), while the properties of Generalized Lorenz Curves, and T5, are set out by Shorrocks (1983). The SWFs implicit in a wide range of inequality measures are derived, and graphed for $n = 3$, by Blackorby and Donaldson (1978).

Index T and its entropy interpretation are given by Theil (1967), while its distance-between-income-shares generalization is derived in papers by Cowell and Kuga (1981a, 1981b). Results demonstrating the relationship between the Generalized Entropy family and decomposability by population subgroup are proved by Bourguignon (1979), Cowell (1980), and Shorrocks (1980) and more generally by Shorrocks (1984). Shorrocks's (1982) paper is the leading theoretical analysis of procedures for inequality decomposition by factor components.

A classic article on the estimation of the Lorenz Curve and the Gini coefficient from grouped data is Gastwirth (1972), but Cowell and Mehta (1984) provide the current state-of-the-art analysis of interpolation methods for a much wider range of measures. The most easily accessible discussion of standard errors and tests of significance for inequality measures is in chapter 5 of Cowell (1977), but even this is frustratingly brief. Easy ways of calculating the indices discussed in this chapter from large microdata sets using standard computer packages such as SPSS^X are given by Jenkins (1988).

References

Atkinson, A. B. (1970) "On the measurement of inequality." *Journal of Economic Theory* 2, 244–63. (Reprinted in Atkinson [1980] with a non-technical appendix, and in Atkinson [1983b] with an additional bibliography of subsequent related work.)

———, ed. (1980) *Wealth, Income and Inequality*, second edition. Oxford: Oxford University Press.

———. (1983a) *The Economics of Inequality*, second edition. Oxford: Oxford University Press.

———. (1983b) *Social Justice and Public Policy*. Cambridge, MA: MIT Press.

———. (1987) "On the measurement of poverty." *Econometrica* 55, 749–64.

Blackorby, C., and Donaldson, D. (1978) "Measures of relative equality and their meaning in terms of social welfare." *Journal of Economic Theory* 18, 58–90.

Bourguignon, F. (1979) "Decomposable income inequality measures." *Econometrica* 47, 901–20.

Cowell, F. A. (1977) *Measuring Inequality*. Oxford: Philip Allan.

———. (1980) "On the structure of additive inequality measures." *Review of Economic Studies* 47, 521–31.

————. (1984) "The structure of American income inequality." *Review of Income and Wealth* 30, 351—75.

Cowell, F. A., and Kuga, K. (1981a) "Additivity and the entropy concept: an axiomatic approach to inequality measurement." *Journal of Economic Theory* 25, 131–143.

Cowell, F. A., and Kuga, K. (1981b) "Inequality measurement: an axiomatic approach." *European Economic Review* 15, 287–305.

Cowell, F. A., and Mehta, F. (1984) "The estimation and interpolation of inequality measures." *Review of Economic Studies* 43, 273–90.

Creedy, J. (1977) "The distribution of lifetime earnings." *Oxford Economic Papers* 29, 412–29.

Dalton, H. (1920) *The Inequality of Incomes*. Routledge, London.

Danziger, S., and Taussig, M. K. (1979) "The income unit and the anatomy of income distribution." *Review of Income and Wealth* 25, 365–75.

Dasgupta, P., Sen, A., and Starrett, D. (1973) "Notes on the measurement of inequality." *Journal of Economic Theory* 6, 180–87.

Deaton, A. S., and Muellbauer, J. (1980) *Economics and Consumer Behaviour*. Cambridge: Cambridge University Press.

Fields, G. S., and Fei, J. C. H. (1978) "On inequality comparisons." *Econometrica* 46, 303–16.

Fisher, F. M. (1987) "Household equivalence scales and interpersonal comparisons." *Review of Economic Studies* 54, 519–24.

Foster, J. E. (1985) "Inequality measurement." In H. P. Young, ed. *Fair Allocation*. Proceedings of Symposia in Applied Mathematics, volume 33, American Mathematical Society.

Gastwirth, J. L. (1972) "The estimation of the Lorenz Curve and Gini index." *Review of Economics and Statistics* 54, 306–16.

Irvine, I. J. (1981) "The use of cross-section microdata in lifecycle models: An application to inequality theory in nonstationary economies." *Quarterly Journal of Economics* 96, 301–16.

Jenkins, S. P. (1988) "Calculating income distribution indices from micro-data." *National Tax Journal* 41, 139–42.

Kolm, S. C. (1969) "The optimal production of social justice." In J. Margolis and H. Guitton, eds. *Public Economics*. London and New York: Macmillan.

————. (1976) "Unequal inequalities I and II." *Journal of Economic Theory* 12, 416–42 and 13, 82–111.

Lambert, P. J. (1989) *The Distribution and Redistribution of Income: A Mathematical Analysis*. Oxford: Basil Blackwell.

Morgan, J. N.; David, M. H.; Cohen, W. J.; and Brazer, H. E. (1962) *Income and Welfare in the United States*. New York: McGraw-Hill.

Musgrave, R. A. (1987) "Short of Euphoria" *Journal of Economic Perspectives* 1, 59–71.

Nygård, F., and Sandström, A. (1981) *Measuring Income Inequality*. Stockholm: Almquist and Wicksell International.

Okun, A. M. (1975) *Equality and Efficiency: The Big Tradeoff*. Washington, DC: The Brookings Institution.

Paglin, M. (1975) "The measurement and trend of inequality: a basic revision." *American Economic Review* 65, 598–609.

Pechman, J. A. (1987) "Tax reform: theory and practice." *Journal of Economic Perspectives* 1, 11–28.

Pen, J. (1971) *Income Distribution: Facts, Theories, and Policies*. New York: Praeger.

Pollak, R. A., and Wales, T. J. (1979) "Welfare comparisons and equivalence scales" *American Economic Review* 69 (Papers and Proceedings), 216–21.

Sen, A. K. (1973) *On Economic Inequality*. Oxford: Oxford University Press.

Shorrocks, A. F. (1978) "Income inequality and income mobility" *Journal of Economic Theory* 19, 376–93.

———. (1980) "The class of additively decomposable income inequality measures." *Econometrica* 48, 613–25.

———. (1982) "Inequality decomposition by factor components." *Econometrica* 50, 193–211.

———. (1983) "Ranking income distributions." *Economica* 50, 3–17.

———. (1984) "Inequality decomposition by population subgroups." *Econometrica* 52, 1369–86.

Shorrocks, A. F., and Foster, J. E. (1987) "Transfer sensitive inequality measures." *Review of Economic Studies* 54, 485–97.

Theil, H. (1967) *Economics and Information Theory*. Amsterdam: North-Holland.

2

Cross-National Comparisons of Inequality and Poverty Position

Timothy M. Smeeding

1. Introduction

The distribution of income, or of economic well-being, between rich and poor, and the relative position of various groups (elderly, children) in the income size distribution has been an important economic and policy issue for quite some time (e.g., Atkinson 1975; Champernowne 1973). Most of the interest in this issue has focused on the lower end of the distribution—on the poverty problem (Rowntree 1901), and most of the research has been confined to studies of poverty within a particular country (Johannson 1973; Townsend 1979; Atkinson 1985; Danziger and Weinberg 1987; Harrington 1963).

Studies of income inequality and poverty have largely remained country specific for one basic reason: lack of comparable cross-national household income microdata. There has been increasing interest in comparing the size distribution of income and characteristics of the low-income population in different countries, with the long-range goal of studying the interrelations between national political and economic systems and problems of low income (Sawyer 1976; Beckerman 1979; Hauser and Nouvertne 1980; Commission of the European Economic Community 1981), but this interest has been frustrated by the necessity to work with inferior data sources and noncomparable tabulations which the researcher cannot control. For instance, most comparisons of the distribution and redistribution of income across countries have had to rely on already-published data, a procedure which has a range of readily apparent weaknesses. Such data

The author thanks the Alfred P. Sloan Foundation, National Science Foundation, and the National Institute for Aging for their financial support, the LIS country sponsors for financial support and use of their data, Lars Osberg and Lee Rainwater for comments, and Brigitte Buhmann, Ryan Smeeding, and John Coder for their assistance with data preparation. All errors of omission, commission, theory, and fact are assumed by the author.

are presented in demographic or geographic groups which may vary from country to country, and which may differ from the groupings which might be desired by a particular researcher. A given choice of income concept (disposable vs. gross income) and of income unit (family individual) may be similarly variable and unsuitable, but predetermined by historical precedent or national agency convention. Moreover, the issues of how to rank incomes and how to weight both income and the income unit do make a difference, because different weights and rankings give different summary measures of inequality but are rarely mentioned (Danziger and Taussig 1979). The restrictions imposed by prestructured data both distort empirical comparisons and render methodological discussion almost futile. Such discussion is, therefore, often neglected. At most, methodological issues tend to be raised as apologetic caveats rather than in the context of analytical choices (O'Higgins, Stephenson, and Schmaus 1988). Even very recent comparative poverty studies have experienced much this same sort of result (Roome 1987).

A key issue then, is the comparability of statistical resources on which cross-national policy studies can be based. The social-science disciplines by their nature rely on inferences drawn from representative population samples (or reports from government statistical and analytical offices which collect such samples). The comparability (or lack thereof) of these data is an important precursor of meaningful analytic cross-national comparisons. This quality varies by the type of data collected, method by which they are collected, and by how they are adjusted for sampling and nonsampling error once collected.

As researchers have begun to be interested in these issues, limited international comparisons using microdata have begun to emerge. Usually two or three researchers derive comparable measures (by exactly specifying certain tabulations ex ante, based on similar income-sharing units, income concepts, rankings, etc.). On the basis of such separately gathered data, joint analyses have then been carried out (see, for example, Smolensky, Pommerehne, and Dalrymple 1979; O'Higgins and Ruggles 1981; Ruggles and O'Higgins 1981; Rainwater, Rein, and Schwartz 1987).

Most recently, the rapidly evolving technology of computerized data banks has provided a challenging opportunity to assemble multinational data bases that provide a common foundation upon which teams of social scientists can build truly long-term, comparative international research programs. These data bases provide the opportunity to define a range of theoretical and substantive problems and to combine analyses of data from different countries into a single paper or book. This is in fact what the Luxembourg Income Study (LIS), upon which this paper is based, is designed to accomplish.

The primary purpose of this paper is to illustrate the usefulness of a database such as LIS for cross-national comparisons of inequality and poverty. Because cross national comparative research is still in its infancy, the possibilities and horizons opened by LIS have only begun to be explored. The appendix to this paper provides the nuts and bolts of LIS: its basic structural elements and design. Section 2 begins to demonstrate the flexibility of LIS by setting the stage for comparisons of several measures of inequality, poverty and relative income position across the ten countries which comprise the LIS database. Choices of income accounting units, income concept, adjustment for family size, inequality measures, etc. are made from alternative possibilities in this section of the paper. Sections 3 and 4 present the results, while the final section (5) summarizes the paper and suggests additional analyses to investigate several of the unresolved issues which have emerged from this brief study.

2. Choices of Perspective: Inequality, Poverty and Relative Position

We intend to illustrate the usefulness of cross-national comparisons using LIS topics:

1. cross-national ranking of household income inequality,
2. cross-national poverty rates, and
3. relative position (level of living) of certain key demographic groups within the income distribution.

To begin this analysis, however, we need to specify the basic elements which go into any cross-sectional analysis of inequality and poverty: the unit of analysis, period to be studied, and measure of income. Only the period to be studied is given by the data: 1979–83. Because of our reliance on relative measure of income, we are not particularly concerned with the exogenous effect of differences in years across our datasets on the results of these analyses. Still readers should be apprised that one of the LIS datasets (the Netherlands) was collected at the trough of the 1982–84 recession, a factor which may independently affect the results.[1]

Because of the availability of the LIS microdata, researchers are allowed a wide degree of breadth in selecting measures of income, demographic units of aggregation, and perspectives for comparison across and within countries. The unit of aggregation chosen here is the family—all persons living together and related by blood, marriage, or adoption. Within LIS all countries have data on the conventional family (as defined above) with little variation.[2] In this paper we have selected both disposable family income (DPI) and DPI adjusted by an adult equivalence scale (ADPI) as our measures of economic well-being. DPI includes all forms of cash and near-cash income including earnings, realized capital income, and government transfers, net of income and payroll taxes.[3] This is the most commonly accepted measure of net ability to consume goods and services.

ADPI makes allowance for the differential needs of different size families by using the median value of the equivalence scale implicit in the poverty lines of eight of the ten countries studied to adjust disposable income for family size.[4] This adjustment is made by dividing the income of a given size unit by the relative number of equivalent adults normalized to a family of size of three. That is, adjusted disposable income (ADPI) is measured by dividing disposable income (DPI) of a given size family by an equivalence factor, where the factor is measured by the family size (S) raised to the power e, where e is the elasticity of need:

$$ADPI = DPI/S^e$$

The equivalence factor, e, varies between 0 and 1. The larger the e, the smaller the economies of scale assumed by the equivalence scale. For this paper, the equivalence scale we have selected has an $e = 0.55$. Hence, a childless couple's income is divided by 0.80, a couple with one child (or a single parent with two children) has its disposable income divided by 1.0, and a family of four by 1.17, five by 1.32, etc.[5] Finally, families are weighted by the number of persons per family (i.e., using person, not family unit weights), the theoretically preferred scheme (Danziger and Taussig 1979).[6]

Inequality. We measure inequality with three well-known and widely used measures:

1. the Atkinson inequality index, with $\varepsilon = 0.5$,[7]
2. the Gini coefficient, and
3. the Theil inequality index.

These all belong to the group of relative inequality measures, and are therefore not sensitive to relative changes in the income scale. But, as indicated by Atkinson (1970) (1975) and Sen (1973), they all imply some a priori value judgments about the distribution itself. For instance, the Atkinson index is sensitive to inequality changes in the lowest part of the income distribution; the Gini coefficient is sensitive to inequality changes around the median; and the Theil index and coefficient of variation are sensitive to changes at the top part of the income distribution (see chapter 1). We present estimates for both DPI and ADPI so that the effect of the equivalence adjustment on inequality patterns and rank order can be estimated.[8]

According to these sensitivities (and hence the implied value judgments), the chosen inequality measures do not all indicate the same inequality difference between two distributions. As long as the Lorenz curves of the distributions do not intersect, they all provide the same qualitative indicator of the direction of inequality change (i.e., increased or decreased). But in the case of crossing Lorenz curves, these one-dimensional measures can even differ in their inferences about the direction of the change in inequality between two distributions. This quasi ordering characteristic of inequality (Sen 1973) produces the result that all statements about inequality differences, measured by one-dimensional indices, have to be confirmed by a test of nonintersecting Lorenz curves.

Relative Economic Status. The second set of results presents estimates of the relative economic status of families with children across the ten LIS countries. Ranking families by the ADPI concept to find the median family, we have divided the population according to the cumulative percent of persons living in families below or above given fractions of median income in each country. We have selected for fractions of median income to represent various levels of living, and have constructed a table which presents estimates for ten groupings of persons in families: all persons in families; five nonelderly groups with heads below age 65 (single persons, childless couples, couples with one child, couples with two or more children, and single parents living with their children)[9]; and four groups of the elderly (heads age 65 or older, married couples with head age 65–74, those with the head 75 or older, and single persons living alone—again 65–74, and 75 or older). These groups were chosen because of widespread policy concern over the economic status of dependent groups in society, i.e., children (and families with children, especially single mothers) and the elderly (particularly elderly single women living alone) (Palmer, Smeeding, and Torrey 1988).

The four levels of living which we have chosen to focus on are as follows:

1. "poor" (adjusted incomes below 0.5 times median income),

2. "near poverty" (adjusted incomes between 0.5 and 0.625 times median income),

3. "middle class" (adjusted incomes between 0.625 and 1.5 times median income),

4. "well-to-do" (adjusted incomes above 1.5 times median income).

The most sensitive policy concern when dealing with the well-being of dependent populations is their degree of economic deprivation or poverty status, and to measure poverty we must specify a poverty line. For the detailed analysis which follows we will define poverty lines as equal to one half of the median ADPI measure. This is a commonly accepted definition of poverty (or low income) and imposes no one country's selected level of poverty on any other one (Bronfenbrenner 1972; Buhmann et al. 1988).

We also selected a near-poverty level to highlight the economically insecure populations who are close to poverty status. Research on the economically insecure elderly in the United States and elsewhere has shown this group to be both quantitatively large and heavily dependent on social retirement income (Smeeding and Torrey 1987; Smeeding, Torrey, and Rein 1988). To the extent that the budgetary pressures of an aging society might lead a government to cut back on the real level of social retirement benefits, large numbers of near-poor units might be pushed into poverty. Similarly, near-poor families with children may be pushed into poverty during economic downturns due to the skewed distribution of the incidence and duration of unemployment coupled with an inadequate social protection system. Hence, the near poor are an important group as well.

The middle-class and well-to-do income levels are designed to show where the population that is neither poor nor at risk of becoming poor is situated in the income spectrum. These categories are important to the budgetary realities of a modern welfare state because growing demands on public entitlements may require either increased taxes or benefit reductions. To the extent that any particular family type, including children and the elderly, are relatively well-to-do, benefit reductions and/or increased taxation among this group might be justified in order to maintain support among those least well off.

The series of inequality results are presented, in section 3, and summarized in Table 2.1. Next, in section 4, the poverty and relative economic position issues are discussed in turn, the numerical results being combined in one table (Table 2.2) which shows all four levels of living.

3. Results: Overall Inequality

We first look at one-dimensional measures of inequality across the ten countries using the different inequality measures and both DPI and ADPI. Table 1 uses the Atkinson index ($\varepsilon = 0.5$), the Gini coefficient, and the Theil index to generate the rank ordering (RO) of each country by each measure, including medians of the RO itself. The overall average level of inequality for each measure is calculated as the simple country mean of the estimates.

According to the Atkinson index, DPI has the highest degree of inequality in the United States, followed by Australia, Canada, and the Netherlands (Panel A). The most equally distributed DPI are found in Sweden and in Norway. Comparing this ranking with other inequality measures, the rank order of countries using DPI remains remarkably stable. The countries are presented according to their median rank order, with the most unequal, geographically larger, more politically and economically diverse, and "newer" countries (United States, Australia, and Canada) at the top and with the Scandinavian countries showing the lowest degree of inequality at the bottom. The other European countries and Israel fall between these extremes. These country rankings are correlated with overall social expenditures as a percent of GDP in 1980, with Australia, Canada, and the United States spending 20 percent on average, European countries spending 26 percent, and Norway and Sweden 30 percent (OECD 1985).

Turning to the ADPI estimates in Panel B, we first note how the equivalence adjustment reduces the overall average (simple mean) level of inequality for each inequality measure. Comparing each country score based on ADPI in Panel B with its DPI score in Panel A, we find that the adjusted distribution is less unequal than the unadjusted distribution in every case, except for Israel. But the rank ordering of countries changes somewhat when going from DPI to ADPI. The United States still has the highest degree of overall inequality, but the Netherlands and Israel have joined Australia and Canada among the most unequal countries. As can be clearly seen by comparing the RO for each ADPI measure, the rankings are not so clearcut or consistent as are those in Panel A.

Several factors may account for these differences. First, Israel has by far the largest family size of all countries. Because of this, the equivalence scales used

Table 2.1

Inequality Measures (×1000) for Disposable Income (DPI) and Adjusted Disposable Income (ADPI) and Rank Order (RO) for Each Measure

Country	Atkinson 0.5 (RO)	Gini (RO)	Theil (RO)	Median (RO)
Panel A: DPI				
United States	99(1)	330(1)	182(1)	(1)
Australia	87(2)	314(2)	165(2)	(2)
Canada	83(3)	306(3)	157(4)	(3)
Netherlands	82(4)	303(4)	159(3)	(4)
Switzerland	79(5)	292(6)	154(5)	(5)
United Kingdom	78(6)	303(4)	153(6)	(6)
Israel	71(7)	292(6)	142(7)	(7)
Germany	66(8)	280(8)	134(8)	(8)
Norway	60(9)	255(10)	114(9)	(9)
Sweden	69(9)	264(9)	114(9)	(10)
Simple Mean	77	294	147	
Panel B: ADPI				
United States	90(1)	315(1)	167(1)	(1)
Netherlands	80(2)	291(3)	153(3)	(2)
Australia	75(4)	292(2)	142(4)	(3)
Israel	76(3)	276(5)	158(2)	(4)
Canada	73(5)	290(4)	141(5)	(5)
Switzerland	70(6)	275(6)	140(6)	(6)
United Kingdom	61(7)	275(6)	124(7)	(7)
Germany	52(8)	249(8)	108(8)	(8)
Norway	44(9)	222(9)	85(9)	(9)
Sweden	36(10)	197(10)	67(10)	(10)
Simple Mean	66	268	129	

Source: LIS database.
Method: Each inequality measure was applied to each country's DPI or ADPI to arrive at an inequality score. The scores were multiplied by 1,000 and ranked from highest (1) to lowest (10).

to calculate ADPI have a larger effect on DPI in Israel relative to other countries. The larger the size (S) the larger the adjustment (S^e), and so large families will artificially depress ADPI relative to DPI. Such an adjustment might particularly affect higher income large families if income and family size are positively correlated. In fact, according to the sensitivity characteristics of these separate indices, one can deduce that the distribution of adjusted income in Israel is relatively unequal in the upper ranges (where the Theil index is second highest) compared to the lower and middle ranges (where the ADPI based Atkinson and Gini scores for Israel rank it 3 and 5, respectively). Of course, because of the change in the rank order for Israel, the ranks of the other countries are also slightly affected by these measures.

A second and different problem may be affecting the Netherlands, whose ADPI ranking is second as compared to fourth using DPI. The year for which we have Netherlands data is 1983—a recession year. At the trough of the business cycle, greater than normal or expected inequality will be experienced and thus both the DPI and ADPI based estimates in Table 2.2 probably overstate the normal level of inequality found in the Netherlands.

Finally, while ranking is useful, it may still obscure the absolute differences between countries. For instance, using the Gini coefficient and ADPI, the United States has clearly the most unequal distribution. But the next three countries (Australia, Canada, and the Netherlands) are very close together indicating that the rank orders are virtually the same. Similarly, the ADPI based Atkinson scores for Australia, Canada, and Israel vary only from 73 to 76.

In general, Canada and Australia tend to have very similar income distributions which are more unequal than average, but not so skewed as that of the United States. Both Canada and Australia have more fully developed their welfare states under the influence of their British heritage than did the United States. Both have active socialist political parties, universal child allowances, national health insurance, and other social equality policies which are not yet present in the United States. But still they are at a lesser level of welfare state development than the United Kingdom and the other European, especially Scandinavian countries.

Even given these anomalies, we conclude that the most equally distributed incomes are found in Sweden and in Norway, followed by Germany, the United Kingdom, and Switzerland. In addition to the fact that these countries tax and redistributively spend a greater proportion of national income than do the others, they tend to have more equal distributions of wages and earnings among the adult workers in their countries as well.

Despite these interesting patterns, one-dimensional measure of inequality can often obscure important differences among population subgroups in society, particularly when the Lorenz curves intersect (which is indeed the case for several of the countries examined). Thus we can make few conclusive statements about relative levels of inequality across countries. In order to more fully examine these issues we need to go "inside" the Lorenz curve and the one-dimensional summary statistics of Table 2.1. We now turn to such an examination.

4. Results: Poverty and Relative Levels of Living

A more complete picture of the relative economic circumstances of various types of families emerges from Table 2.2, where we separate families by type and by level of living. We begin our analysis by comparing poverty (Panel A) and near poverty (Panel B) status across groups and countries, moving finally to the middle (Panel C) and well-to-do (Panel D) levels of living.

Poverty and Near Poverty. Large differences in relative poverty status (persons in families with incomes below half of the median ADPI) emerge across groups and among countries in Panel A of Table 2.2. Because of the widely differing tax and transfer policies in these ten countries, differences across countries should come as no surprise to those who have studied cross-national social policy. But the differences in group poverty rates within countries should surprise most analysts.

With respect to overall poverty in general, and child poverty in particular, the countries fall into roughly four groups: The Scandinavians (Norway, Sweden) and Germany with the lowest poverty rates, near 5 percent overall, and lower for persons in two parent (couple) families with children. These are followed by the Swiss and Dutch in the 8 percent range but still below the overall average rate of 10.1 percent. Slightly above average are the third group: The Canadians, Israelis, Australians, and the United Kingdom, all in the 11–13 percent range. The United States has by far the highest overall rate at 16.6 percent.

In all countries, childless couples and couples with children have below average poverty rates. In fact, if we only look at couples with children, the United Kingdom joins the below average group while the Dutch move closer to the group average. In families with two or more children, three countries have double digit poverty rates, with the United States again highest, but more closely followed by Canada and Australia than in the overall figures. Again, consistent with previous descriptions, countries with large geographic boundaries and with diverse economic conditions across the fiscal subjurisdictions of those boundaries (e.g., United States, Canada, Australia) are more likely to have high poverty rates than smaller, more homogeneous countries like those in Scandinavia and Western Europe.

In general, and as expected, persons in single parent families with children have relative poverty rates which are at least twice as high and up to eight to ten times as high, as persons living in married couple families. On average, 28.6 percent of persons in single parent families are poor, compared to rates of less than 7 percent for two parent families with two or more children. While single parenthood creates a severe economic burden on the persons involved, and while these families are poorer than other families with children, some countries cope better with poverty and single parenthood than do others. For instance, consider the United States, Canada, and Australia with single parent rates near or above 50 percent. They do measurably less well than the Netherlands, United Kingdom, Israel, or Switzerland which are below average but still in the 20–30 percent range. The Scandinavian countries and Germany do best, with rates below 10 percent. This result is in large part due to differences in the social protection systems and in the labor force behavior of single parents across these

Table 2.2

Relative Economic Position of Persons Living in Various Demographic Groups^a

| | Total | | | Nonelderly^j | | | Elderly^j | | | |
| | | | | Couples^e | | | Couples^e | | Single persons | |
	All persons^b	Single persons^c	Lone parent with children^d	0 child	2 child	2+ children	65–74	75+	65–74	75+
A. Poor^f										
United States	16.6	19.6	54.0	3.9	6.1	12.1	15.0	22.5	39.6	43.4
Australia	11.4	17.8	55.4	2.3	6.9	10.3	7.3	3.5	30.1	35.4
Canada	12.3	19.9	46.3	3.9	5.7	11.5	12.0	9.4	32.0	40.1
Netherlands	7.5	18.6	21.0	0.9	3.2	3.7	2.3	3.9	2.0	7.1
Switzerland	8.2	15.1	21.2	1.9	2.1	6.0	4.0	6.8	16.9	23.9
United Kingdom	11.7	12.6	29.3	1.1	2.5	7.5	23.6	32.1	51.5	59.7
Israel	11.0	9.3	22.6	2.6	2.6	9.8	13.2	24.1	23.4	35.1
Germany	4.9	9.9	7.2	1.4	1.1	1.3	8.6	11.0	12.9	22.4
Sweden	5.0	14.0	9.8	2.3	2.5	4.6	0.6	0.0	0.9	1.3
Norway	4.8	12.9	8.1	1.7	2.0	1.9	2.9	5.8	4.9	11.3
Average^k	9.4	15.4	28.6	2.2	3.6	6.7	8.9	11.6	21.4	28.0
B. Near Poor^g										
United States	7.6	7.4	13.0	3.1	6.3	9.0	9.2	12.5	15.8	19.1
Australia	9.8	6.4	10.1	2.7	4.6	9.2	24.7	33.5	41.0	39.9
Canada	8.7	8.4	12.7	2.5	5.7	9.0	12.5	26.7	24.9	28.9
Netherlands	6.7	3.3	23.5	0.7	4.7	10.6	4.6	3.7	1.2	0.7
Switzerland	7.7	8.1	14.1	1.6	4.6	10.2	10.1	14.8	12.5	21.1
United Kingdom	9.7	6.7	14.8	1.0	5.8	10.0	19.1	22.3	26.4	30.0
Israel	10.6	9.1	15.1	3.5	3.6	7.0	12.1	20.0	21.0	26.1
Germany	7.7	8.6	5.7	0.1	3.7	10.6	9.2	16.5	16.7	17.2
Sweden	5.5	5.6	9.4	1.4	3.7	3.5	3.5	6.7	7.4	30.4
Norway	8.4	9.4	9.2	1.3	2.0	1.9	11.3	21.0	31.7	47.2
Average^k	8.2	7.2	12.5	1.8	4.5	8.0	11.7	17.8	19.8	26.1

C. Middle Class[h]

United States	53.7	48.0	31.2	44.2	63.8	66.7	55.4	52.0	36.6	31.2
Australia	56.0	48.7	31.1	33.4	66.7	71.9	53.3	50.7	23.4	21.5
Canada	58.5	47.3	39.1	44.7	68.7	70.1	57.6	55.0	31.3	24.9
Netherlands	62.5	51.0	45.1	37.5	74.2	75.1	50.3	56.4	78.4	77.3
Switzerland	67.2	56.2	53.2	55.7	76.6	76.4	63.5	58.3	58.6	45.4
United Kingdom	58.5	55.7	47.8	43.9	75.5	74.7	47.7	40.1	19.9	8.4
Israel	54.2	43.4	59.2	42.8	69.4	66.0	55.7	43.3	49.8	32.4
Germany	70.1	57.1	77.8	55.4	83.7	79.2	60.9	53.3	35.5	52.5
Sweden	79.0	75.7	79.7	55.9	70.6	85.7	89.9	91.8	90.3	67.9
Norway	73.4	59.9	74.5	37.6	76.4	88.3	69.2	68.4	56.2	38.8
Average[k]	62.8	54.3	53.9	45.0	72.6	75.4	60.3	57.0	48.0	40.0

D. Well-to-Do[i]

United States	22.1	25.0	1.8	48.8	23.9	12.2	20.4	13.0	8.8	6.2
Australia	22.6	27.1	3.3	61.6	21.9	8.7	14.6	12.3	5.4	3.2
Canada	20.6	24.4	1.9	48.9	19.9	9.4	17.9	8.8	11.8	6.1
Netherlands	23.3	27.1	10.4	60.9	17.9	10.6	22.9	21.7	18.4	14.9
Switzerland	16.9	20.6	12.4	40.8	16.7	7.4	22.4	20.1	12.0	9.6
United Kingdom	20.2	25.0	8.0	54.0	16.3	7.8	9.5	5.5	19.9	8.4
Israel	24.2	38.2	3.1	51.1	24.4	17.2	19.0	12.6	5.8	6.4
Germany	17.3	24.4	14.3	43.2	11.5	8.9	21.2	19.1	4.8	7.8
Sweden	10.5	4.7	1.1	40.4	15.2	6.3	6.0	1.5	1.4	0.4
Norway	13.4	17.8	8.2	59.4	19.6	7.9	16.6	4.9	7.2	2.7
Average[k]	19.4	23.4	6.4	50.9	18.8	9.7	17.0	12.0	9.5	6.6

a Table ranks all persons in families by adjusted family incomes according to family type.
b All persons includes all persons in families.
c Single persons living alone under age 64.
d Lone parent includes children living in families with one adult under age 65 and no other adults in the household.
e Couples include married couple households with both spouses present and unmarried couples living together as married in Sweden, Norway, and the Netherlands.
f Poor are persons in families with adjusted incomes below 0.5 median adjusted income.
g Near poor are persons in families with adjusted incomes between 0.5 and 0.625 median adjusted income.
h Middle class are persons in families with adjusted incomes between 0.626 and 1.5 times median adjusted income.
i Well-to-do are persons in families with adjusted incomes above 1.5 times the median.
j Nonelderly are families headed by a person age 64 or younger; elderly heads are 65 or older.
k Average is simple mean of each column.

countries. The highest earnings among single parents occur in countries which rely least heavily on means-tested income transfers (Smeeding and Torrey 1988).

As compared to the other groups, it is much harder to characterize the elderly. On average (bottom line of Panel A), older couples have lower average poverty rates than do single elderly persons living alone. And the younger elderly, whether couples or singles, have lower rates than do the oldest. Moreover, single elderly alone have much higher than overall average poverty rates, while couples of all ages are closer to average. But these relationships do not hold in all countries. For instance, both aged couples and singles have above-average rates of poverty in Israel and Britain, but below-average rates in the Netherlands and Sweden. The United Kingdom rises from a below-average poverty situation for families with children to the highest poverty rates for both types of older units, particularly for the single elderly living alone.

Looking across nonelderly family types more closely, the decision to have one child (as opposed to none) appears to only slightly increase the poverty rate for couples, from 2.2 to 3.6 percent on average. Families which then have additional children find that their chances of poverty increase to 6.7 percent. Explanations for poverty among large families are numerous. Among married couple families with children, economic conditions in labor markets, i.e., unemployment, relative wage levels, and the like, are liable to influence low income as much as, or more than, tax and transfer policy. While the availability and generosity of family allowances and child tax credits have some effect on the extent of poverty among children, they are not so important as are these other factors (Smeeding, Torrey, and Rein 1988). One major factor to consider is labor force participation. The earnings levels of married women in LIS drop precipitously in virtually all countries when two or more children are present, hence reducing family money income. While we have no evidence on trends in husband vs. family earnings in other countries, Levy (1987) has recently documented the falling relative wages of husbands and the necessity of having two earner families to maintain a middle class standard of living in the United States. The figures in Table 2.2 suggest that such a pattern may extend to poverty and near poverty as well in the United States. Countries with stronger union involvement, countries which may be said to be more concerned with the "family wage" and hence having more equal wage structures (e.g., Germany and Scandinavia) tend to have the lowest poverty rates among larger families.

A key factor in predicting poverty rates for all family types is the depth and breadth of the social insurance and income transfer systems. For instance, the only country studied which does not have a child allowance (or child tax credit) as a part of their social policy system is the United States. Among poor families with children, the United States has the lowest level of overall benefits per poor family and the lowest percentage of families receiving social insurance transfers such as unemployment compensation. Thus the high U.S. poverty rates for children observed earlier can in large part be attributed to low levels of transfers

(Smeeding and Torrey 1988). Turning to the elderly, the relative and absolute generosity of a country's social insurance system is a key factor in explaining poverty, particularly among older (75+) single elderly living alone. Over 70 percent of this category are very elderly widows who depend heavily on social retirement income (Smeeding and Torrey 1987). While elderly couples tend to be younger and have a wider mix of income sources (including earnings, property income and occupational pensions), levels of social retirement benefits are the key to explaining the relative position of single older women. In countries with high minimum benefits in their social retirement systems, e.g., Sweden, Norway, and the Netherlands, elderly widows are much less likely to be poor than in countries with less generous minimum social retirement benefits, e.g., the United Kingdom, or those with heavily earnings related benefit structures, e.g., Canada or the United States (Smeeding and Torrey 1987; Smeeding, Torrey, and Rein 1988).

The topic of generational equity (Preston 1984; Palmer, Smeeding, and Torrey 1988) suggests that we compare relative poverty rates of the old to the young. However, the poverty figures in Table 2.2, and other analyses, indicate that the least well off groups cannot be categorized as young or old: children in single parent families among the young, and elderly women among the old are more likely to be relatively poor and/or disadvantaged than are other groups. For instance, both have overall average poverty rates of 28 percent. Thus instead of young vs. old, perhaps we should characterize the dichotomy as one of women (young and old) vs. men (young and old).

The second panel (B) of Table 2.2 indicates the percentage of persons who live in families with ADPI which are not quite at poverty levels, but are within 25 percent of the poverty line. The overall average figures in the bottom row indicate that there are actually more elderly near poor couples than poor couples, and nearly as many near poor single elderly as poor single elderly. As with their poor counterparts, these people rely heavily on social transfer income to avoid poverty. In the United States for instance, the near poor elderly have money incomes which are three quarters or more social retirement (U.S. House Ways and Means Committee 1988). Similarly, larger fractions of couples with children are found among the near poor than among the poor. While a much larger fraction of lone parents are poor than are near poor, this group is overrepresented among the near poor as well. These estimates should underline our caution regarding the sensitivity of poverty levels to the point where the poverty line is drawn. On average the near poor (8.2 percent) are almost as large a group as are the poor (9.4 percent).

If we compare the overall inequality rankings in Table 2.1 with the all-person poor and near poor groupings in Table 2, the country rankings are in rough correspondence. The United States, Australia, and Canada are above average, the Scandinavian countries are below average. The remaining countries are more difficult to categorize. For instance, the Netherlands has below average poverty (and near poverty) rates, but ranks fourth highest in terms of overall inequality. Hence, it is possible for a country to have high inequality *and* an effective safety net for prevention of poverty. Israel is just the opposite: relatively high poverty and low overall inequality.

Of course, looking beyond the overall averages and focusing on groups of individuals allows us to identify policy-relevant concentrations of poverty and near poverty which can be addressed by public policy makers. Thus cross-national data analyses such as those evident in Table 2.2 allow the investigator to compare groups across countries and to highlight significant similarities, such as the relatively high poverty and near poverty rates of single elderly women and single parents; and also significant differences, such as elderly poverty in the United Kingdom and child poverty in the United States.

Middle Class and Well-to-Do. While one must take careful note of the variance in poverty rates across family types and countries and their explanation, cross-national patterns of living standards for various family types classified as middle class (Panel C) and well-to-do (Panel D) seem to be more consistent, with a much smaller range across countries. For instance, all countries have at least 54 percent of their populations classified as middle class according to our ADPI rankings, with an overall cross-country average of 63 percent. If we exclude single elderly persons and childless couples, all groups average at least 50 percent of their members among the middle class. The percent of the population classified as middle class is below 50 for the single elderly because of their overrepresentation among the poor and near poor (Panels A, B) and for childless couples because of their overrepresentation among the well-to-do (Panel D).

On average the most heavily represented middle class group, but (excluding single parents and single elderly) the least heavily represented well-to-do group, are two-parent families with a large number of children. This finding is most interesting and may provide an explanation for the declining birth rates among majority families in all western nations. On average more than half of all childless couples (50.9 percent, to be exact) are well-to-do as measured by ADPI. This is at least twice as high a fraction as for any other group (younger single persons are next with 23.4 percent well-to-do), perhaps because of double-earner-no-kids families who are either young ("yuppies") or perhaps later middle aged ("empty nest").

Perhaps most apparent and surprising, however, is the cost of having large families. As expected, single parents have a very small chance of being well-to-do, less than 7 percent, on an ADPI basis. Only in the European countries (Switzerland, Germany, the Netherlands), where child support and alimony payments are both high and strictly enforced do we find a figure above 10 percent (Smeeding, Torrey, and Rein 1988). For couples with children, the average odds of being well-to-do fall from 51 to 19 percent with one child and all the way to 10 percent if two or more children are present. Again the pattern is continuous and consistent across each of the countries studied. Excluding the outliers—

Israel, due to its high birth rate and relatively high child subsidies, an anomalous country to begin with; and Sweden, where equality is the norm—the percentage of large two parent families which are well-to-do varies only from 7.4 to 12.2 percent across the remaining eight countries. While larger two parent families were much more likely to be poor or near poor than were smaller families (Panels A, B), they were still below the comparable rates of most other groups in society.

Hence, we conclude that while having two or more children does not seem to push traditional two parent families into poverty in the countries examined, it severely reduces one's ability to live in relative affluence in modern societies such as those studied here.

In contrast, elderly couples are on average more likely to be affluent than are large families. The proportion of younger elderly couples who are well-to-do looks much like the overall average figures for a society, except for Sweden and Britain where heavy reliance on relatively flat social retirement pensions and low property incomes tend to depress inequality at the upper end of the distribution. In every country studied, except Sweden, 65–74 year old elderly couples were more likely to be affluent than were larger two parent families. Elderly couples (both the younger and older groups among them) are also well entrenched in the middle classes of most countries. Excluding the United Kingdom and very elderly Israeli couples, between 50 and 90 percent of elderly couples were found to have adjusted incomes in the middle class range. Moreover, elderly couples are among the highest wealth groups in society (Greenwood and Wolff 1988), further reinforcing the pattern of relative affluence found in Table 2.2. Whereas only thirty years ago the elderly were almost synonymous with the poor (Myles 1983), their climb to middle class and higher levels of living is perhaps the singular most impressive outcome of modern western private and social retirement systems over the past several decades.

Yet, before we pat ourselves on the back for the gains of the elderly couples, let us not forget the single elderly persons living alone. With the exception of the Netherlands, single elderly living alone are always less likely to be well-to-do or middle class than are elderly couples. The single elderly group are less likely to have earnings, occupational pensions and other income sources which elderly couples have. This consistent pattern of increased relative deprivation among single older persons, three out of four of whom are women, has led several countries to reexamine their survivor and widow social pension schemes in recent years (Gibson 1987).

5. Summary and Conclusion

This brief survey of inequality, poverty, and relative levels of well-being across countries has perhaps raised more questions than it has answered. One notable result is that delving beneath comparisons of simple one-dimensional measures of inequality such as those in Table 2.1 can be much more enriching and satisfying, particularly from a policy standpoint. Moreover, by focusing on different group levels of living (near poverty rates and higher levels of living) there was again an evident depth of understanding which would not be apparent if we only focused on overall country poverty rates. While some patterns were robust, e.g., greater inequality and poverty in large countries and below average inequality and poverty in Scandinavian nations, others were more tenuous and/or were found to have several exceptions.

As we explored the economic status of different groups as measured by their distribution across adjusted income levels within and across countries, some striking differences emerged. For instance:

—large differences in poverty and near poverty status emerge for children as compared to elderly as we moved from country to country,

—sex of family head emerges as much more likely than age or presence of children to be correlated with relative poverty and affluence,

—while having a large family does not carry with it a high chance of being poor or near poor in most countries, the income cost of having children, in terms of reduced chances to be well-to-do, is large in most countries.

But even these results call for additional explanation and analyses. While our investigation hinted at some of the causes, we were not able to systematically explore them in the space provided here. Additional study of the labor market institutions and income tax and transfer benefit structures is needed to fully understand the pattern of results in Table 2.2. In closing, we would like to urge other researchers to amplify these findings and to add to the rich harvest of cross-national understanding which LIS and related databases now make possible.

Appendix

Over the last fifteen years, social scientific use of household income survey data for economic policy analysis within both academia and government has increased dramatically. The capacity to describe the effects of existing policy and simulate the effects of changes in policy is well established in most modern nations, especially those with elaborate welfare states. Microsimulation models in individual countries provide policy makers with increasingly detailed analytic insights into the impacts of policy changes on participant behavior (labor supply, savings), on public budgets, and on family well-being (poverty status). However, while the techniques used in Canada, Germany, and the United States are similar, the analyses are almost always limited to one country. It seems reasonable that the next step in improving policy analysis comes from moving to a cross-national focus using comparable household income surveys in a number of countries. This is, in fact, the accomplishment of LIS, the Luxembourg Income Study. That is, LIS has assembled a databank of household income surveys that can be used by scholars and policy analysts to study the effects of different kinds of programs on poverty, income adequacy in retirement, and the distribution of economic well-being generally.

Under the sponsorship of the government of Luxembourg, the LIS experiment was begun in April 1983. The purpose of the project was to gather in one central location, the Center for Population, Poverty and Policy Studies (CEPS) in Walferdange, Luxembourg, sophisticated microdata sets which contain comprehensive measures of income and economic well-being for a set of modern industrialized welfare states. From its inception, LIS was to be a researcher-led project with a flexible nonbureaucratic administrative structure. Because of the breadth and flexibility afforded by microdata, researchers are free to make several choices of perspective (definition of unit, measure of income, population to be studied) within the same research project. This truly comparable international microdata creates a rich resource for economic and policy research.

As of January 1, 1989, the LIS data bank contained data sets from ten countries: Australia, Britain, Canada, Germany, Israel, the Netherlands, Norway, Sweden, Switzerland, and the United States. Table 2.A-1 gives an overview of these data sets by country, data-set name and size, income year, data sampling frame, and representativeness of the population.

The data base consists of annual household income microdata sets prepared according to a common plan, based on common definitions of income by source; taxes, by type; and family and household composition and characteristics. The forty-two income variable categories for each country allows the researcher to construct any of several separate definitions of income: factor or market income (including employment related fringe benefits, if desired); several sources of private and public income transfers; three types of pensions: social retirement (OASI), employment related pensions for private sector workers and for public sector workers; and a set of noncash income components. The several categories of transfer allow for detailed breakdown of means-tested benefits, employment related social insurance entitlements, and universal benefits such as child allowances. In most countries realized capital gains (realized lump-sum income) is also recorded. Finally, spouses' earnings and average annual wage rates—earnings divided by hours worked—are separately recorded as well.

The LIS dataset also contains a set of thirty demographic variables for each household or family unit, including several sources of separate information (age, education, occupation, industry work and disability status) for both spouses in married couple households. A "relatedness" variable allows the researcher to choose the "household" (all persons having the same living arrangements regardless of relatedness) or "family" (all related persons sharing the same unit) as the unit of analysis. Separate information on earnings for heads and spouses allows for separation of contributions of each to family income. Additional information on the basic rules used to construct the LIS data base is contained in Smeeding, Schmaus, and Allegrezza (1985).

Table 2.A-1

An Overview of LIS Datasets

Country	Dataset name, income year (and size[a])	Population coverage[c]	Basis of household sampling frame[h]
Australia	*Income and Housing Survey* 1981–82 (17,000)	97.5[d]	Dicennial census
Canada	*Survey of Consumer Finances* 1981 (37,900)	97.5[d]	Dicennial census
Germany	*Transfer Survey* 1981[b] (2,800)	91.5[g]	Electoral register and census
Israel	*Family Expenditure Survey* 1979 (2,300)	89.0[e]	Electoral register
Nether-lands	*Survey of Income & Program Users* 1983 (4,833)	99.2	Address register of the postal and telephone companies
Norway	*Norwegian Tax Files* 1979 (10,400)	98.5[d]	Tax records
Sweden	*Swedish Income Distribution Survey* 1981 (9,600)	98.0[d]	Population register
Switzer-land	*Income and Wealth Survey* 1982 (7,036)	95.5[i]	Electoral register and central register for foreigners
United Kingdom	*Family Expenditure Survey*[b] 1979 (6,800)	96.5[f]	Electoral register
United States	*Current Population Survey 1979 (65,000)*	97.5[d]	Dicennial census

[a] Dataset size is the number of actual household units surveyed.

[b] The U.K. and German surveys collect subannual income data which is normalized to annual income levels.

[c] As a percent of total national population.

[d] Excludes institutionalized and homeless populations. Also some far northern rural residents (Inuits, Eskimos, Laps, etc.) may be undersampled.

[e] Excludes rural population (those living in places of 2,000 or less), institutionalized, homeless, people in kibbutzim, and guest workers.

[f] Excludes those not on the electoral register, the homeless, and the institutionalized.

[g] Excludes foreign-born heads of households, the institutionalized, and the homeless.

[h] Sampling frame indicates the overall base from which the relevant household population sample was drawn. Actual sample may be drawn on a stratified probability basis, e.g., by area or age.

[i] Excludes nonresident foreigners but includes foreign residents and the institutionalized.

The LIS project and data set are permanently housed at the CEPS Center in Luxembourg. The data are stored on the government of Luxembourg's central computers, which are accessed via several computer terminals at CEPS under the strict rules of the government of Luxembourg's data access and privacy laws. Once research papers or reports are prepared from the LIS, the researcher is required to make the results available as a LIS-CEPS Working Paper. In this way we can document previous LIS research by those interested in furthering the use of our network and we can provide for a statistical review of results by LIS member-country central statistical offices. The first step in using LIS is to request the Information Guide (Coder, Rainwater, and Smeeding 1988) which provides a basic description of LIS and its many features and functions, from LIS at the following address: John Coder, LIS at CEPS/INSTEAD, B.P. #65, L-7201 Walferdange, Luxembourg.

Notes

1. Of the ten datasets comprising LIS, only three are not for either 1979 or 1981, i.e., the Netherlands (1983), Switzerland (1982). Readers who feel that relative poverty or inequality in these countries is strongly influenced by the business cycle or by secular or structural demographic trends, e.g., too high unemployment, may want to take this issue into account when evaluating the results presented below.

2. In the Netherlands, Norway and Sweden, unmarried adults age eighteen or over not living as married with someone of the opposite sex are counted as separate family units. Unmarried adults living together as married are counted as families. Thus an adult child or elderly parent living with a middle age couple would be counted as two separate units in Norway and Sweden, but as members of a larger family in the other countries. Further, a man and a woman who live together (cohabit) and share resources and living space are counted as married. In every LIS country researchers have attempted to define the family unit as the prime income and resource sharing or consumption unit. The LIS procedure is to begin with the natural resource sharing unit as defined by each country, but to provide the opportunity for the user to further aggregate (or disaggregate) these units into households (or individuals, primary families) wherever possible. The family unit as defined in the paper and as qualified here is the most common and consistent unit for comparing all ten current LIS countries.

3. Our income measure also includes a set of "near-cash" benefits: transfers which are nominally defined as in kind, but which have a cash equivalent value (Hicksian equivalent variation) equal to their market value. For instance, near-cash benefits include cash housing allowances in the United Kingdom and Sweden and food stamps in the United States. See Smeeding, Schmaus, and Allegrezza (1985) for additional detail.

4. These include all countries but Israel and Norway which do not have national estimates of poverty lines or low income cutoffs.

5. Other equivalence scales could be and have been used and the results shown below may be somewhat sensitive to this choice. The comparison of Panels A and B in Table 2.1 gives the reader some idea of the sensitivity of results to this choice. For more on this topic the reader should consult Buhmann et al. (1988).

6. Income ranks are also grouped according to the number of persons per unit so that, for instance, 20 percent of persons are found in the lowest quintile of the income distribution. The reason for these choices is as follows: the individual is the basic unit of analysis

in neoclassical welfare economics. If it is assumed that all persons share equally in household economic well-being, then a weighting scheme which counts the income of each person as a per capita share of household income—adjusted or not adjusted—has been shown to be preferred to a weighting scheme which counts each family or household as a separate unit regardless of the number of persons which it contains. Analysis based on this latter scheme would count families as the basic unit of analysis using family weighting and ranking by a scheme which had 20 percent of families in each quintile of the distribution. See Danziger and Taussig (1979) for an in depth analysis of this issue.

7. The Atkinson index is defined in Atkinson (1970).

8. See Buhmann et al. (1988) for a more complete discussion of this issue.

9. Of this group, 90 percent or more are mothers living alone with their children.

References

Atkinson, A.B. 1970. "On the Measurement of Inequality." *Journal of Economic Theory*, 2:244–63.

———. 1975. *The Economics of Inequality*. Oxford: Clarendon Press.

———. 1985. "How Should We Measure Poverty? Some Conceptual Issues." Presented to the Symposium on Statistics for the Measurement of Poverty organized on behalf of the EEC by the German DIW, Berlin.

Beckerman, W. 1979. *Poverty and the Impact of Maintenance Programmes in Four Developed Countries*. Geneva: International Labor Organization.

Bronfenbrenner, M. 1972. *Income Distribution Theory*. Chicago: Aldine/Atherton.

Buhmann, B., L. Rainwater, G. Schmauss, and T. Smeeding. 1988. "Equivalence Scales, Well-Being, Inequality and Poverty: Sensitivity Estimates Across Ten Countries Using the LIS Database." *Review of Income and Wealth* June 1988: 115–42.

Champernowne, D.G. 1973. *The Distribution of Income*. Cambridge: Cambridge University Press.

Coder, J., L. Rainwater, and T. Smeeding. 1988. "Information Guide to LIS." LIS-CEPS Working Paper No. 7. Walferdange, Luxembourg: LIS at CEPS/INSTEAD.

Commission of the European Economic Community. 1981. *Final Poverty Report*. Brussels: European Economic Community.

Danziger, S., and M. Taussig. 1979. "The Income Unit and the Anatomy of Income Distribution." *Review of Income and Wealth Series 25*, pp. 365–75.

Danziger, S., and D. Weinberg. 1987. *Fighting Poverty: What Works*. Cambridge, MA: Harvard University Press.

Gibson, M.J. 1987. *Income Security and Long Term Care for Women in Midlife and Beyond: U.S. and Canadian Perspective*. Proceedings of a U.S. Canadian Expert Group Meeting on Policies for Midlife and Older Women. Washington, DC: American Association of Retired Persons.

Greenwood, D., and E. Wolff. 1988. "Relative Wealth Holdings of Children and the Elderly." In Palmer, Smeeding, and Torrey (1988).

Harrington, M. 1963. *The Other America*. New York: Basic Books.

Hauser, R., and U. Nouvertne. 1980. "Poverty in Rich Countries." SB3 Discussion Paper No. 39. University of Frankfurt, Germany.

Jenkins, Stephen. 1989. "The Measurement of Income Inequality." This volume.

Johannson, Sten. 1973. "Approaches to the Study of Poverty in the United States." In Vincent T. Corello (ed.), *Poverty and Public Policy*. London: G.H. Hale.

Levy, F. 1987. *Dollars and Dreams*. New York: Russell Sage Foundation/Basic Books.

Myles, J. 1983. *Old Age in the Welfare State*. Toronto: Little, Brown and Company.

OECD. 1985. *Social Expenditure: 1960–1990*. Paris: OECD.

O'Higgins, M., and P. Ruggles. 1981. "The Distribution of Public Expenditures and Taxes among Households in the United Kingdom." *Review of Income and Wealth* 27.3:298–326.

O'Higgins, M., G. Stephenson, and G. Schmaus. 1988. "Income Distribution and Redistribution." LIS-CEPS Working Paper No. 3.

Palmer, J., T. Smeeding, and B. Torrey (eds.) 1988. *The Vulnerable: America's Children and Elderly in an Industrial World.* Washington, DC: Urban Institute Press.

Preston, S. 1984. "Children and the Elderly in the U.S." *Scientific American* 251.6:44–49.

Rainwater, L., M. Rein, and J. Schwartz. 1987. *Income Packaging in the Welfare State.* London: Oxford University Press.

Roome, G. 1987. "New Poverty in the European Community." Mimeo. University of Bath, United Kingdom.

Rowntree, B.S. 1901. *Poverty: A Study of Town Life.* London: Macmillan.

Ruggles, P., and M. O'Higgins. 1981. "The Distribution of Public Expenditure among Households in the United States." *Review of Income and Wealth* 27.2:137–64.

Sawyer, M. 1976. *Income Distribution in OECD Countries.* Paris: OECD.

Sen, A.K. 1973. *On Economic Inequality.* Oxford: Oxford University Press.

Smeeding, T., G. Schmaus, and S. Allegrezza. 1985. "Introduction to LIS." LIS-CEPS Working Paper No. 1. Walferdange, Luxembourg: LIS at CEPS/INSTEAD.

Smeeding, T., M. O'Higgins, and L. Rainwater, eds. 1988. *Poverty, Inequality and Income Distribution in International Perspective.* London: Wheatsheaf Books.

Smeeding, T., and B. Torrey. 1987. "Comparative Economic Status of the Elderly in Eight Countries: Policy Lessons from the Luxembourg Income Study and the International Database on Aging." LIS/CEPS Working Paper No. 9. LIS at CEPS/INSTEAD, November.

———. 1988. "Poor Children in Rich Countries." *Science,* Volume 242, pp. 873–77, November 11.

Smeeding, T., B. Torrey, and M. Rein. 1988. "Levels of Well-Being and Poverty Among the Elderly and Children in the U.S. and Other Major Countries." In Palmer, Smeeding, and Torrey (1988).

Smolensky, E., W. Pommerehne, and R. Dalrymple. 1979. "Postfisc Income Inequality: A Comparison of the United States and West Germany." In J.R. Moroney, ed., *Income Inequality: Trends and International Comparisons.* Lexington, MA: Lexington Books.

Townsend, Peter. 1979. *Poverty in the United Kingdom.* London: Penguin Books.

U.S. House Ways and Means Committee. 1988. *Background Material and Data on Programs with the Jurisdiction of the Committee on Ways and Means.* Washington, DC: U.S. Government Printing Office, March 24.

3

Global Economic Inequality
and Its Trends Since 1950

Albert Berry, François Bourguignon,
and Christian Morrisson

Poverty and economic inequality are, in any context, cause for deep social and ethical concern. Much of that concern finds expression in the context of nation states, since these are the main loci of the decision making which does or could affect poverty and inequality. But poverty tends to be very concentrated in certain countries, and much of the inequality among the world's citizenry taken as a group is the result of differences in economic well being *among* countries rather than *within* countries. Since the division of the world into political jurisdictions is essentially arbitrary, there is no very clear ethical or other reason to distinguish poverty by where it occurs. There are, indeed, practical reasons for placing much emphasis on inequalities within nation states, since poverty-redressal policies, like other social and economic policies, are almost always national in scope. But those practical considerations should not be allowed to cloud the moral questions. Nor can one afford to be too pessimistic with respect to the possibility that international relationships may increasingly take account of world economic inequality as something which calls for attention both on moral grounds and on grounds of systemic self-preservation.

Some sense for the extent of world income inequality and its intra- and inter-country components can be derived from Table 3.1, which shows raw figures (i.e., not adjusted in ways employed below for later tables) on the per-capita income and the internal inequality of selected countries.

Average per-capita income is estimated to be 152 times greater in the United States than in Ethiopia and 62 times greater than in India. Meanwhile, the average income of the top 10 percent of households in a given country can be as high as 50 times that of the bottom 20 percent, as in Brazil, or as low as 5 times, as in Japan. Evidently both intercountry and intracountry income differentials are very large. When one considers that the richest people in the developed countries have incomes several times the American average and the poorer people in countries like Ethiopia and Bangladesh or India have incomes of no more than a quarter or a third of their extremely low national averages, the enormous gap between the world's richest and its poorest is painfully evident. Although some needed refinements to the above estimates do imply somewhat smaller "true" gaps (see below), the picture they paint is broadly accurate.

Not surprisingly, trends in the world distribution of income have been the subject of much recent discussion. The issue of increasing economic inequality among nonsocialist countries in the postwar period has been central to the debate about the New International Economic Order. In 1969 the Pearson Commission Report pointed to the "widening gap between the developed and developing countries" as a "central issue of our time," and proposed the reduction of that gap as the main objective of international cooperation.[1] Morawetz (1978) found that the gap between the two sets of countries rose from 12.6-fold in 1950 to 13.2-fold in 1975. Other authors saw a more complicated picture; Atkinson (1975), for instance, argued that although the share of poor countries in world income probably declined between 1950 and 1970, that of the countries at the middle of the world distribution probably increased. In the view of authors like Amin (1974), Emmanuel (1972), and Frank (1978) the capitalist mode of development necessarily leads to the rich countries of the "center" becoming richer and poor countries of the "periphery" becoming poorer, to a degree depending on their involvement in international trade, so a widening gap between developed and developing countries is simply the statistical confirmation of an unavoidable consequence of the national and international capitalist system.

Estimating *trends* in the world income distribution necessarily involves methodological, statistical, and conceptual problems which prevent firm, precise conclusions. We attempt in section 1 to provide some feel for the major sources of imprecision in our estimates. When socialist countries are included, no unambiguous trends emerge from our detailed estimates for the period 1950–77 as a whole, regardless of whether income or consumption is the indicator of economic welfare. Among nonsocialist countries there was some clear worsening over the longer period 1950–86 for which we have data, especially in the distribution of private consumption (section 2).

World economic performance in the 1980s has been different from that of the previous three decades; the incomplete data do not at this time point to any general loss in share for the poorest deciles over this period, but a large subgroup of the low-income countries which were losing ground over the previous decades continued to do so, especially those in sub-Saharan Africa.

Section 3 provides a decomposition of changes in world inequality over the subperiods distinguished between 1950 and 1977, based on the elasticities of decomposable inequality measures like the Theil coefficient and the mean logarithm deviation (MLD). Most significant changes in world inequality are essentially explained by the economic performance of the few countries which are large either in terms of population (India, China) or income (United States), and

Table 3.1

Average Per-Capita Income and Distribution of Income, Selected Major Countries

Country	Per-capita income in 1985 (U.S. $)	Gini coefficient	Share of income accruing to					
			Lowest 20%	Second 20%	Third 20%	Fourth 20%	Highest 20%	Highest 10%
Ethiopia	110							
Bangladesh	150	0.324	6.6	10.7	15.3	22.1	45.3	29.5
Zaire	170							
Burma	190							
India	270	0.402	7.0	9.2	13.9	20.5	49.4	33.6
Kenya	290							
Tanzania	290							
China	310							
Pakistan	380							
Indonesia	530	0.424	6.6	7.8	12.6	23.6	49.4	34.0
Philippines	580	0.445	5.2	8.9	13.2	20.2	52.5	37.0
Egypt	610	0.396	5.8	10.7	14.7	20.8	48.0	33.2
Ivory Coast	660	0.567	2.4	6.2	10.9	19.1	61.4	43.7
Nigeria	800							
Thailand	800	0.444	5.6	9.6	13.9	21.1	49.8	34.1
Peru	1,010	0.575	1.9	5.1	11.0	21.0	61.0	42.9
Turkey	1,080	0.495	3.5	8.0	12.5	19.5	56.5	40.7
Colombia	1,320							

Brazil	1,640	0.599	2.0	5.0	9.4	17.0	66.6	50.6
Hungary	1,950	0.280	6.9	13.6	19.2	24.5	35.8	20.5
Malaysia	2,000	0.495	3.5	7.7	12.4	20.3	56.1	39.8
Yugoslavia	2,070	0.311	6.6	12.1	18.7	23.9	38.7	22.9
Mexico	2,080	0.515	2.9	7.0	12.0	20.4	57.7	40.6
Argentina	2,130	0.434	4.4	9.7	14.1	21.5	50.3	35.2
Korea, Republic of	2,150	0.371	5.7	11.2	15.4	22.4	45.3	27.5
Venezuela	3,080	0.487	3.0	7.3	12.9	22.8	54.0	35.7
Spain	4,290	0.313	6.9	12.5	17.3	23.2	40.0	24.5
Italy	6,520	0.359	6.2	11.3	15.9	22.7	43.9	28.1
United Kingdom	8,460	0.322	7.0	11.5	17.0	24.8	39.7	23.4
France	9,540	0.353	5.5	11.5	17.1	23.7	42.2	26.4
Australia	10,830	0.397	5.4	10.0	15.0	22.5	47.1	30.5
Germany Federal Republic	10,940	0.304	7.9	12.5	17.0	23.1	39.5	24.0
Japan	11,300	0.277	8.7	13.2	17.5	23.1	37.5	22.4
Sweden	11,890	0.320	7.4	13.1	16.8	21.0	41.7	28.1
Canada	13,680	0.337	5.3	11.8	18.0	24.9	40.0	23.8
Norway	14,370	0.312	6.0	12.9	18.3	24.6	38.2	22.8
United States	16,690	0.336	5.3	11.9	17.9	25.0	39.9	23.3

Source: World Bank (1987), pp. 202–3, pp. 252–53. The Gini coefficients have been calculated from the income shares shown in the table and, given the small number of income categories used, understate the true Ginis by a percentage point or so.

Note: Figures refer to households, and generally to the most recent year in which such data were available, usually sometime during 1975–85 but occasionally during 1970–75.

are found towards one or the other end of the ranking by per-capita income. Section 4 provides a brief summary.

1. Methodology and Data

A number of methodological and conceptual problems involved in estimating world income distribution at a point of time have been dealt with in Berry et al. (1981a). Here we discuss points which seem particularly relevant to trends over time.

Computation of the World Income Distribution from National Data

Estimates of world income distribution for a given year, t, are based on three pieces of data for each country, i, included in the analysis: population P_{it}; average income *per capita* at constant United States purchasing power Y_{it}; and percentage distribution of income by deciles of individuals d, v^d_{it} ($d = 1, \ldots, 10$). Alternative computational procedures are possible.[2] Note that although our discussion is in terms of the distribution of income among individuals, the underlying data from countries refer almost always to the distribution among households (see note 24). This fact creates several methodological problems to which we return below; the major one, which implies that our figures understate inequality both within countries and at the world level, is the absence of data on intrafamily inequality and especially inequality between males and females. The fact that our data refer to annual rather than lifetime incomes also tends to understate differences in economic well-being.

Sources of Changes in the World Distribution

World inequality reflects both intracountry and intercountry income differences. Were the former the preeminent source of world inequality, it would be appropriate to leave to national governments the responsibility for redistribution, anticipating that different countries might ''choose'' different levels of internal inequality. The greater the importance of intercountry differences as a source of world inequality the less satisfactory that route, and the more emphasis needed on mechanisms to achieve progressive redistribution of income among countries. Direct observation gives many people a feel for the serious inequality characterizing most countries in both the developed industrial world and in the less developed countries; there is no clear relationship between the degree of intracountry inequality and the level of development or per-capita income and many poor countries also suffer severe internal inequality. Intercountry inequality, while apparent enough, is perhaps harder to assess intuitively at a world level.

The decomposition of world inequality into an intracountry component and an intercountry component is a necessary prelude to any discussion of how best to attack world poverty and inequality. Thus, as well as considering trends in world inequality, we attempt to see how they reflect disparities across countries in economic and demographic growth, such as the economic performance of newly industrialized countries (Brazil, Korea, etc.) or the demographic growth of the Indian subcontinent. We have computed the elasticities of the two decomposable inequality measures (Theil's entropy coefficient and the mean logarithmic deviation)[3] with respect to national populations, national per-capita incomes and intracountry inequalities.[4] The "elasticity" of any variable with respect to changes in another related variable is the percent change in the affected variable resulting from a one percent change in the independent variable. In the present context, therefore, the elasticity of some indicator of world inequality (e.g., the Theil coefficient) with respect to internal inequality in Brazil would be defined as the percent change in the world Theil coefficient resulting from a one percent change in Brazil's Theil coefficient.

Data and Assumptions

Three time series are necessary at the national level: population, a measure of *per-capita* economic welfare, and a measure of intracountry economic inequality. The last two involve some statistical and conceptual difficulties. The variable traditionally used in international welfare comparisons is GNP *per capita* (i.e., output per capita), but one must convert values from national currencies to some international standard, and it is well recognized that use of the exchange rate for this purpose may lead to large errors. Empirical work on this issue, especially by Kravis and associates, has recently made it possible to use purchasing power parities (or reasonable approximations to them) for this purpose.[5] The main source of the inadequacy of the exchange rate as a converter is the existence of different price vectors in different countries. The exchange rate tends to provide a good approximation to relative purchasing power for goods which countries trade, but is much poorer for untraded goods and especially for untraded services. (The effect of excluding services from comparisons of relative per-capita expenditures is apparent in the figures of Table 3.2.) For example, countries may provide different services free (i.e., at a zero price) to their populations, a fact which complicates the comparison of capitalist and communist countries.

When binary (two-country) comparisons of average income levels are made, one cannot isolate a "correct" purchasing power parity between the two currencies, but it is possible under the assumption of the same utility function in the two countries to conclude that the true purchasing power parity lies between two values: those resulting from the application of the price vector of each country to the consumption (or absorption) baskets of both. Although the availability of directly calculated purchasing power parities represents a great improvement over the use of exchange rates, those parities may be quite sensitive to which

Table 3.2

Relative Per-Capita Expenditures of Selected Countries vis-à-vis the United States Including and Excluding Services, for Various Weighting Systems, 1970 (U.S. expenditures per capita = 100)

	GDP (1)	GDP, excluding government (2)	GDP, excluding government, education, recreation, and medical services (3)
Kenya			
U.S. weights	8.6	7.3	6.1
Kenya weights	4.0	4.0	3.6
International weights of Kravis et al.	6.3	5.8	5.5
India			
U.S. weights	8.5	8.0	7.2
India weights	4.3	4.3	4.3
International weights	6.8	6.6	6.8
Colombia			
U.S. weights	21.5	23.4	23.6
Colombia weights	11.8	11.9	12.3
International weights	18.1	18.7	19.8
Italy			
U.S. weights	53.5	57.8	55.9
Italy weights	42.7	45.8	42.2
International weights	49.2	48.8	46.4
Hungary			
U.S. weights	48.4	51.4	45.4
Hungary weights	32.8	34.4	29.8
International weights	42.7	44.9	40.9

Source: Column (1) is taken directly from, and Columns (2) and (3) are calculated on the basis of, data presented in Kravis et al. (1978b).

country's value weights are chosen (or what other price vector is adopted to compare real incomes). Relative per-capita incomes between poor countries and the United States can differ by as much as 2:1 according to whether United States prices are used or those of the poor country. Kravis et al. (1978a)(1978b), by using an ''international price vector'' (average relative prices in the world, therefore giving high weight to the rich countries), come up with an intermediate result, usually somewhat closer to the use of United States weights. (See Table 3.2).

When one wishes to aggregate across more than two countries, the fact that the true relative income per capita between two countries would, assuming the same preference system in each country, lie between that calculated using one country's prices and that calculated using prices of the other country is of less value. At a world level, and ignoring some conceptual complexities,[6] one might anticipate that use of a Kravis et al. type of "international" price vector would provide a downward biased estimate of world inequality;[7] a probably upward biased estimate might result from a procedure where it is assumed that the relative per-capita income of each country vis-à-vis the United States is given by a conversion using its own price vector. These two approaches are used here to provide benchmark Estimates 1 and 2 respectively, shown in Table 3.3.[8] The overall level of income inequality reported in Estimate 1 is virtually identical (the Gini coefficient is 0.65) to that reported by Whalley (1979) for 1972, using a similar methodology. As expected, the inequality associated with Estimate 2 (where purchasing power parities of each country vis-à-vis the United States are based on that country's price vector) is somewhat greater, though not as great as that which results if country incomes are converted using exchange rates.

The distribution of world consumption is somewhat less unequal than that of world income for two reasons; principally because the savings rate is below average in many of the poorer countries (though the relationship between depressed inequality measures based on consumption and a low savings rate is far from close when the socialist countries, and in particular China, are taken into account); and secondarily because the intracountry distribution of consumption is generally less unequal than the income distribution since the marginal propensity to consume falls with income and the high income families therefore do most of the savings.[9] The greater role of the first factor reflects the reality that the dominant source of worldwide inequality is the variance between countries, not intracountry variance, whether of income or consumption.[10] Inequality is somewhat higher for the set of nonsocialist countries than for the world.[11]

These figures indicate that about 50 percent of the world's goods and services go to the top 10 percent of persons (46–53 percent according to which column of Table 3.3 we use) while the bottom 20 percent get only 1.4 to 2.5 percent; on a per-capita basis the top decile thus fares about 40–70 times as well as the bottom quintile. The Gini coefficient ranges between 0.60 and 0.69 and the Theil coefficient between 0.68 and 0.92. This degree of inequality is probably not equalled within any country, even those with the worst inequality.

While the above figures could err for many reasons, the probable margins of error are fairly small. Accurate country price vectors are not available for all countries and in any case the true vectors change over time, creating possible errors and/or instability in world distribution estimates. However, although cross-country comparisons of per-capita income may be somewhat sensitive to the international price vector chosen, and estimates not based on price data for the country in question may involve considerable error, these appear not to be

Table 3.3

Estimates of World Personal Income and Consumption Distribution in 1970
(124 socialist and non-socialist countries)

	Income (GDP)		Consumption	
	Estimate 1[a]	Estimate 2[b]	Estimate 1[a]	Estimate 2[b]
Income or consumption shares (%):				
Decile 1	0.72	0.51	1.01	0.73
Decile 2	1.22	0.89	1.51	1.12
Decile 3	1.65	1.17	2.09	1.51
Decile 4	2.14	1.55	2.59	1.89
Decile 5	2.69	1.91	3.75	2.41
Decile 6	2.95	3.01	4.72	3.67
Decile 7	7.02	6.29	7.58	7.13
Decile 8	11.81	11.34	12.30	11.61
Decile 9	19.45	20.62	19.02	20.29
Second 5% from top	15.47	16.58	14.86	16.16
Top 5%	33.88	36.13	30.97	33.50
Inequality measures:				
Gini	0.649	0.693	0.609	0.659
Theil	0.797	0.923	0.685	0.814
Mean log deviation	0.845	1.043	0.702	0.885
Atkinson 1 ($\varepsilon = 0.75$)	0.472	0.543	0.413	0.487
Atkinson 2 ($\varepsilon = 0.50$)	0.345	0.399	0.299	0.355
Atkinson 3 ($\varepsilon = 0.25$)	0.187	0.217	0.161	0.192
Variance log	1.580	1.985	1.296	1.656
$\dfrac{\text{Mean of top 5\%}}{\text{Mean of bottom 20\%}}$	94.1	141.7	61.3	91.8
$\dfrac{\text{Mean World}}{\text{Mean U.S.}}$	0.247	0.233	0.255	0.238

[a] National figures converted to a common base using the purchasing power parity conversion rates estimated by Kravis et al. (1978a) for capitalist countries and World Bank estimates for the socialist countries.
[b] Country values converted to U.S. dollars using own country weight.

serious problems for the estimation of world income distribution, partly because price vectors are on average fairly stable, and partly because some errors tend to be mutually offsetting.[12]

The sensitivity of the world Theil coefficient to income and distribution data for individual countries is very low, except for some large countries like India, China, and the United States.[13] With the exception of China it seems improbable that errors in specific county estimates of income per capita or its distribution would significantly bias the world measure. China, however, is clearly an exception, being the country with the most uncertain data and the greatest possible impact on world inequality. A 20 percent error in the income estimate is perhaps possible in which case the Theil coefficient corresponding to Estimate 1 in Table 3.3 would change by 3.2 percent, i.e., rising to 0.822 in the case of a 20 percent reduction of the Chinese income.[14] Even in this extreme case, the order of magnitude of the potential bias is hardly dramatic.

Other possible sources of inaccuracy include differences in age structure across countries (making per-capita income overestimate income per adult equivalent in some countries relative to others), the failure to allow for intrafamily income disparities (about which we still know relatively little), and the differential impact of the range of goods and services included in measures of national product.[15]

Each of these is potentially remediable with more complete information. Less tractable is the ultimate and difficult question of how well a person's (or a country's) annual income reflects his (its) well-being. One aspect of well-being is length of life, which is on average markedly longer in rich than in poor countries and for richer than poorer people in the same country. By allowing only for the distribution of income in a finite, fixed period, the traditional measures of inequality thereby tend for each point of time to understate inequality more satisfactorily defined. Note however that world lifetime income inequality has been falling since the life expectancy gap between rich and poor countries has narrowed in the post-war period.[16] It would be interesting to assess trends in the intrafamily welfare gap between the genders but not much can be done to rectify this other major deficiency in our data.

If we leave aside the issues of how life expectancy should be treated in the analysis of inequality and if we neglect intra-family income differences, the correlation of GNP per capita with a more appropriate definition of national economic well-being is probably quite high, given relatively stable national and international price structures. But given our objective of assessing trends over time a country's income per-capita series differs from an output per-capita series (like GNP per capita) due to changes in its international terms of trade. Working with a per-capita output series for the oil-producing countries, for example, is equivalent to ignoring the international transfer of purchasing power to them due to the increases in oil prices since 1973. Since calculation of constant price per-capita income series for all the countries in the sample was difficult, we have preferred to do the analysis at a double level, using on the one hand GNP per capita and on the other private consumption per capita. While the latter does not fully capture changes in national purchasing power, it does reflect them in part and its trend may better reflect changes in current well-being than do the trends in either GNP per capita or national income per capita.[17]

Inclusion of the socialist countries creates some problems due to their difference in national accounting procedures vis-à-vis the capitalist countries, and in some cases their weak data.[18] These difficulties are perhaps not too important for the USSR and the East European countries, all of which belong to the intermediate deciles of the world distribution. Their growth was regular and substantially above the world mean throughout the whole 1950–77 period, and they probably induced a small ambiguous reduction[19] in world inequality over that period.[20]

But the lack of solid data on China is a different matter. Given its size and low rank in the world income scale, the assumptions made about its economic and demographic growth are crucial in the estimation of world distribution trends. Two alternative estimates of Chinese economic growth over 1950–77 are used in the computations which follow in section 2; in both cases Chinese per-capita GNP is taken to be about 5 percent below that of India in 1970.[21] In alternative A, China's cumulative growth of per-capita GNP between 1950 and 1977 is 220 percent (4.4 percent annually), starting 40 percent below India in 1950. In alternative B, the starting point is 25 percent below India and the cumulated growth is 130 percent (3.1 percent annually). The difference leads to distinct conclusions about world distribution changes.

2. Changes in the World Distribution of GNP and of Consumption

Figure 3.1 shows the evolution of inequality over 1950–77 for the world and over 1950–86 in the nonsocialist countries alone, using GNP per capita (in 1970 United States dollars) as the measure of income. Because of computational costs and data gaps, the year by year evolution is reported only for the Theil and Mean Log Deviation inequality measures starting in 1950. The Gini coefficient and the absolute poverty index (number of persons with income less than U.S. $200, of 1970)[22] are given for the three decade years 1950, 1960, 1970, and selected years thereafter.

Under assumption A (high growth in China) 1950–77 showed three distinct subperiods in the evolution of the world GNP distribution (Figure 3.1 and Table 3.4). A clear-cut improvement took place in the 1950s with the bottom four deciles and the upper middle ones (especially 9) increasing their share of world income at the expense of the top decile. All summary measures of inequality fell and the world Lorenz curve unambiguously shifted upward. Then two significant increases in inequality took place between 1960 and 1968, substantially attributable to events in China.[23] First came the disastrous crop of 1961 and the failure of the "Big Leap Forward" policy; GNP per capita plunged by 22 percent. The second setback occurred in 1968, as a consequence of the Cultural Revolution. Other poor countries also fared relatively less well than in the 1950s. The upper-middle deciles again increased their share of world income but this time at the expense of the bottom deciles, while the top decile maintained its share close to the 1960 level. The Lorenz curve shifted downward and in the early 1970s all the

Figure 3.1. **The Evolution of Economic Inequality**

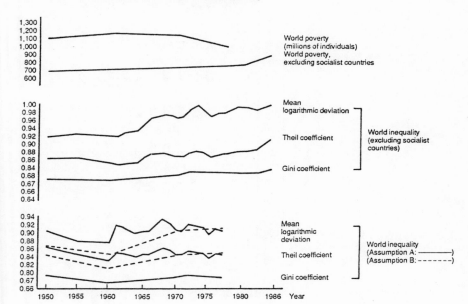

Notes: Estimates are reported for years 1950, 1960, 1970, and 1977 for poverty measures, Gini coefficients, and other inequality measures under Assumption B (slower estimate of growth in China). Estimates are reported for 1950, 1955, and every year after 1960 for the Mean logarithmic deviation and Theil coefficient under Assumption A (higher estimate of growth in China).

inequality measures were back around their 1950 levels. Between 1972 and 1977 another reversal occurred. The Lorenz curve shifted upward, largely because of Chinese growth, and the inequality measures showed a moderate decline.

When one compares 1950 and 1977, no unambiguous conclusions can be drawn; inequality measures are more or less at the same level. The two Lorenz curves cross twice, the upper-middle deciles (8–9) and the four bottom deciles gaining at the expense of both the top decile and the lower-middle deciles (5–7). World absolute poverty, however, dropped significantly from 1.18 billion individuals in 1950 to 1.04 billion in 1977, most of the change occurring in China over the last seven years (world poverty had increased by approximately 50 million between 1950 and 1970).

Under Assumption B, with a slower growth of China's per-capita GNP (3.1 percent per year), there is again no clear trend in the world distribution although some indicators (e.g., MLD) show a measurable increase in inequality (Figure 3.1). The absolute number of poor people is more or less stable throughout the whole period and the same is approximately true for the relative income of the poorest to the richest half of the world population, which fluctuates around 1:12.

Table 3.4

World Distribution of GNP and Consumption Including Socialist Countries: Selected Years
(Assumption A—Upper Estimate of Economic Growth in China)

	GNP										Consumption					
	1950		1960		1970		1972		1977		1950		1960		1977	
Decile shares in world income or consumption (%)	Shares	CS*	Shares	CS	Shares	CS	Shares	CS	Shares	CS	Shares	CS	Shares	CS	Shares	CS
Decile 1	0.7	0.7	0.7	0.7	0.7	0.7	0.6	0.6	0.7	0.7	0.8	0.8	0.9	0.9	0.8	0.8
2	1.0	1.7	1.1	1.8	1.1	1.7	1.0	1.7	1.1	1.7	1.2	2.1	1.4	2.3	1.2	2.0
3	1.3	3.0	1.5	3.3	1.4	3.2	1.4	3.1	1.5	3.2	1.6	3.6	1.7	4.0	1.6	3.6
4	1.8	4.8	1.9	5.2	1.8	5.0	1.8	4.9	1.9	5.1	2.2	5.8	2.2	6.2	2.1	5.7
5	2.6	7.4	2.6	7.8	2.4	7.3	2.3	7.2	2.4	7.5	3.1	8.9	3.1	9.3	2.7	8.4
6	4.1	11.5	4.0	11.8	3.7	11.0	3.6	10.8	3.6	11.2	4.7	13.6	4.6	13.9	4.0	12.4
7	6.7	18.2	6.9	18.7	6.5	17.5	6.4	17.2	6.4	17.6	7.3	20.9	7.4	21.3	6.7	19.1
8	11.0	29.3	11.5	30.3	11.9	29.4	11.7	28.9	11.7	29.3	11.0	31.9	11.6	32.9	11.7	30.8
9	18.1	47.4	19.1	49.4	20.1	49.5	20.2	49.0	20.2	49.4	18.3	50.2	18.8	51.7	19.3	50.2
10	52.6	100.0	50.6	100.0	50.5	100.0	51.0	100.0	50.6	100.0	49.8	100.0	48.3	100.0	49.8	100.0
Top 5%	36.2		34.7		34.6		35.0		34.8		34.1		33.0		34.5	

Summary inequality measures							
Gini	0.670	0.659	0.667	0.671	0.667	0.642	0.631	0.652
Theil	0.867	0.828	0.844	0.858	0.846	0.785	0.750	0.807
MLD	0.919	0.879	0.918	0.936	0.915	0.809	0.775	0.848
Atkinson (ε = −1.0)	0.726	0.711	0.727	0.734	0.726	0.681	0.665	0.697
Atkinson (ε = −1.5)	0.791	0.778	0.792	0.799	0.792	0.753	0.737	0.766
Atkinson (ε = −2.0)	0.828	0.816	0.829	0.836	0.831	0.795	0.780	0.807
Summary inequality measures assuming no intra-country inequality							
Gini	0.574	0.554	0.559	0.564	0.558	0.533	0.515	0.536
Theil	0.579	0.538	0.553	0.564	0.548	0.489	0.455	0.503
MLD	0.625	0.582	0.616	0.633	0.609	0.515	0.478	0.543
Poverty							
Absolute (millions of individuals with less than U.S. $200)	1,178	1,249	1,226	1,177	1,043	1,297	1,478	1,666
Relative (%)	48.5	42.4	34.2	31.6	25.5	53.4	50.2	40.8

*CS = cumulated shares

The evolution of the world distribution of private consumption expenditures generally follows that of GNP,[24] but the worsening between 1960 and 1972 is much more pronounced with the result that the 1977 distribution is unambiguously more unequal than that of 1950 (see Table 3.4). The main source of this difference with the GNP distribution trend lies in differences across countries in the behavior of the private consumption to GNP ratio. After 1960 that ratio decreased markedly in almost all nonsocialist developing countries (the average for this group of countries fell from 72.0 percent in 1960 to 67.5 percent in 1977) while remaining relatively stable in most developed countries, and rising in the United States from 60.5 percent in 1960 to 63.8 percent in 1977. The equalizing effect on the world distribution of the higher consumption to GNP ratio in the developing world was thus largely eroded during this period.

An important issue, then, in deciding whether the trends in the distribution of private consumption expenditures are more or less relevant than those of GNP over 1950–77 is the interpretation given to the evolution of the private consumption/GNP ratio in the less developed countries. The decline in the share of private consumption is approximately matched by an increase in the share of gross domestic investment. By 1978 the gross investment to GNP ratio in lower-income countries had about caught up with that of the industrialized countries (at 0.21 or 0.22), though still lagging behind that of middle-income developing countries (0.25).[25] This could have provided grounds for hope that the worsening of the world distribution of private consumption observed since 1960 would reverse itself in the future, though the continuing loss of ground by poorer nonsocialist countries (see below), even in the 1970s when their investment levels were high, indicated that this was far from obvious. Also, public consumption expenditures in these latter countries had risen in relation to GNP and in the 1970s the foreign resource balance became more negative. In any case, in terms of our direct objective of measuring trends in economic inequality between 1950 and 1977 the distribution of private consumption is probably a better measure than that of GNP,[26] so the likelihood that a meaningful worsening occurred is high.

The preceding conclusions on the evolution of world inequality over the period through the 1970s emerge more clearly for the nonsocialist world by itself. Rapid economic growth in China was, under Assumption A, a strong equalizing factor in the world distribution, and the source of the sharp fluctuations observed in 1961 and 1968 (see Table 3.5 and Figure 3.1). With the exclusion of China and the industrialized communist countries, the 1950s and early 1960s exhibit a relative stability, possibly a slight decline, in inequality; between 1964 and 1972 there was a substantial worsening; during the rest of the 1970s there was again no trend despite a sharp fluctuation in 1975. For the period as a whole, distribution seems to have worsened somewhat, with the change concentrated in the sub-period 1964 to 1972. The 1980s (up to 1986) saw a new twist. For the bottom half of the world's nonsocialist population income share was unchanged. Meanwhile the top decile gained at the expense of the sixth, seventh, and eighth. Though changes were, not surprisingly, rather different across sub-periods, it is true that for 1950–86 as a whole there was an unambiguous worsening of income distribution. The top two deciles gained, albeit not dramatically, the next decile's share was unchanged and each of the bottom deciles lost, especially those in the middle (fourth to seventh). The share of the bottom seven deciles fell from 12.7 percent to 15.3 percent. The loss of the bottom five appears to have been gradual but chronic: at no time did any of them show significant gains, and each saw its share fall by 15 percent or thereabouts. For the middle deciles, especially the seventh and eighth the marked gains of the 1950s and 1960s were canceled out by the losses of the 1970s and (especially) the 1980s.

In terms of relative consumption too, this was a "devil take the hindmost" period in the nonsocialist world. Table 3.5 shows a substantial unambiguous worsening between 1950 and 1986, with the two upper deciles increasing their share of world consumption from 68.5 percent to 71.6 percent at the expense of all seven lower deciles.

We have been unable, thus far, to incorporate recent (post-1977) figures for the socialist countries in our calculations, so it is only possible to speculate as to how the world distributions of income and consumption have evolved since then. For the quarter century 1950–77 the impact of the inclusion of the socialist countries was to offset the tendency within the group of nonsocialist countries for the lowest deciles to lose share. Since there has in any case been no loss of share between the mid-1970s and the 1980s by the bottom deciles in the non-socialist world, the addition of the socialist countries and in particular of China, whose presence weighs heavily in the trends of the lower deciles, could well produce increasing income and consumption shares for the lower several deciles during this decade. In that case, the net changes over 1950–86 would probably include (with some differences in detail between the income and consumption distribution trends) a slight gain for the top deciles, a net loss for a group of deciles in the middle, and the just noted gain at the bottom. If the distribution of income within China has worsened significantly over the last decade, a possibility whose quantitative dimensions we are not able to judge at this time, there might be no gain at the very bottom (e.g., the lowest two deciles) but the bottom half of the distribution would still probably have gained over the thirty-six years.

Growth was slower over 1980–85 for most countries except China, the South Asian countries and a very few others. The fact that China and South Asia have done extremely well over this period has, per se, had a positive impact on world distribution, given their low average incomes. More generally, China and all of the South Asian countries (India, Pakistan, Bangladesh, Sri Lanka, and Nepal) have registered faster GDP growth over 1980–85 than over 1965–80 (Table 3.6), and some (especially China) have gained ground substantially vis-à-vis both the industrial market economies at the top of the world distribution and the

Table 3.5

World Distribution of GNP and Consumption Excluding Socialist Countries: Selected Years

Decile shares in world income (%)

	GNP												Consumption							
	1950		1960		1970		1972		1977		1986		1950		1960		1977		1986	
	Shares	CS*	Shares	CS	Shares	CS	Shares	CS	Shares	CS	Shares	CS	Shares	CS	Shares	CS	Shares	CS	Shares	CS
Decile 1	0.6	0.6	0.6	0.6	0.6	0.6	0.5	0.5	0.5	0.5	0.5	0.5	0.8	0.8	0.8	0.8	0.6	0.6	0.6	0.6
2	0.9	1.5	0.9	1.5	0.8	1.4	0.8	1.3	0.8	1.3	0.8	1.3	1.2	2.0	1.2	2.0	1.0	1.6	1.0	1.6
3	1.4	2.9	1.4	2.9	1.2	2.6	1.2	2.5	1.2	2.5	1.2	2.5	1.7	3.7	1.6	3.6	1.4	3.0	1.4	2.9
4	1.9	4.8	1.9	4.8	1.7	4.3	1.6	4.1	1.7	4.2	1.6	4.1	2.4	6.1	2.4	6.0	2.0	5.0	2.0	4.9
5	2.6	7.4	2.6	7.4	2.4	6.7	2.3	6.4	2.4	6.6	2.2	6.3	3.3	9.4	3.2	9.2	2.7	7.7	2.6	7.5
6	4.1	11.5	4.1	11.5	3.8	10.5	3.7	10.1	3.8	10.4	3.3	9.6	4.6	14.0	4.7	13.9	4.2	11.9	3.8	11.3
7	6.2	17.7	6.5	18.0	6.3	16.8	6.3	16.4	6.3	16.7	5.7	15.3	6.8	20.8	6.8	20.7	6.6	18.5	6.1	17.4
8	10.4	28.1	10.8	28.8	11.4	28.2	11.3	27.7	11.2	27.9	10.6	25.9	10.8	31.6	11.2	31.9	11.4	29.9	10.9	28.3
9	19.8	47.9	20.0	48.7	20.8	49.0	20.9	48.5	20.7	48.5	20.8	46.7	19.3	50.9	19.3	51.2	19.8	49.6	19.8	48.1
10	52.1	100.0	51.3	100.0	51.0	100.0	51.5	100.0	51.6	100.0	53.3	100.0	49.2	100.0	48.8	100.0	50.5	100.0	51.8	100.0
Top 5%	34.5		33.8		33.8		34.2		34.3		35.5		32.7		32.2		33.9		34.9	

Summary inequality measures										
Gini	0.671	0.669	0.677	0.683	0.681	0.694	0.639	0.637	0.662	0.672
Theil	0.857	0.846	0.864	0.881	0.877	0.924	0.767	0.759	0.826	0.865
MLD	0.930	0.933	0.987	1.016	1.002	1.043	0.803	0.804	0.909	0.940
Atkinson ($\varepsilon = -1.0$)	0.733	0.736	0.757	0.768	0.763	0.773	0.681	0.683	0.728	0.738
Atkinson ($\varepsilon = -1.5$)	0.801	0.804	0.822	0.832	0.828	0.835	0.756	0.757	0.798	0.807
Atkinson ($\varepsilon = -2.0$)	0.839	0.842	0.858	0.866	0.864	0.869	0.801	0.802	0.839	0.848
Summary inequality measures assuming no intra-country inequality										
Gini	0.557	0.332	0.560	0.567	0.563		0.508	0.503	0.534	
Theil	0.545	0.327	0.343	0.557	0.546		0.445	0.432	0.487	
MLD	0.581	0.579	0.627	0.656	0.638		0.454	0.449	0.545	
Poverty										
Absolute (millions of individuals with less than U.S. $200)	682	702	723	733	748	859	772	862.1	978	1,092
Relative (%)	42.7	36.3	30.5	29.7	27.5	26.4	48.3	44.6	36.0	33.3

Note: Figures for 1986 are from Bourguignon et al. (1988); for some earlier years figures of that source differ very slightly from those presented here.

*CS = Cumulated shares

Table 3.6

Average Annual GDP Growth during 1965–80 and 1980–85, by Regions

Regions	1965–80	1980–85	GNP per capita, (U.S. $ of 1985)	Population 1985 (millions)
Low-income countries[a]	4.8	7.3	270	2439.4
China	6.4	9.8	310	1040.3
India	3.8	5.2	270	765.1
Other South Asia[b]	3.9	5.0	263	229.1
Other	2.9	1.7	326	404.8
Other, excluding socialist			224	
countries and Uganda	3.3	–0.1		306.8[e]
Lower-middle income[c]	6.3	1.6	820	674.6
Upper-middle income[d]	6.6	1.7	1,850	567.4
Industrial market economics	3.7	2.3	11,810	737.3
Industrial nonmarket economics	5.4[f]	3.6		340.7

[a] 1985 per capita income below $400 U.S.
[b] Pakistan, Bangladesh, Sri Lanka, and Nepal.
[c] 1985 per capita income of $400–1600 U.S.
[d] 1985 per capita income of $1600–7500 U.S. but not classified as industrial or as high-income oil exporters (Libya, Saudi Arabia, United Arab Emirates).
[e] Estimate.
[f] Refers to 1969–80.

middle-income less-developed countries (LDCs). These latter middle income countries, meanwhile, lost ground relative to both the industrial countries (whether market-oriented or socialist) at the top of the distribution and the lower-income countries as a group. Among the lower-income countries a major divergence of performance arose; while the growth of China and South Asia accelerated compared to the previous fifteen years, other nonsocialist low-income countries suffered a drastic decline, from 3.3 percent over 1965–80 to zero over 1980–85 (Table 3.6).

Most of these countries are in sub-Saharan Africa, increasingly the focus of concern and pessimism given the currently very low income levels and the unpromising prospects for the future. This part of the world now has a faster growing population than anywhere else, an agriculture thus far bypassed by the green revolution, and a foreign debt to GDP ratio significantly worse than most of the developing world's biggest and best known debtors.[27] It has been the site of the worst episodes of famine and starvation in the 1980s. It should be emphasized that this sub-Saharan crisis is somewhat hidden in our data since the region has a relatively small share of world population.

3. A Decomposition Analysis of Changes in World Inequality, 1950–77

Though it would be of interest to attach countries to deciles of the world distribution, intracountry dispersion is normally wide enough so that a given world decile cannot be associated even approximately with specific countries, nor does a change in the share of a world decile simply reflect the fact that a particular set of countries is doing better or worse than the world average. Nevertheless, a look at changes in the country composition of some world deciles helps one understand the sources of changes in the world distribution. Table 3.7 provides such information over the period 1950–77 for selected countries and for groups of countries with similar GNP per capita, geographical or historical conditions, or rates of economic growth.[28] It shows, most notably: the increasing share of world poverty found in the poor (nonsocialist) countries and the decreasing share in China (China, under hypothesis A, and the Indian subcontinent having exactly opposite evolutions in this respect);[29] the substantial fall of the United States share of the world's rich, though this is due in large part to the falling share of the United States in world population; and the increasing weight of China, developing, newly industrialized, and OPEC countries in the world middle-income deciles.

Decomposition based on the elasticities of Theil and MLD coefficients with respect to countries' income per capita and population helps to identify the various proximate sources of change in world inequality.[30] On the income side, there are two unambiguous pairs of conflicting forces on world inequality. The slow economic growth of the poorest countries, and in particular the heavily populated countries of the Indian subcontinent, increases inequality whereas that of the United States, the richest country, does the opposite.[31] Among the relatively fast growers it is again those most distant from the world mean income which are most likely to affect world inequality in a substantial way. China's growth performance is by far the major equalizing factor in the world distribution (under Assumption A).[32] At the other end of the per-capita income spectrum, the nonsocialist industrialized countries other than the United States and Japan were the main disequalizing factor; although their average per-capita income growth was not much above the world mean, their weight and their rank in the world distribution are sufficient to produce a significant worsening.

Between these cited extremes we find three types of situations. The fast growth of the newly industrialized and OPEC countries contributed only moderately, although unambiguously, to world equality. The economic performances of the East European countries, USSR and Japan have a different impact on world inequality depending on what measure, i.e., what underlying social utility function, is selected. Finally, the evolution of other country groups has a negligible effect on the world distribution, either because their per-capita GNP increase was too close to the world mean or because they are too small.

The direct[33] effects of demographic phenomena on world inequality are sim-

Table 3.7

Country Composition of Selected Quantiles of the World Distribution of GNP, 1950 and 1977

Countries and groups of countries*	Poor (GNP per capita less than U.S. $200)		Bottom 60%		Top 10%		World population	
	1950	1977	1950	1977	1950	1977	1950	1977
Socialist economies	*42.1*	*28.3*	*37.0*	*36.6*	*8.9*	*17.9*	*34.2*	*33.5*
China**	41.8	28.3	36.3	36.5	0.0	0.0	22.5	24.0
USSR	0.0	0.0	0.0	0.0	3.8	13.4	7.4	6.3
East European countries	0.3	0.0	0.7	0.1	5.1	4.5	4.3	3.2
Market economies	*57.9*	*71.7*	*63.0*	*63.4*	*91.1*	*82.1*	*65.8*	*66.5*
Poor countries								
Indian subcontinent	26.9	40.8	28.1	30.0	0.0	0.0	18.4	19.6
Nigeria and Indonesia	8.0	6.9	7.6	7.9	0.0	0.0	4.8	5.2
Other	8.4	14.1	7.9	8.8	0.3	0.0	5.1	5.8
Developing countries	7.1	7.0	8.2	9.8	3.0	3.2	7.3	9.1
Newly industrialized countries	3.4	1.7	5.1	3.8	2.3	5.5	4.6	5.8
Oil-exporting countries	1.9	0.6	2.1	1.6	0.9	1.8	1.7	2.3
Semi-industrilized countries								
European	0.8	0.0	1.3	0.4	1.2	2.0	2.0	1.5
Other	0.4	0.5	0.4	0.7	1.9	0.8	1.3	1.4
Industrialized countries	*1.1*	*0.0*	*2.3*	*0.2*	*82.6*	*68.7*	*20.4*	*16.1*
United States	0.0	0.0	0.0	0.0	41.3	30.9	6.3	5.3
Largest five West European countries	0.4	0.0	0.9	0.2	30.0	23.8	8.3	6.1
Japan	0.7	0.0	1.2	0.0	1.7	7.3	3.4	2.8
Other	0.0	0.0	0.2	0.0	9.6	6.7	2.4	1.9

*See composition of country groups in Table 3.A-1
**Under Assumption A (see section 2).

pler. Population has grown much faster in poor and middle income countries than in rich countries. This necessarily shifts the bottom of the Lorenz curve upward and the top of the curve downward so that the net effect on world distribution is ambiguous. Since the Theil coefficient is more sensitive to changes at the top of the curve, it is raised sharply, whereas the MLD is almost unaffected.

In synthesis, the main proximate sources of change in the distribution of world GNP between 1950 and 1977 were: (i) the faster demographic growth in poor and developing countries producing an ambiguous effect on the Lorenz curve and inequality measures; (ii) the slow economic growth of poor countries apart from China—India being by far the most important—and the above average growth of nonsocialist developed countries, United States excluded, increasing inequality; (iii) the below average growth of the United States and the fast growth of China and some developing countries (the OPEC and NIC groups), lowering world inequality. Under Assumption A (fast economic growth in China) the third effect dominates the second. But, because developments in other countries have ambiguous effects, no clear conclusion can be reached as to how world inequality changed over this period.[34] This is the more true if Assumption B (of slower Chinese growth) is retained.

Although technically the same ambiguity remains when the analysis of this period is restricted to nonsocialist countries, many welfare criteria (including those implicit in all the summary measures we use) indicate a worsening in that case.[35] And if one focuses on absolute poverty the conclusion is unambiguous. The slow economic growth of the poorest countries, associated with the rapid increase of their populations, led to an increase in the absolute number of poor persons (income below 1970 U.S. $200) from about 680 million in 1950 to about 750 million in 1977 and to 860 million in 1986 (Figure 3.1). While the share of total population in poverty does show a marked decline (42.7 percent in 1950 to 27.5 percent in 1977 and 26.4 percent in 1986), it is alarming to see that the absolute number of poor was growing even between 1972 and 1977, let alone during the 1980s. Likewise, the increasing gap between the lower and the upper halves of the nonsocialist world is worrying. Although it has leveled off since 1972, it moved from 1:12.5 in 1950 to 1:14.6 in 1972.[36]

For the period 1980–85, with the world economy growing at about 3 percent (when country GDP is converted to U.S. dollars using purchasing power parities), the major forces unequivocally tending to raise world inequality were the relatively rapid growth of the industrialized nonmarket economies (per-capita GDP rising at nearly 3 percent, vs. a world average of about 1.25 percent per year) and the slow economic growth and fast population growth of the low income countries excluding China and South Asia—a group including much of sub-Saharan Africa. The economic and demographic trends in this latter group were the dominant force pushing up the absolute level of poverty over this period; whether the previous downward trend in the share of world population living in poverty has been significantly slowed in the 1980s will not be clear until Chinese data and those for the other socialist countries can be incorporated into the picture. The major factor working to lower the level of world inequality and poverty in the 1980s has been the fast economic growth of China and of the Indian subcontinent. Since about 70 percent of poverty was located in these regions as of 1977, the accelerated growth there and the considerable decline in the rate of population growth in China have no doubt permitted some further lowering of the share of world population in poverty. For the nonsocialist countries our data indicate virtually no change since 1977 in the share of people in poverty, as the marked gains in the Indian subcontinent have been offset by the accentuation of the poverty crisis in Sub-Saharan Africa. The sorry performance of the middle-income developing countries does not greatly affect most indicators of world distribution, precisely because they are around the middle of the distribution. Per-capita income growth in the industrialized market economies was not far from the world average and hence had no significant effect on world distribution.

4. Summary

The estimation of world income distribution for any point of time is plagued by many conceptual and statistical problems. It appears, fortunately, that estimates of trends in world distribution are rather less sensitive to these issues/problems than are point of time estimates.

Both the level and trends in world inequality can, in any case, be shown to depend mainly on intercountry differences in per-capita income and their trends. World inequality cannot, therefore, be seriously dealt with by national policy alone, important as that may be. Over the quarter century 1950–77 our summary measures indicate that the distribution of world GNP was essentially unchanged, while that of private consumption became more unequal. The difference between the two patterns reflected the decreasing private consumption to GNP ratios in the lower-income countries as a group. The 1950s saw improvement, 1960–72 worsening and 1972–77 a slight improvement. Developments in China were the main factor underlying these differences across subperiods, and the rapid growth of this country was a major equalizing factor for the quarter century as a whole. Within the nonsocialist camp, there was some increase in the inequality indicators for GNP, and a larger increase in those for consumption; the big gainers were the eighth and ninth deciles, while the bottom six deciles all lost. The slow growth of per-capita income in the Indian subcontinent was the main single factor in this latter development, while the rapid growth of such middle income countries as Japan, Russia, and (at a lower level) Brazil underlay the gains by the middle against both the top and the bottom.

Significant changes in the pattern of growth and a general slowdown for much of the world have occurred in the 1980s. The previously negative influence yielded (both on world inequality and on the level of poverty) by the sluggish growth of the Indian subcontinent was exactly reversed, at least for the time being, and together with the continued dynamism of China constituted a powerful positive factor. Other low-income countries as a group, however, fared much worse than before, contributing to a probably sharp increase in the level of poverty in Africa. The other dramatic reversal was in the cessation of the strong growth registered by the middle income developing countries, where poverty has also risen in the 1980s.

Taking the full period 1950–86, there was an unambiguous worsening in the distributions of income and consumption in the nonsocialist countries, a significant decrease in the share of people in poverty and a significant increase in the absolute number of people in poverty. For the world as a whole, we can conjecture, despite our inability to incorporate recent figures for the socialist countries, that there has been little overall change in the standard inequality indicators, a result of some gains for the bottom half and for the top decile or so, with losses for the intermediate group.

Appendix A. Note on Elasticities of Theil and MLD Coefficients

Let v_i and w_i be the shares of country i in world income and population respectively. Theil and MLD coefficients write:

$$(1) \qquad T = \sum_i v_i T_i + \sum_i v_i \log (v_i / w_i),$$

$$(2) \qquad L = \sum_i w_i L_i + \sum_i w_i \log (w_i / v_i),$$

where T_i and L_i are respectively Theil and MLD coefficients for the distribution of income within country i. Then v_i and w_i can be expressed as the following functions of population sizes, n_i, and mean incomes, y_i:

$$(3) \qquad v_i = n_i y_i / \sum_j n_j y_j$$

$$w_i = n_i / \sum_j n_j.$$

Differentiating now, (1), (2) and (3) with respect to the n_i, y_i, T_i, and L_i, yields the following elasticities of T and L.

$$(4) \qquad \varepsilon_{y_i}^T = \frac{v_i}{T} (T_i + \log v_i / w_i - T) \qquad \varepsilon_{y_i}^L = \frac{1}{L} (v_i - w_i),$$

$$\varepsilon_{n_i}^T = \frac{v_i}{T} (T_i + \log v_i / w_i - T) + \frac{1}{T} (w_i - v_i),$$

Table 3.A-1

Countries Included in the Analysis

I. Non-Socialist Countries

Poor countries

Indian subcontinent	Oil-producing Countries	Other poor countries
Bangladesh	Nigeria	Afghanistan
India	Indonesia	Botswana
Pakistan		Burma
Sri Lanka		Burundi
Nepal		Cambodia
		Central Africa
		Chad
		Ethiopia
		Gambia
		Lesotho
		Madagascar
		Malawi
		Mali
		Mauritania
		Rwanda
		Somalia
		Sudan
		Tanzania
		Togo
		Uganda
		Upper Volta
		Zaire

Developing Countries

Barbados	Malaysia	Senegal
Bolivia	Mauritius	Sierra Leone
Cameroon	Morocco	Swaziland
Chile	Nicaragua	Syria
Colombia	Panama	Thailand
Costa Rica	Papua	Trinidad
Dominican Republic	Paraguay	Tunisia
Egypt	Peru	Turkey
Ecuador	Philippines	Zambia
Fiji	Salvador	Zimbabwe
Ghana		
Guatemala		
Guyana		
Honduras		
Ivory Coast		
Jamaica		
Jordan		
Kenya		
Lebanon		
Liberia		

Newly industrialized countries

Brazil	Mexico	Taiwan
Hongkong	Singapore	South Korea

Oil exporting countries

Algeria	Kuwait	Qatar
Gabon	Libya	Saudi Arabia
Iraq	Oman	Venezuela
Iran		

Semi-industrialized countries

European		*Other*
Cyprus	Malta	Argentina
Greece	Portugal	South Africa
Ireland	Spain	Uruguay
Israel		

Developed Countries

United States	Canada	Australia	Japan
	France	Austria	
	Italy	Belgium	
	United Kingdom	Denmark	
	West Germany	Finland	
		Iceland	
		Netherlands	
		New Zealand	
		Norway	
		Sweden	
		Switzerland	

II. Socialist Countries

China	Bulgaria
	Czechoslovakia
	East Germany
	Hungary
	Poland
	Romania
	Soviet Union
	Yugoslavia

$$\varepsilon_{n_i}^L = \frac{w_i}{L} (L_i + \log w_i / v_i - L) + \frac{1}{L} (v_i - w_i) ,$$

$$\varepsilon_{T_i}^T = v_i \frac{T_i}{T} \qquad \varepsilon_{L_i}^L = w_i \frac{L_i}{L} .$$

Ignoring within-country inequalities (T_i, L_i), income elasticities, $\varepsilon_{y_i}^T$ and $\varepsilon_{y_i}^L$ are positive for countries with mean income sufficiently high with respect to the world mean $(\bar{y})$. The ratio v_i/w_i is equal to $y_i/\bar{y}$, so that $\varepsilon_{y_i}^L > 0$ if $y_i > \bar{y}$. For the Theil coefficient, the value above which $\varepsilon_{y_i}^T > 0$ is higher because this requires $\log y_i/\bar{y}$ to be larger than the world average of $\log y_i/\bar{y}$ weighted by the v_i's. So $\varepsilon_{y_i}^T$ is still negative for $y_i = \bar{y}$.

The sign of population elasticities is less easy to determine. They include two terms with eventually opposite signs. So for a high $y_i / \bar{y}$, the first term of $\varepsilon_{n_i}^T$— which is in fact $\varepsilon_{y_i}^T$ is positive but the second is negative, whereas the opposite is true for $\varepsilon_{n_i}^L$. This comes from the fact that a population increase at any extreme of a distribution implies a Lorenz curve which necessarily crosses the original one. So, the sign of population elasticities is ambiguous for low and high income countries. In formulae (4), it is clear that, when the ratio $y_i/\bar{y}$ goes from zero to infinity, the elasticities ε_{ni} are successively positive, negative and, positive again. Empirically, the preceding points seem to remain valid when internal inequalities T_i and L_i are taken into account.

Notes

1. Commission on International Development (1969).

2. The method used here consists of ranking the elementary groups defined above into a restricted number of income brackets, selected so that none of them include a significant percentage of the world population. A geometric progression of approximately one hundred brackets with appropriate rate and initial value proved sufficient for no bracket to include more than 2 percent of the world population in the low income range and 1 percent in the high income range (most inequality measures are particularly sensitive to high income values). Using decomposable inequality measures, the loss of precision implied by this method has always been less than 0.2 percent. For further details see Berry et al. (1983a).

3. Other measures could have been used but the decomposability property makes computation much easier. An unfortunate disadvantage of the mean logarithmic deviation as a measure of inequality is its failure to obey the principle of transfers over the entire income range (see chapter 1).

4. Let $\varepsilon_P^i, \varepsilon_Y^i$ and ε_T^i respectively be those elasticities for country i (their analytical expression is given in Appendix A). A first order approximation of the change in world inequality, as measured by the Theil coefficient, T, is:

(1) $$\delta T = \sum_i (\varepsilon_P^i P_i + \varepsilon_Y^i Y_i + \varepsilon_T^i \delta T_i) ,$$

where δ is the growth rate operator, and T_i is the Theil coefficient for country i. The decomposition formula (1) measures the contribution of economic and demographic growth in country i to changes in world inequality assuming zero growth in all other countries. The inequality measures which are used being homogeneous of degree zero in population and income, we know that

$$\sum_i \varepsilon_P^i = \sum_i \varepsilon_Y^i = 0 \; ;$$

hence (1) is equivalent to:

(2)
$$\delta T = \sum_i [\varepsilon_P^i (\delta P_i - \delta P^0) + \varepsilon_Y^i (\delta Y_i - \delta Y^0) + \varepsilon_T^i \delta T_i] \; ,$$

where δP^0 and δY^0 are arbitrary constants. The more general formula (2) does the same as formula (1), but under the assumption that rates of growth are respectively δP^0 and δY^0 for population and income *per capita* in all countries. The calculated decomposition of changes in world inequality varies with the reference rates (δP^o and δY^0) chosen. This choice is essentially arbitrary—it depends on the question one wishes to ask. Here we adopt reference rates equal to the mean world population and *per-capita* income growth rates over the whole 1950–77 period; the arbitrary nature of the choice must be kept in mind.

5. For noncommunist countries the conversion rate used in our calculations of world income are from Kravis et al. (1978a). For most socialist countries the rates are based on a variety of sources, discussed in Berry et al. (1981a), Annex 4a. A useful discussion of some of the conceptual and other difficulties involved in these comparisons is Marris (1979).

6. Especially the fact that there is no obvious interpretation of any comparison of incomes of two groups not based on the relative prices of one of them.

7. There appears no reason to believe that the true purchasing power parity between two countries would systematically lie closer to the limit defined by one country's prices than to that defined by the other country's prices.

8. For further details see Berry et al. (1983b).

9. A third factor, the difference between consumption purchasing power parities and income purchasing power parities, appears to have a mild tendency to increase inequality of world consumption relative to that of world income.

10. For example, in Estimate 1 of world income distribution, the Theil coefficient would be 0.51 even if distribution was perfectly equal within each country, while the actual Theil coefficient was 0.80.

11. The range given by Estimates 1 and 2 for the Gini coefficient of the income distribution of the nonsocialist countries is 0.68–0.71, whereas it was 0.65–0.68 when socialist countries were included.

12. For further details see Berry et al. (1981a).

13. See Berry et al. (1981a). The small income elasticity for the USSR comes from its standing roughly at the middle of the world income distribution.

14. Different sources vary considerably in their local currency estimates of per capita income or output. A recent discussion is Perkins (1980). Further, estimating the purchasing power parity of the Chinese currency is more difficult than for most countries.

15. See Berry et al. (1981a).

16. Thus between 1960 and 1986 average life expectancy in the group classed in World Bank (1988a) as low income rose by 46 percent (from 41.5 to 60.5) while for the industrial market economies the increase was only 8 percent (70.5 to 76 years).

17. The population, GNP per capita and consumption per capita series used for our detailed analysis of the period 1950–77 are from *World Tables 1976* and *World Tables*

1980 (World Bank 1976, 1980a), complemented by our own estimates for some countries in early years (1950–55) and by recent issues of the *World Bank Atlas, World Development Report* (World Bank 1976, 1980a, 1988a, 1988b), and by Summers and Heston (1984, 1988).

The 1970 local currency values have been converted to 1970 U.S. dollars by the purchasing power parity indices estimated by Kravis et al. (1978b) for most nonsocialist countries in the analysis. The 1970 dollar values for other years are based on the growth rates of GNP and consumption in constant local prices between 1970 and the year in question.

For most socialist countries, we estimated the purchasing power parity with the U.S. dollar using a variety of sources and attempting to maintain a methodological parallel with the figures of Kravis et al. The validity of estimates for earlier years is lessened by the fact that the basket of goods used in the estimation of purchasing power parity may be more and more inappropriate as one moves away from 1970. The same limitation plagues the measurement of national growth rates, however, since many countries change their base years quite infrequently; not much can be done to alleviate either problem.

The intracountry inequality data we use are estimates made circa 1970 of the household income distribution, which is usually quite similar to the distribution of per capita household income among individuals (the distribution we are conceptually most interested in). They are the same data underlying Table 3.3 above. We disregard changes which may have occurred over the 1950–77 period. For most developed countries reasonably good data indicate that those changes have been minor. In developing countries lack of adequate data is a major problem. We had at our disposal reasonably good income distribution estimates at two points of time (usually about 1960 and 1970) for some twenty countries at various levels of development and representing 70 percent of the population of the nonsocialist developing world. In one experiment we equated the change in the distribution of any given country to the average change observed in those of the twenty above-mentioned countries at the same level of development; in another we assumed unchanged distribution in each of the missing countries; in each case the effect of these intracountry changes in inequality on trends in world distribution was almost negligible, less than 0.5 percent for the Gini and Theil coefficients. Given this and the weak evidence on intracountry distribution trends in less developed countries, we elected to assume inequality constant in each country at its 1970 level (or as close to that year as possible). In the case of countries for which no reasonably good data exist on distribution, we have estimated the level of inequality on the basis of that in similar countries. (See Berry et al. 1981b.) The constancy assumption may lead to a slight downward bias in the estimated trend of world inequality, but sensitivity analysis indicates that reasonable alternative assumptions would not much alter the conclusions. Note that keeping national distributions constant is not equivalent to assuming intracountry inequality away. Intracountry inequalities give some inertia to world inequality and countries' contributions to changes in world inequality, as described by equation (2) for instance, depend very much on their own income distribution. A final assumption is that the distribution of private consumption in a given country is the same as that of income; whereas in Table 3.3 our objective was to contrast the income and consumption distributions so we estimated the latter somewhat crudely with the limited data at hand, in the present context our main concern is with over-time trends.

18. These problems are discussed in detail in Berry et al. (1981a).

19. Following the theoretical literature on inequality (for instance, Sen 1973), a change in the world distribution will be described as "unambiguous" if it lowers or raises the whole Lorenz curve. If the whole Lorenz curve does not shift in one direction, the change will be described as "ambiguous" even though the various summary measures of inequality may indicate a worsening or an improvement of the distribution.

20. Their rate of growth of per capita income has been 3.8 percent versus 2.6 percent for the whole world. Increases in the relative income of intermediate deciles tend to produce an ambiguous shift in the Lorenz curve. The ranking of socialist countries in the world distribution is such that in terms of conventional inequality measures, this shift is slightly equalizing.

21. See the discussion in Berry et al. (1981a).

22. This definition is that used recently by the World Bank. See for instance, Ahluwalia et al. (1979).

23. Hence neither shows up in the series for nonsocialist countries.

24. As noted above, our assumption for purposes of the trend analysis that the distribution of private consumption is the same as that of income in each country leads to an upward bias in our estimates of world inequality of consumption; the bias is unlikely to change much over time, however, so there is no reason to believe that the trends we estimate would be significantly affected by use of this assumption. Since public expenditures also contribute to the current well-being of a country's citizens, it would have been better to consider total instead of only private consumption expenditures, especially since the ratio of public to private consumption does vary across countries and in particular between socialist and capitalist countries. Lack of information on the distribution of the benefits of public consumption severely hampers any such attempt. The available information on the rate of growth of public consumption by groups of countries does suggest that its inclusion would not alter the results significantly.

25. See World Bank (1980b), Table 5.

26. One may wonder to what degree private consumption figures reflect the income changes associated with phenomena like the sharp change in terms of trade associated with the oil crisis. The answer seems to be "only partially." OPEC countries did increase their consumption considerably faster than their GNP over 1972–77, taking advantage of the gain in their terms of trade. The increase was, however, far from reflecting the size of their additional oil income which, in fact, has been partly transferred to or invested in other countries and, in particular, rich countries.

27. End of 1987 data show a ratio of 0.69 for sub-Saharan Africa compared to 0.48 for the fifteen biggest debtors in the Third World (IMF 1988, p. 182).

28. The country composition of the groups is given in Appendix B.

29. In the period since 1977, however, the Indian subcontinent's share of poverty has declined significantly, so that its behavior has been similar to though less extreme than that of China. Meanwhile the decline in the share of Indonesia and Nigeria has been reversed with the sharp fall in Nigeria's per-capita income in the 1980s, and the increase in the share of the other poor market economies has continued and probably accelerated.

30. For further details see Berry et al. (1983a).

31. For further details see Berry et al. (1983a, Table 4).

32. Under Assumption B (slower increase in China's income per capita), China's contribution to changes in world Theil and MLD would fall respectively to about −1.8 percent and about −2.9 percent. Though still having the largest single negative effect of any country on MLD and a comparable effect to that of the United States on the Theil coefficient, China's experience is much less dominant under this assumption.

33. "Direct" in the sense that no account is taken of the caused interactions between population growth and growth of per capita income. A full causal analysis would require a model of the relationship in each country between population growth and the growth of per capita GNP. With such a model, formula (2) can once again be employed. Consider the impact of a slower rate of population growth in the Indian subcontinent, for example a growth of 1.2 percent per year instead of the actually observed 2.2 percent. If one assumed an output elasticity of population growth of 0.33 percent, the 1 percent lower rate

of population would lower the growth of output by 0.33 percent per year, and raise the growth of per capita output by 0.67 percent per year. Whereas the above average growth of population in the Indian subcontinent could be said to be the ''cause'' of a 0.4 percent increase in the world Theil coefficient—were there no causal relation between that growth rate and per capita income growth (this figure is from Berry et al. 1983, Table 4)—with an output elasticity of population growth of 0.33 it could be blamed for an increase of about 0.7 percent. Our figures thus understate the negative impact of fast population growth in the poor countries on world inequality.

For a full discussion of demographic effects, see Bourguignon et al. (1988).

34. Of the six summary measures we use, three (Gini, Theil, and MLD) fell, two were essentially unchanged, and one Atkinson, ($\varepsilon = -2.0$) rose. But all the changes were quite small.

35. As discussed earlier, for the longer period 1950–86 there is no ambiguity of the sort referred to here; the data indicate an unequivocal worsening.

36. As noted above, this gap remains approximately constant when socialist countries are included.

References

Adelman, I. (1984). ''The World Distribution of Income.'' In *Problemen und Perspektiven der Weltwirtschaftlichen Entwicklung*. Berlin: Dunckert Humblot, pp. 575–93.

Amin, S. (1974). *Accumulation on a World Scale*. New York: Monthly Review Press.

Ahluwalia, M., N. Carter, and H. Chenery (1979). ''Growth and Poverty in Developing Countries.'' *Journal of Development Economics* 6:299–342.

Atkinson, A. (1975). *The Economics of Inequality*. Oxford: Clarendon Press.

Berry, A., F. Bourguignon, and C. Morrisson (1983a). ''Changes in the World Distribution of Income between 1950 and 1977.'' *Economic Journal* 93:331–50.

——— (1983b). ''The Level of World Inequality: How Much Can One Say?'' *Review of Income and Wealth*, Series 29, 3:217–41.

——— (1981a). ''How Unequal are Material Standards of Living Within and Between Countries?'' Mimeo, Laboratoire d'Économique Politique, École Normale Supérieure, Paris.

——— (1981b). ''Data for the Analysis of the World Distribution of Income,'' Working Paper No. 39, LEP, École Normale Supérieure, Paris.

Bourguignon, F. (1979). ''Decomposable Income Inequality Measures.'' *Econometrica* 47:901–20.

Bourguignon, F., C. Morrisson, and A. Berry (1988). ''The World Distribution of Income: Evolution over the Recent Period and Effects of Population Growth.'' Mimeo.

Commission on International Development (1969). *Partners in Development*. New York: Praeger.

Emmanuel, A. (1972). *Unequal Exchange: A Study of the Imperialism of the Imperialism of Trade*. New York and London: Brian Pearce, Trans.

Frank, A.G. (1978). *Dependent Accumulation and Underdevelopment*. London: Macmillan.

International Monetary Fund (1988). *IMF Survey*. Washington: International Monetary Fund.

Kravis, I., A. Heston, and R. Summers (1978a). ''Real GDP Per Capita for More Than One Hundred Countries.'' *Economic Journal* 88:215–42.

——— (1978b). *United Nations International Comparison Project: Phase II; International Comparisons of Real Product and Purchasing Power*. Baltimore: Johns Hop-

Marris, R. (1979). "A Survey and Critique of World Bank Supported Research on International Comparisons of Real Product." *World Bank Staff Working Paper No. 365.*

Morawetz, D. (1978). *Twenty-Five Years of Economic Development: 1950–75.* Washington: World Bank.

Perkins, D. (1980). "Issues in the Estimation of China's National Product." In Alexander Eckstein, ed., *Quantitative Measures of China's Economic Output.* Ann Arbor: University of Michigan Press.

Sen, A. (1973). *On Economic Inequality.* Oxford: Clarendon Press.

Shorrocks, A. (1980). "The Class of Additively Decomposable Inequality Measures." *Econometrica* 48:613–25.

Summers, R., and A. Heston (1984). "Improved International Comparisons of Real Product and Its Composition, 1950–1980." *Review of Income and Wealth*, Series 30, 2:207–62.

———— (1988). "A New Set of International Comparisons of Real Product and Prices: Estimates for 130 Countries, 1950–1985." *Review of Income and Wealth*, Series 34, 1:1–26.

Summers, R., B. Irving, I. Kravis, and A. Heston (1981). "Inequality among Nations: 1950 and 1975." *Disparities in Economic Development Since the Industrial Revolution.* P. Bairoch and M. Levy-Leboyer, eds. London: Macmillan, chapter 2.

Theil, H. (1967). *Economics and Information Theory.* Amsterdam: North-Holland.

———— (1979). "World Inequality and Its Components." *Economic Letters*, 2:8–14.

Whalley, J. (1979). "The Worldwide Income Distribution: Some Speculative Calculations." *Review of Income and Wealth*, Series 25, 3:261–76.

World Bank (1976). *World Tables.* Washington, DC: John Hopkins University Press for the World Bank.

———— (1980a). *World Tables.* Washington, DC: John Hopkins University Press for the World Bank.

———— (1980b). *World Development Report 1980.* Washington, DC: Johns Hopkins University Press for the World Bank.

———— (1987). *World Development Report 1987.* Washington, DC: Johns Hopkins University Press for the World Bank.

———— (1988). *World Development Report 1988.* Washington, DC: Johns Hopkins University Press for the World Bank.

———— (1988). *World Bank Atlas.* Washington, DC: Johns Hopkins University Press for the World Bank.

4

The Distribution of Household Wealth: Methodological Issues, Time Trends, and Cross-Sectional Comparisons

Edward N. Wolff

1. Introduction

There has been renewed interest in the subject of wealth distribution in North America and Western Europe in the last several years. In the United States, for example, there has been a virtual explosion of surveys on household wealth over the last ten years. Results from these surveys have appeared in newspapers and magazines around the country and generated considerable controversy and attention.

In this paper, I will focus on methodological and factual issues connected with the distribution of household wealth: (1) What is the proper definition of wealth? (2) What are the most effective methods for estimating the size distribution of wealth from available data? (3) Has there been any historical movement towards greater equality in the distribution of household wealth? (4) Is it proper to include measures of retirement wealth in the household balance sheet and, if so, how do such assets affect overall inequality in the size distribution of household wealth? (5) Since families tend to accumulate wealth over time, how important, empirically, is age in explaining differences in household wealth? (6) Do there appear to be significant differences in the concentration of wealth among industrialized countries? There are four findings of particular note that emerge from this survey. First, the degree of wealth inequality among households declined from the early 1920s through the 1970s. This observation is based on data for Sweden, the United Kingdom, and the United States, the only countries for which such long time-series information is available. The share of total household wealth held by the top 1 percent of wealth holders declined from 50 percent in 1920 to 21 percent in 1975 in Sweden, from 61 percent in 1923 to 23 percent in 1974 in Great Britain, and from 38 percent in 1922 to 19 percent in 1976 in the United States. Second, since the mid-1970s or so, the degree of wealth inequality has remained relatively constant in the United Kingdom and has risen in Sweden and the United States. Third, despite the decline in wealth inequality since the early part of this century, household wealth is still highly concentrated today. In the mid-1970s, the richest 1 percent held a quarter of all household wealth in France and the United States, over 30 percent in the United Kingdom, and about a fifth in Sweden. Indeed, household wealth is considerably more concentrated than household income. Fourth, attempts to account for the high degree of wealth inequality in these countries on the basis of age and other demographic factors have yielded very little. This suggests major modifications in formal models of household wealth accumulation to include more behavioral and institutional factors.

The remainder of this paper is divided into four parts. The first of these, section 2, discusses several important methodological issues involved in the estimation of household wealth inequality. As will become apparent in this discussion, the problems involved in wealth estimates are much more severe than those related to income estimates. Section 3 presents results on time trends in household wealth for three countries, Sweden, the United Kingdom, and the United States. The discussion is limited to these three nations, because they are the only ones for which long time series are available on wealth inequality. Section 4 considers cross-sectional comparisons of household wealth inequality within a single country among different demographic groups and for different concepts of household wealth. Since much of this literature considers age as a principal factor, a brief discussion of the so-called "life cycle" model will also be included. In addition, some relatively tentative international comparisons of wealth inequality are also presented. The last part presents some concluding comments and discusses some broader implications of the survey.[1]

2. Methodological Issues

In most industrialized countries today, there are now official estimates of the size distribution of household income. In the United States, for example, the census bureau conducts an annual survey in March, called the Current Population Survey, which provides detailed information on individual and household earnings and income. On the basis of these data, the U.S. Census Bureau constructs its estimates of both family and household income inequality. Moreover, the Current Population Surveys have been conducted in the United States for more than twenty years. As a result, there exists a consistent time-series on household income distribution for the United States which covers more than two decades.

Unfortunately, there do not exist comparable data on the size distribution of household wealth for the United States or, for that matter, for any other country in the world. As a result, researchers in this field have had to make estimates of household wealth inequality from a variety of sources, which are often inconsistent and, indeed, contradictory. Compounding this problem is the fact that household wealth is much more heavily concentrated in the upper percentiles of the distribution than income. Thus, unless surveys or data sources are especially designed to cover the top wealth groups in a country, it is quite easy to produce biased estimates of the size distribution of wealth. The net result is that estimates of household wealth distribution are much less reliable than those of income distribution.

There are, correspondingly, many more methodological problems associated with household wealth data than with income data. These include: (1) the definition of household wealth, (2) the unit of observation, (3) the treatment of retirement assets, (4) underreporting biases, (5) sampling problems, (6) asset coverage, (7) institutional differences in wealth ownership over time, and (8) the statistical measurement of wealth distributions. I shall discuss the first three issues and the last in separate sections below. However, the underreporting, sampling, and asset coverage problems one encounters depend very much on the type of data one is using as the basis of the estimates, and, as a result, I shall organize the discussion of these three methodological issues by data sources.

A. Definition of Wealth

A theme that regularly emerges in the literature on household wealth is that there is no unique concept or definition of wealth that is satisfactory for all purposes. There are six that can be identified in the literature: (i) the accounting notion of wealth as the market value of assets (less liabilities) that are directly tradable; (ii) the neoclassical notion of wealth as the present value of the future stream of income; (iii) the potential future consumption represented by the stock of wealth; (iv) a liquidity notion of wealth as the ability to circumvent financial constraints that would otherwise be binding; (v) the Marxian notion of wealth as a measure of the power and influence that can be exercised; and (vi) wealth as the potential advantages transmitted to future generation of heirs. Each concept is important in a different theoretical construct.

Household disposable wealth. The conventional or traditional definition of household wealth includes assets and liabilities that have a current market value and that are directly or indirectly marketable (fungible). A typical list of assets includes owner-occupied housing and other real estate; consumer durables and household inventories; cash, checking and savings accounts; bonds, and other financial instruments; corporate stocks or shares; the equity in unincorporated businesses; trust funds; and the cash surrender value of life insurance policies and pension plans. I refer to this measure as "household disposable wealth," or HDW, since it represents those assets over which the family or individual has control (see, for example, Wolff 1983, for further discussion). This notion corresponds to wealth as a store of value and is used in the standard national accounting framework.

Augmented wealth. A wider definition of household wealth will often add some valuation of pension rights, from both public and private sources, to disposable wealth. Such a measure provides a better gauge of potential future consumption. A still wider definition will also include human capital or some comparable measure of future earnings possibilities. This is the concept of wealth that is most consistent with neoclassical theory, since it represents the present value of the discounted stream of future net income flows. In principle, all forms of future income should be included in computing "augmented wealth." These include property income, labor earnings, private pension income, and government transfers such as social security benefits, unemployment benefits, welfare payments, disability payments, medical payments, food stamps, and the like. The first four are by far the biggest and, for simplicity, I shall ignore the others.[2] The first component of augmented wealth, the present value of the future stream of net income from household assets (less liabilities), is presumably already captured in HDW. That is to say, if all capital markets are perfect (a typical neoclassical assumption), then the current market value of household assets (liabilities) should equal the present value of their corresponding income (payment) flows.[3] HDW thus, in theory, capitalizes the future net income flows emanating from disposable assets and liabilities.

The second component of augmented wealth is the capitalized value of future labor earnings, usually referred to as "human capital." Unlike disposable assets, there are no capital markets to assign a market value to human beings based on expectations of their future earnings. However, by making certain assumptions about the future state of the economy, one can estimate human capital for current workers.

The other two components are pension and social security wealth—or, more properly, pension and social security "entitlements." Pension entitlements are defined as the present value of discounted future pension benefits less the present value of discounted future pension contributions.[4] In similar fashion, social security entitlements are defined as the present value of the discounted stream of future social security benefits less the present value of future social security contributions. Future entitlements for both pensions and the social security program depend on many factors, such as the health (and survival) of a company, productivity growth and other macroeconomic variables, and future legislation. Thus, estimating the value of these two forms of wealth is, to a large extent, arbitrary, particularly for the younger age cohorts.[5]

The concept used in computing pension and social security wealth is their *net* value. The gross value of each is defined as the capitalized value of future benefits. The net value is the difference between this and the capitalized value of future contributions. The net value is used instead of the gross value in order to be consistent with the neoclassical notion of wealth that requires the capitalized value of the net addition to the future income stream from the various sources of income. If benefits were exactly determined by contributions (as in a defined contribution pension plan), there would be no net addition to wealth, since the future benefits would already be captured in human capital. To include the future benefits in this case would be to double-count. Thus, the only addition to this form of wealth from the private pension or the social security system would occur if a given group of retirees received a "bonus" over and above their accumulated contributions. For the social security system, this has been histori- cally true, at least up to now, through legislative fiat. The underlying economic conditions that allowed this were labor force participation patterns, the age distri- bution, the start-up of the system in 1937, sustained productivity growth since World War II, and the pay-as-you-go nature of the social security system. Cer- tain defined benefit pension plans also have this feature, where benefits are determined by a formula involving years of service and company earnings his- tory, rather than by the worker's contributions into the pension fund. In this regard, the social security system is treated as a defined benefit plan.

There are, of course, many methodological issues and problems associated with the inclusion of both pension and social security wealth in the household portfolio, as well as that of human capital. Since such items are not directly marketable (neither future pension and social security benefits nor human capital can be transferred or used as collateral for a loan) nor under the direct control of the household or individual, it is questionable whether they should even be considered household wealth. Moreover, the argument which is used to justify the inclusion of social security and pension wealth in household wealth also implies that human capital should be included as part of the household portfolio. Most studies include only social security and pension wealth in the household balance sheet. In addition, many simplifying assumptions are required in order to estimate expected income paths. Besides the ones mentioned above, the re- searcher must project the interest rate, the future growth of earnings, and future retirement transfers. Moreover, tractability entails limiting such projections to representative population groups, thus underestimating the true variance in the distribution of future income flows. As a result, estimates of augmented wealth should be viewed with considerable caution and interpreted with care.

Narrow wealth concepts. Some authors have also used definitions that are narrower than disposable wealth. In previous work (see Wolff 1981), I proposed a division of household wealth into two components. The first, which I called "life cycle wealth," consists of net equity in owner-occupied housing (the gross value less the mortgage debt), consumer durables, household inventories, cash and demand deposits, and the cash value of life insurance and pensions less consumer debt. The second, called "capital wealth," is the residual, defined as the sum of time and savings deposits, bonds and securities, corporate stock, business equity, net equity in investment real estate, and trust fund equity. I called the first set of wealth components life cycle wealth, because in previous work (Wolff 1981) it was found that the distribution of this form of wealth among households was better accounted for by the life cycle model of savings than the distribution of total household wealth (see below for a discussion of the life cycle model). Households which do accumulate wealth over the life cycle do so mainly for their own use (housing, durables, inventory), liquidity (currency and demand deposits), and retirement (pensions and life insurance cash surrender value). In a sense, this form of wealth is accumulated for its service flows or "use-value," to use a Marxian term.

In contrast, capital wealth is accumulated as a store of value or for its "exchange value." These assets are directly associated with the ownership of the means of production and are held primarily for their income-producing potential. It is this form of wealth which confers economic and social power on a family rather than disposable or life cycle wealth measures. These assets are held almost exclusively by the upper wealth classes and are often transmitted to succeeding generations. From the standpoint of political economy, it is capital wealth which is of direct relevance for the division of society into economic classes—particularly, capitalists, landlords, and workers.

Another measure that is sometimes used in the literature is liquid wealth, defined as financial assets less unsecured debt. This form of wealth can be almost immediately converted into cash (which is what is meant by "liquidity") and thus has the most direct relevance for consumption behavior. This measure of wealth is used quite often in analyses of the consumption behavior of young and poor families.

B. Unit of Observation

Another definitional issue revolves around the proper unit of observation. As we shall discuss below, there are three basic units of observation in primary wealth data: the family (or household), the individual, and the taxpaying unit. However, in general, the proper unit for either welfare or behavioral analysis will not directly correspond to the observational unit. In regard to welfare, family wealth, family per capita wealth, and some combination of the two has each been used as a measure of welfare in the literature. Family wealth is employed most frequently, since families are the primary unit of consumption. However, smaller families are probably better off than larger families who have the same level of family wealth. This recommends a family per capita wealth measure. Greenwood (1987), for example, adjusts her inequality measure for household size. Yet, there are economies of consumption, so that family per capita wealth may actually understate the welfare level of large families. An alternative approach is to divide household wealth by an "equivalence scale" which adjusts family size for actual consumption needs. Radner and Vaughan (1987), for example, use the U.S. poverty line levels as an equivalence scale to obtain a household wealth welfare measure. A similar approach is employed by Greenwood and Wolff (1988) and Haveman, Wolfe, Finnie, and Wolff (1988) for various analyses of the change in family welfare for specific demographic groups over the 1962–83 period in the United States.

From a behavioral point of view, the family is used most often as the unit of analysis, since families tend to make wealth decisions jointly and accumulate wealth over time for future consumption needs. Yet, over time, the family is not a stable unit. Children leave families to set up independent family units. Moreover, it is quite common for married couples to separate or divorce, and, as a result, for family wealth to be split. From this standpoint, it may also be appropriate to base behavioral models on individual wealth accumulation decisions.[6]

C. The Role of Retirement Systems

Another major concern in the literature is the role of retirement systems in household wealth accumulation. One of the major developments in the postwar period among industrialized countries has been the enormous growth in both public and private pension systems. Even though such pension funds are not in the direct control of individuals or families, they are a source of future income to families and thus may be perceived as a form of family wealth. Moreover, as Feldstein (1974) has argued, insofar as families accumulate "traditional" wealth to provide for future consumption needs, the growth of such pension funds may have offset private savings and hence traditional wealth accumulation.

Two different treatments of pensions are represented in the literature. The first, and most common, is a "wealth" approach, where various attempts are made to estimate both public and private pension wealth. These imputations are based on varying assumptions about the future growth in earnings and pension benefits. Such estimates are then included as part of household wealth. In some analyses, cross-sectional comparisons are provided of the distribution of such wider notions of wealth and that of traditional measures of household wealth (see Feldstein 1976 and Wolff 1987, for example). In other analyses, time-series trends are compared for the concentration of expanded household wealth and that of conventional wealth measures (see Shorrocks 1987 and Wolff and Marley 1987, for example). The second is an "annuity" approach, where retirement income flows are projected from both public and private pensions on the basis of varying assumptions regarding future benefit growth. These estimated benefits are then included along with expected income flows from traditional household wealth to compute post-retirement income. Analyses are then possible regarding the "adequacy" of retirement income with respect to pre-retirement income (see Wolfson 1987, for example).

D. Data Sources

There is extensive discussion in the wealth literature concerning the measurement problems and biases inherent in the various sources of household wealth data. There have been five principal sources of data for developing household wealth estimates: (i) estate tax data; (ii) household survey data; (iii) wealth tax data; (iv) income capitalization techniques; and (v) synthetic data sources. I shall begin the discussion with estate tax data, since it was the first major source of data used for wealth analysis.

 1. *Estate tax data.* Estate tax records are actual tax returns filed for probate. Such data have a great degree of reliability, since they are subject to scrutiny and audit by the state. Their main limitation, in the United States at least, is that the threshold for filing is relatively high, so that only a small proportion of estates (typically, one percent or so) are required to file returns.[7] Another difficulty with these data is that the sample consists of decedents. As a result, various assumptions must be used to construct "estate multipliers" in order to infer the distribution of wealth among the living. Insofar as mortality rates are inversely correlated with wealth (that is, the rich tend to live longer), the resulting multipliers can be biased. Moreover, the resulting estimated distribution of wealth is by individual, rather than by family. Changing ownership patterns within families (for example, joint ownership of the family's house) can affect estimated wealth concentration. In addition, various assumptions must be made to infer family wealth from estimates of individual wealth holdings.

 Another problem involves underreporting and nonfiling for tax avoidance. Though the returns are subject to audit, the value of cash on hand, jewelry, housewares, and business assets are difficult to ascertain. Their value is typically understated in order to reduce the tax liability of the estate. Moreover, *inter vivos* transfers, particularly in anticipation of death, can bias estimates of household wealth among the living. Estate tax data have been extensively used by Atkinson and Harrison (1978) and Shorrocks (1987) for the United Kingdom, and Lampman (1962), Smith (1984, 1987), and Wolff and Marley (1989) for the United States. The long-term time-series concentration estimates for Britain and the United States are based on estate tax data and the individual unit of account.

 2. *Household survey data.* The second principal source is the field survey. Its primary advantage is that it provides considerable discretion to the interviewer about the information requested of respondents. However, its major disadvantage is that information provided by the respondent is often inaccurate, and, in many cases, the information requested is not provided at all. Another problem is that because household wealth is extremely skewed, the very rich (the so-called "upper tail" of the distribution) are often considerably underrepresented in random samples. An alternative is to use stratified samples, based typically on income tax returns, which oversample the rich. However, studies indicate that response error and nonresponse rates are considerably higher among the wealthy than among the middle class. Two major surveys for the United States, the 1962 Survey of Financial Characteristics of Consumers and the 1983 Survey of Consumer Finances, are described in detail in Projector and Weiss (1966) and Avery, Elliehausen, and Kennickell (1988), respectively.

 3. *Wealth tax data.* A third source is wealth tax return data. A few countries,

such as Sweden and, recently, France, assess taxes not only on current income but also on the stock of household wealth. Though there is typically a threshold for paying wealth taxes, their coverage of the population can be considerably greater than that of estate tax returns. However, the measurement problems are similar to that of estate tax data. The filer has a great incentive to understate the value of his assets, or even not to report them, for tax avoidance. Moreover, the assets subject to tax do not cover the full range of household assets (for example, consumer durables are often excluded). In addition, the observational unit is the tax return unit, which does not necessarily correspond to the family unit. Wealth tax data have been used extensively by Spånt (1987) for an analysis of wealth trends in Sweden.

4. *Income capitalization techniques.* The fourth type of wealth data is based on "income capitalization" techniques, which are usually applied to income tax return data. In this procedure, certain income flows, such as dividends, rents, and interest, are converted into corresponding asset values based on the average asset yield. This source also suffers from a number of defects. First, only assets with a corresponding income flow are covered in this procedure. Thus, owner-occupied housing, consumer durables, and idle land cannot be directly captured. Also, in the United States, state and local bonds cannot be estimated, because this source of interest income is exempt from federal income taxes. Second, the estimation procedure rests heavily on the assumption that asset yields are uncorrelated with asset levels. Any actual correlation between asset holdings and yields can produce biased estimates. Third, the observational unit is the tax return, which is not strictly comparable to the individual or family. Various assumptions must be imposed in order to construct family wealth estimates from tax unit wealth. The earliest study using this technique on U.S. data was that of Stewart (1939).

5. *Synthetic data sources.* Another source of data comes from the use of various eclectic approaches. These involve combining two or more basic sources of data, as well as merging and matching of datasets. There are two principal examples of this approach for the United States. First, Wolff (1980, 1982, and 1983) matched U.S. tax return data from the Internal Revenue Service with U.S. Census household survey data. Income capitalization was then applied to the tax return data to obtain values of corresponding assets, and the Census data were used to supply values for some of the missing assets, such as the value of owner-occupied housing. Second, Greenwood (1983, 1987) used a specially constructed dataset in which individual income tax records were matched to family records in the 1973 Current Population Survey. Income capitalization was also applied to income flows to obtain corresponding asset values. This approach has the advantage of combining the strengths of the basic data sources. However, the major disadvantage is that the joint distributions of noncommon variables in the two data sources, imputed from statistical matches, are statistically unreliable.

E. Inequality Indices

Though not a major focus of this survey, issues regarding the measurement of household wealth inequality require a brief mention as a background for sections 3 and 4 below. Because much of the data used in wealth analysis is limited to the upper percentiles of the wealth distribution, the most common concentration measures are the shares of the top one, two, or five percent of the wealth distribution. Where wealth data for representative samples are available, the most common measure is the Gini coefficient (see chapter 1). Gini coefficients, by construction, range from a low of zero to a high of unity. Gini coefficients for household wealth are typically of the order of 0.7 to 0.8. In comparison, those for income are typically in the neighborhood of 0.4. Several attempts have also been made to adjust the Gini coefficient for sources of inequality related strictly to life cycle factors (see Greenwood 1987, for example).

3. Long-Term Time Trends in Household Wealth Inequality

There are three countries for which long-term time-series are available on household wealth inequality: the United Kingdom, Sweden, and the United States. The most comprehensive data exist for the United Kingdom, and I will discuss the findings for that country first.

A. The United Kingdom

A 1987 paper by Anthony Shorrocks summarizes results of several previous studies of long-term trends in household wealth inequality in the United Kingdom, and I will use his work as the basis of this discussion.[8] The principal finding of his study is that there was a dramatic decline in the degree of household wealth inequality in the United Kingdom from 1923 to 1974 but little change thereafter. Based on a conventional definition of wealth, the share of the top 1 percent of wealth holders fell from 61 percent in 1923 to 23 percent in 1974; the share of the top 5 percent declined from 82 to 43 percent; and the share of the top 10 percent dropped from 89 to 57 percent. However, between 1974 and 1980, the last date for which these series are available, there was virtually no change in the concentration of household wealth.

Details are provided in Table 4.1 (also see Figure 4.1). The decline in wealth concentration was not continuous during this period. Between 1923 and 1930, there was relatively little change in the share of wealth held by the top wealth holders. However, between 1930 and 1950, there followed a significant decline in inequality, with the share of the top 1 percent falling by 10 percentage points and that of the top 5 percent by 5 percentage points. Another substantial decline in inequality occurred between 1950 and 1962, with the share of the top 1 percent dropping from 47 to 31 percent and that of the top 5 percent from 74 to

Table 4.1

Shares of Total Household Net Worth Held by Richest Individual Wealthholders in the United Kingdom, 1923–80

	England and Wales			United Kingdom[a]		
	Top 1%	Top 5%	Top 10%	Top 1%	Top 5%	Top 10%
A. Traditional (disposable) wealth						
1923	61%	82%	89%			
1924	60	82	88			
1925	61	82	88			
1926	57	80	87			
1927	60	81	88			
1928	57	80	87			
1929	56	79	86			
1930	58	79	87			
1936	54	77	86			
1938	55	77	85			
1950	47	74	—			
1951	46	74	—			
1952	43	70	—			
1953	44	71	—			
1954	45	72	—			
1955	45	71	—			
1956	45	71	—			
1957	43	69	—			
1958	41	68	—			
1959	41	68	—			
1960	34	60	72			
1961	37	61	72			
1962	31	55	67			
1964	35	59	71			
1965	33	58	72			
1966	31	56	69	33%	56%	69%
1967	31	56	70	—	—	—
1968	34	58	72	—	—	—
1969	31	56	68	—	—	—
1970	30	54	69	—	—	—
1971	28	52	68	31	52	65
1972	32	56	70	—	—	—

Year				
1974	—	23	43	57
1975	—	24	44	58
1976	—	24	46	61
1977	—	23	44	58
1978	—	23	44	58
1979	—	24	45	59
1980	—	23	43	58

B. Estimates including entitlements to occupational pensions[b]

Year			
1971	27%	46%	59%
1974	19	38	52
1975	20	38	52
1976	21	40	53
1977	19	38	51
1978	19	39	52
1979	20	38	51
1980	19	37	50

C. Estimates including entitlements to occupational and state pensions[c]

Year			
1971	21%	37%	49%
1974	15	31	43
1975	13	27	37
1976	14	27	37
1977	12	25	35
1978	13	25	36
1979	13	27	37
1980	12	25	35

Source: Shorrocks (1987, Tables 2.1 and 2.2).

[a] Based on Series C Estimates, *Inland Revenue Statistics 1980, 1982.*
[b] Based on Series D Estimates, *Inland Revenue Statistics 1980, 1982.*
[c] Based on Series E Estimates, *Inland Revenue Statistics 1980, 1982.*

Figure 4.1. **Share of Total Wealth Held by the Top 1 Percent, 1920–81**
(based on traditional wealth measures)

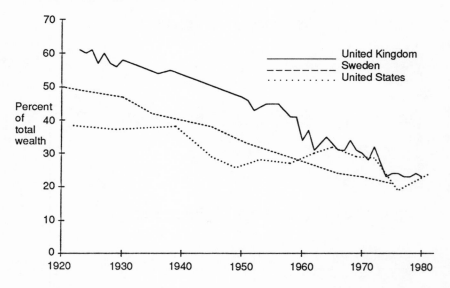

55 percent. Very little trend in inequality is apparent during the next ten years or so. However, the period from 1971 to 1974 was characterized by another sharp decline in inequality, with the share of the top 1 percent falling by 8 percentage points and that of the top 5 percent by 9 percentage points. Then, as noted above, there was no change in wealth concentration between 1974 and 1980.

The results reported in this paper are based on estate duty data. Such information refers to individuals and is, as a result, sensitive to changes in ownership patterns within families. In particular, any tendency to share legal title to various household assets between husband and wife, such as the family home or automobile, will lead to a reduction in the share of wealth held by the richest individuals, even if there is no change in the distribution of family wealth. Shorrocks believes that part of the decline in the share of the top 1 percent of wealth holders in Britain is attributable to this factor. In evidence, he cites the fact that the share of total wealth held by the top 10 percent declined substantially less than that of the top 1 percent. Indeed, the share of total wealth held by those in the top decile, but outside the top percentile, actually increased from 28 percent in 1923 to 38 percent in 1972.

Shorrocks presents two additional series on household wealth distribution, which use a wider notion of household wealth defined as conventional wealth plus rights to private and state pension plans (see the bottom two panels of Table 4.1 and Figure 4.2). The shares of the top wealth holders are considerably lowered by the addition of retirement wealth, since the latter is more equally distrib-

Figure 4.2. **Share of Total Wealth Held by the Top 1 Percent, 1920–81**
(including government and private pension wealth)

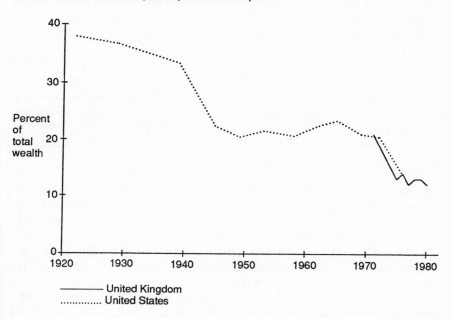

United Kingdom
.... United States

uted than disposable wealth. In 1980, for example, the share of disposable wealth held by the top one percent was 23 percent, while the share of expanded wealth was only 12 percent. Moreover, since pension entitlements have grown enormously since 1900, the inclusion of pension wealth in household wealth serves to strongly reinforce the downward trend observed for wealth inequality. Between 1971 and 1980 (the only period for which such data are available), the share of total augmented household wealth, including entitlements to both occupational and state pensions, fell by 9 percentage points for the top 1 percent and by 12 percentage points for the top 5 percent.

Another factor responsible for the equalizing trend in household wealth is the widespread ownership of homes and the rapid appreciation of house values. Shorrocks estimates that a home valued at 50,000 pounds, net of mortgage, would have placed the holder among the top three percent of wealth holders in 1980.

Several problems with the estate data source and methodology for the United Kingdom are discussed by Shorrocks. First, the estate multiplier method is likely to lead to some bias in estimated wealth shares because of the positive correlation between wealth and life expectancy (wealthier individuals tend to live longer within age-sex groups). Second, the value of household goods and small businesses are likely to be understated in estate data, since their value is considerably greater when in use than when put up for sale. Third, the value of life insurance policies are considerably greater in estates, since they are fully paid out, than comparable policies in the hands of the living. Fourth, except for life insurance policies, the total value of assets based on estate tax data falls far short of national balance sheet figures for the household sector.

B. Sweden

A paper by Roland Spånt in 1987 investigates time trends in wealth concentration in Sweden from 1920 through 1983. The analysis is confined to the distribution of disposable wealth. The data for the period from 1920 through 1975 are based on actual tax returns. The results for 1983 are computed from projections based on relative asset price movements from 1975 through 1983.

Tax return data are subject to error, like other sources of wealth data. The principal problem with tax return information is underreporting due to tax evasion and legal tax exemptions. However, some assets, such as housing and stock shares, are extremely well covered, because of legal registration requirements in Sweden. Also, the deductibility of interest payments from taxable income makes it likely that the debt information is very reliable. On the other hand, bank accounts and bonds are not subject to similar tax controls, and it is likely that their amounts are considerably underreported.

In 1975, owner-occupied housing comprised close to 40 percent of gross assets, and other real estate about a fourth. Bank deposits accounted for 14 percent and stock shares 5 percent of gross assets. However, household wealth in Sweden was not always dominated by real estate. Indeed, the relative holdings of different asset types have changed dramatically in Sweden. Between 1945 and 1975, the share of owner-occupied housing and secondary dwellings in household assets rose from 18 to 44 percent. During this period, stock shares as a proportion of household assets declined from 12 to 6 percent, while the value of farms and unincorporated businesses fell from 30 to 20 percent. However, liabilities have remained almost proportional to total assets over this period.

The major finding of this study is the dramatic reduction in wealth inequality in Sweden between 1920 and the mid-1970s and a subsequent increase in the early 1980s. Based on the years for which data are available, the decline appears to be a continuous process between 1920 and 1975 (see Table 4.2 and Figure 4.1). Over the whole period, the share of the top percentile declined from 50 percent to 21 percent of total household wealth in tax value terms. In market price terms, the top 1 percent held 17 percent of total wealth in 1975. On the other hand, the share of the bottom 95 percent increased from 23 to 56 percent of total wealth. Moreover, the percent of households that declared any taxable wealth increased from one-fifth in 1920 to three-fourths in 1975. Indeed, because of differential underreporting by asset type, the concentration of wealth is probably even more equal in 1975 than the official figures indicate. Still, wealth is considerably less equally distributed than income. Whereas the richest decile

Table 4.2

Shares of Total Household Taxable Net Worth Held by Richest Households in Sweden, 1920–83

	Top 0.01%	Top 0.03%	Top 0.1%	Top 0.5%	Top 1%	Top 5%	Top 10%
1920	9%	15%	24%	40%	50%	77%	91%
1930	—	13	21	37	47	74	88
1935	6.5	11	18	33	42	70	84
1945	—	9	15	29	38	66	82
1951	—	7	12	25	33	60	76
1966	3.6	5.5	9	18	24	48	64
1970	3.3	5	8.5	17	23	46	62
1975	3.0	4.7	8	15	21	44	60
1975 (at market prices)	2.2	3.7	6	12.5	17	38	54
1983 (at market prices)	—	—	8	14.5	19.5	—	—

Source: Spant (1987, Tables 3.7, 3.8, and 3.11).

of income earners received 20 percent of total disposable income in 1975 in Sweden, the top decile of wealth holders owned 55 percent of total wealth.

Spant estimates that the concentration of wealth in Sweden increased between 1975 and 1983. The 1983 results are based on asset price series from 1975 through 1983. The extrapolation assumes that the composition of asset holdings remained constant across wealth groups. During this period, real estate prices tended, on average, to lag behind the inflation rate. The same was true of savings accounts, bonds, and other financial assets. Liabilities, which amounted to 30 percent of total assets, were halved in real terms. However, stock share prices almost doubled in real terms over this period. Since stock shares are held by the very wealthy (the top percentile owned half of all stock shares in 1975), while real estate and financial assets are more evenly distributed, the net effect has been increased concentration of wealth. Spant estimates that the share of the top percentile in market price terms increased from 17 percent in 1975 to almost 20 percent in 1983.

C. The United States

Information available on household wealth distribution in the United States over the twentieth century is based mainly on estate data for the very wealthy collected from national estate tax records for selected years between 1922 and 1982 and cross-sectional household surveys for selected years starting in 1953. In addition, there are synthetic data bases, such as Wolff's 1969 MESP sample (see Wolff 1980), and Greenwood's 1973 database (see Greenwood 1983), which have been constructed using income tax data merged with census files, estate files and other sources.

1. *Estate tax data*. Estate tax estimates of household wealth concentration are available for the United States over the period from 1922 to 1981. There are three principal studies which have constructed time-series from these data. The first, by Lampman (1962), covers the years from 1922 through 1953; the second, by Smith (1984, 1987), provides concentration figures for the period from 1953 to 1976; and the third, by Wolff and Marley (1989), constructs new estimates for the 1922–81 period. The Lampman data and the Smith data are each internally consistent, using the same accounting conventions and the same set of national balance sheet estimates. The Wolff-Marley study attempts to provide a consistent accounting framework and consistent set of national balance sheet totals in order to reconcile the Lampman and Smith estimates.

There are two principal findings which emerge from the estate data series. First, the share of wealth held by top wealth holders fell between 1922 and the mid-1970s, particularly during World War II and the 1970s, and then rose thereafter. This time pattern in twentieth century wealth inequality is consistent with that found by other researchers, including Lampman (1962) and Williamson and Lindert (1980).

Second, the downward trend in wealth inequality from the estate data series remains robust to many different choices of adjustment procedures and wealth concepts. However, there are two factors which influence the trend in measured inequality. The first is the addition of expected social security wealth, which increases the decline in concentration over the sixty-year period. The second factor is the transformation of the estate data series, which is based on the individual as the unit of observation, into corresponding household estimates of concentration. The household-based series shows less of a decline in inequality during and after World War II.

Table 4.3 reports Lampman's and Smith's original concentration estimates for the top 0.5 percent of the population from 1922 through 1976. These estimates show a high concentration of wealth throughout the period. Over 20 percent of total wealth was owned by the top 0.5 percent in each of these years except 1949 and 1976. However, the results also indicate a significant decline in concentration over the century, from a maximum share of 32.4 percent for the top 0.5 percent in 1929 to 14.3 percent in 1976. In particular, there was a substantial decline in the top wealth holders' share during World War II and another large fall in the mid-seventies, as indicated in Smith's results.

Lampman's results show, in particular, almost no trend in wealth concentration between 1922 and 1939. There is a peak in 1929, just at the start of the

Table 4.3

Shares of Total Household Net Worth or Total Assets Held by Richest Individual Wealthholders in the United States, 1922–81

	Share of net worth		Share of assets (traditional)			Share of assets (incl. pension wealth)	
			individuals		house-holds	individuals	
	Lamp-man[a]	Smith[b]	Wolff-Marley[c]		Wolff-Marley[d]	Wolff-Marley[e]	
	Top 0.5%	Top 0.5%	Top 0.5%	Top 1%	Top 1%	Top 0.5%	Top 1%
1922	29.8%	—	30.3%	38.3%	25.5%	29.9%	37.9%
1929	32.4	—	33.2	37.2	30.7	32.7	36.7
1933	25.2	—	—	—	—	—	—
1939	28.0	—	29.1	38.1	25.3	25.6	33.4
1945	20.9	—	22.6	28.9	20.7	17.7	22.4
1949	19.3	—	20.2	25.7	18.8	16.3	20.5
1953	22.7	22.0%	22.9	28.1	21.7	17.9	21.6
1958	—	21.4	22.0	27.0	20.0	16.4	20.7
1962	—	22.2	24.2	30.1	22.1	17.6	22.5
1965	—	25.4	26.2	31.9	23.9	18.7	23.4
1969	—	21.8	23.4	29.0	21.6	16.4	21.0
1972	—	21.9	23.0	28.6	20.2	15.9	20.5
1976	—	14.4	14.4	18.9	12.7	10.1	13.8
1981	—	—	17.8	23.6	—	—	—

[a] *Source*: Lampman (1962, p. 202), based on his so-called "basic variant" for the wealth holdings of the top one-half percent.

[b] *Source*: Smith (1984, p. 422).

[c] *Source*: Wolff and Marley (1989, Table 6). The results are based on the W2 series, where W2 is defined as the cash surrender value of total assets less liabilities and is a measure of the wealth currently available to the household or individual. The assets include owner-occupied housing, other real estate, all consumer durables, demand deposits and currency, time and savings deposits, bonds and other financial securities, corporate stock, unincorporated business equity, trust fund equity (valued at full reserve value), and the cash surrender value of insurance and pensions. Liabilities include mortgage debt, consumer debt, and other debt.

[d] *Source*: Wolff and Marley (1989, Table 7). The results are based on lower bound estimates for W2.

[e] *Source*: Wolff and Marley (1989, Table 6). The results are based on the W4 series, where W4 is defined as W2 plus the total value of pension reserves less the cash surrender value of pensions (which is included in W2) plus the expected present value of future social security benefits.

Great Depression, and a trough in 1933, during its depth. However, the 1933 concentration level is almost the same as it was in 1922. There followed a substantial drop in wealth concentration between 1939 and 1945, and almost no trend during the ensuing decade.

Smith's data resume where Lampman's series ends. He investigates time trends in wealth concentration in the United States from 1958 through 1976 based on estate tax data. The series from 1958 through 1976 is consistent with respect to the categorization of assets, the estate multiplier technique in use, and the aggregate balance sheet estimates. Smith's data show that the share of wealth held by the richest half percent and the richest one percent of the population remained essentially unchanged between 1958 and 1972, with the share of the top percentile fluctuating between 27 and 31 percent of total net worth. However, between 1972 and 1976, the share of the top half percentile fell from 22 to 14 percent and the share of the top percentile declined from 28 to 19 percent. The main reason for the decline in concentration is the sharp drop in the value of corporate stock held by the top wealth holders. The total value of corporate stock owned by the richest one percent fell from $491 billion in 1972 to $297 billion in 1976. Moreover, this decline, according to Smith, is directly attributable to the steep decline in share prices, rather than a divestiture of stock holdings.

The estate files represent the wealth of the deceased. The wealth estimates for the living population are derived using the estate multiplier method which divides the population by age and sex and weights the deceased in each group by the reciprocal of the survival probability for each group. The survival probabilities used are higher than those for the population at large, due to the longer expected life span of the wealthy. This method represents a point estimate which can have a very large variance, particularly for the young, since there are very few in the sample. In fact, the multipliers for those under 50 approach 2,000. Estate estimates have been criticized by Atkinson (1975) and Shorrocks (1987) as overestimating the decline in inequality. The reason is that estate estimates are based on the individual rather than the household unit and over the century marital customs and relations have changed. Married women now inherit more wealth and have higher wealth levels than they did in 1900 or 1930. This reduces individual concentration even if household wealth inequality does not change. For example, between 1929 and 1953, Lampman reported that the percentage of married women among top wealth holders increased from 8.5 percent to 18 percent.

The estate files used by Lampman and Smith do not include all assets and the authors used different assumptions concerning pensions and trusts. For example, in Smith's estimates pensions are included only at their cash surrender value and a large percentage of trusts, those that were not directly under the control of the deceased, are measured at their actuarial value since that is how they are measured in the estate files. On the other hand, Lampman used a wealth measure that includes the full value of pensions as well as trusts. Because of the fraction of trusts not included, Smith's reported concentration estimates are biased downward in relation to Lampman's. Another asset, life insurance, is overstated in the estate files, a problem that both Lampman and Smith recognized and made adjustments for. Another difference is that Lampman's concentration estimates are based on estimates of aggregate household wealth prepared by Goldsmith (1962). In contrast, Smith's estimates are based on aggregate data from Ruggles and Ruggles (1982).

In order to derive a more consistent series on household wealth concentration, Wolff and Marley (1989) made a series of adjustments to the Lampman and Smith figures. First, they used consistent aggregate household balance sheet totals to derive the concentration estimates. Second, imputations were provided for the assets that were left out of the estate files, particularly trusts. The Wolff-Marley series is also shown in Table 4.3. The results are quite similar to the original ones of Lampman and Smith. However, an important addition to the Lampman and Smith data is the inclusion of an estimate for 1981 based on Schwartz (1983). The 1981 estimates show an increased concentration of wealth between 1976 and 1981, with the share of the richest 1 percent increasing from 19 to 24 percent.

As mentioned above, estate files record wealth for the individual while the more interesting unit for welfare analysis is the household. Moreover, the increased tendency to divide wealth equally between household members will reduce the individual estate concentration estimates without changing household wealth concentration. In order to change the estate data to a household base, certain assumptions are required about the division of wealth within households. One series is shown in Table 4.3, based upon the set of assumptions which yielded the smallest concentration estimates (see Wolff and Marley 1989 for details).

The results indicate that a proportion of the decline in individual wealth concentration over the period 1922–53 was due to changes in the wealth of married women. The share of total assets of the top 1 percent of households declined four percentage points over this period, in contrast to a 10 percentage point drop in the share of the wealthiest 1 percent of individuals. During the period from 1958 to 1976 Wolff and Marley estimated on the basis of Smith's data that the percentage of married women among the wealthy remained relatively constant at 18 percent.[9] Thus, for this period, there is relatively little difference in the concentration estimates between the top 1 percent of households and the top 1 percent of individuals.

The extent to which wealth concentration is lessened when retirement wealth is included in the household balance sheet is indicated by concentration estimates for the Wolff-Marley W4 series, shown in Table 4.3. W4 includes full pension reserves which are reported in the aggregate data sources, as well as imputations for social security wealth. However, one major difficulty is that there is very little information concerning the percentage of total pensions owned by the top wealth holders. In the Wolff-Marley paper, alternative assumptions were made about this share, ranging from a maximum of 15 percent to a minimum of 3 percent for the top one percent of wealth holders. The different assumptions had little effect on total wealth concentration. In the estimates reported in Table 4.3 it was assumed that the share of total pension wealth held by the top percentile of wealth holders declined over the twentieth century because of the growth of pensions over the period. The addition of pension wealth has had a minor effect on concentration, due to its relatively small size in relationship to total assets. On the other hand, the addition of social security wealth significantly lowered the degree of inequality, because of its relatively large magnitude. The share of net worth of the top percentile dropped between 4 and 8 percentage points from the inclusion of social security wealth. The resulting series shows a somewhat different time path than that based on traditional wealth. Wealth concentration declined gradually between 1922 and 1939, and then fell sharply during World War II. However, during the postwar period there appears to be very little trend, except for a sharp drop in 1976.

2. *Inequality estimates based on 1962 and 1983 survey sources.* I next compare estimates of household wealth inequality based on various sources of household survey data. As much as inconsistencies plague estate tax data estimates, problems are even more severe when different survey sources are involved. However, in two studies, considerable effort was expended on making two survey data sources consistent (see Wolff 1987a, and Wolff and Marley 1989). I first report results based on the 1962 Survey of Financial Characteristics of Consumers (SFCC) and the 1983 Survey of Consumer Finances (SCF). Two sets of results are shown. The first set is based on the original survey data, while the second uses adjusted estimates that have been aligned to national balance sheet totals for the household sector. In addition, in the adjusted estimates, imputations are provided for assets missing from the survey data—most notably, consumer durables and household inventories.

Results are shown in Table 4.4. The first line indicates that the Gini coefficient for original, unadjusted household wealth in 1962 is 0.772 and the share of the top percentile is 32 percent. The change in inequality that results from adding an asset to the household portfolio is a function of three factors: (i) the degree of concentration of the asset, (ii) the relative magnitude of the asset; and (iii) its covariance with other components of net worth (see Wolff 1987c, for example). The addition of other consumer durables (a category which comprises 6 percent of total balance sheet assets and is distributed equally) to original unadjusted net worth causes the Gini coefficient to decline from 0.77 to 0.70. This decline is primarily due to the increasing shares of the bottom two quintiles. The further addition of household inventories has a similar effect, with the Gini coefficient declining from 0.70 to 0.68.

The adjustment and alignment of the original components of household wealth in the SFCC to the national balance sheet causes an increase in the Gini

Table 4.4

Inequality Measures for Different Concepts of Household Wealth, Based on Both Unadjusted and Adjusted U.S. Data, 1962 and 1983

	1962 SFCC			1983 SCF		
	Gini coeffic.	Shares of		Gini coeffic.	Shares of	
		Top 1%	Top 5%		Top 1%	Top 5%
A. Unadjusted estimates						
1. Original wealth components	0.772	32.4%	52.5%	0.788	34.5%	56.2%
2. Line 1 + other durables	0.701	29.5	48.0	0.740	32.4	53.0
3. Line 2 + inventories	0.679	28.4	46.5	0.729	31.8	52.1
4. Line 1 less autos	0.798	33.9	54.5	0.806	35.7	57.9
B. Measures adjusted to align with the national balance sheets						
5. Original components only	0.793	33.3%	54.6%	0.781	32.8%	54.6%
6. W2 = line 5 + other durables	0.731	31.8	50.1	0.739	30.9	51.8
7. W2 + inventories	0.715	29.3	48.9	0.728	30.4	51.0
8. W2 less all durables	0.805	33.4	55.0	0.800	34.0	56.3
C. Augmented measures of household wealth with retirement wealth						
9. W5 = W2 + social security and pension wealth[a]						
g = 0.0	0.624	23.8%	40.8%	0.607	20.6%	39.1%
g = 0.01	0.607	22.9	39.5	0.592	20.0	37.9
g = 0.02	0.586	21.9	38.0	0.572	19.0	36.4
g = 0.03	0.563	20.6	36.1	0.550	17.8	34.7

Sources: Wolff and Marley (1989, Tables 13 and 15). The 1962 results are based on the 1962 SFCC and the 1983 results on the 1987 Federal Reserve Board tape for the 1983 SCF. This version contains imputations for missing values from nonresponse and corrections of inconsistencies in the data.
[a] The parameter *g* is the assumed rate of growth mean real security benefits over time. See Wolff and Marley (1989) for details.

coefficient from 0.77 to 0.79 (line 5). Most of the increased concentration occurs in the upper quintile, since the most underreported items were those held by the upper part of the distribution. However, the addition of other consumer durables to produce wealth-measure W2 causes a sharp reduction in measured inequality and the further addition of household inventories causes another reduction in measured inequality. The net effect of including missing items and aligning with the national balance sheets is a *reduction* in measured inequality, and the reduction is quite substantial, with the Gini coefficient falling from 0.77 (line 1) to 0.72 (line 7). Most of the change is due to gains by the bottom two quintiles, and, indeed, the share of the top percentile was reduced relatively little. Finally, lines 4 and 8 compare unadjusted and adjusted estimates of what might be called "fungible net worth"—W2 less all consumer durables. The distributional estimates are almost identical, 0.798 compared to 0.805. For fungible wealth, alignment makes almost no difference in measured concentration.

Table 4.4 also shows the 1983 estimates of overall household wealth inequality before and after alignment to the national balance sheet totals. The pattern of results is similar to those based on the 1962 SFCC. Based on unadjusted wealth figures, the inclusion of other consumer durables and household inventories in the household portfolio causes a substantial reduction in measured inequality, in this case from a Gini coefficient of 0.79 (line 1) to 0.73 (line 3). As with the 1962 data, alignment to the national balance sheet totals of the original wealth components in the SCF had less of an impact on measured inequality than adding other consumer durables and inventories. However, the direction of change is different for the 1983 data. In this case, the Gini coefficient declines slightly from 0.79 (line 1) to 0.78 (line 5). The total effect of both the imputation of missing assets and the alignment to the national balance sheet totals is to cause a decline of the Gini coefficient from 0.79 to 0.74 (line 6) and a fall of the share of the top percentile from 35 percent of total wealth to 31 percent.

Pension and social security wealth were also imputed to the household balance sheet. Pension wealth is defined as the present value of discounted future pension benefits. In similar fashion, social security wealth is defined as the present value of the discounted stream of future social security benefits. There are, of course, many methodological issues and problems associated with the inclusion of both pension and social security wealth in the household portfolio, which were discussed in section 2 above. Despite these problems, I include such estimates here, since it has now become fairly standard to do so. However, these various cautions should be kept in mind when interpreting the results (see Wolff 1987c and forthcoming for more discussion of the methodological issues involved).

The imputation of both pension and social security wealth involves a large number of steps, which I will not discuss here (technical details can be found in Wolff 1988). Line 9 of Table 4.4 shows results on the distribution of W5, defined as the sum of W2 plus pension and social security wealth.[10] The addition of retirement wealth to traditional wealth causes a marked reduction in measured inequality. Gini coefficients for W5 in 1962 range from 0.56 to 0.62, while those for 1983 vary between 0.55 and 0.61.[11]

In summary, on the basis of the adjusted and aligned household wealth estimates, there appears to be very little change in household wealth inequality between the two years. The Gini coefficients for the original components alone (line 5), for the sum of line 5 and other consumer durables, and for the sum of the latter and inventories show a slight increase, while the coefficient for fungible wealth (line 8) shows a small decline. Lines 5 and 6 show a modest decline in

Table 4.5

Share of Total Net Worth of Richest Households in the United States: Estimates from Survey Data, 1962–84

	1962 SFCC[a]	1969 MESP[b]	1973 Green wood data-base[c]	1979 ISDP survey[d]	1979 Pension survey[e]	1983 SCF[f]	1984 SIPP survey[g]
Percent of richest households	1.0	1.0	1.0	1.5	1.0	1.0	1.9
Percent of net worth based on sample totals	N/A	30.8	32.6	26.0	16.2	N/A	26.0
Percent of net worth based on national balance sheet totals	32.4	N/A	24.0	17.0	8.4	34.5	N/A

Source: Wolff and Marley (1989), Table 9.

[a] Estimates based on the original data in the 1962 SFCC (not aligned to national balance sheet totals).

[b] From Wolff (1983), based on the MESP file, a synthetic database created by matching income tax return data to the 1970 Census Public Use Sample.

[c] From Greenwood (1987). The database is derived from a synthetic match of estate data records with income tax returns.

[d] From Radner and Vaughan (1987), based on the Income Survey and Development Program. The share of wealth of the top 1.5 percent of households is estimated using a Pareto distribution.

[e] From Cartwright and Friedland (1985), based on the pension survey conducted by the President's Commission on Pension Policy.

[f] Estimates based on the original data in the 1983 SCF (not aligned to national balance sheet totals).

[g] From Lamas and McNeil (1986), based on the Survey of Income and Program Participation. The estimates shown above were provided to us by John McNeil.

the share of the top 1 percent, while lines 7 and 8 show a slight increase. Finally, the Gini coefficient for augmented household wealth, defined as the sum of traditional wealth (W2) and pension and social security wealth, shows a modest decline between the two years, while the share of the top 1 percent falls by about 3 percentage points.

3. *Inequality trends based on estimates from other survey sources*. Table 4.5 reports some concentration estimates from other sources. The results suggest that many surveys do not sufficiently over-sample the rich to capture the upper tail of the distribution. For example, the 1979 ISDP survey captured only 66 percent of

the total net worth based on national balance sheet data and the 1979 pension survey estimated an aggregate household wealth which was only 52 percent. In comparison, the (unadjusted) 1962 SFCC captured 79 percent and the (unadjusted) 1983 SCF captured 89 percent of aggregate net worth.[12] The resulting concentration estimates from each survey vary with the degree of underreporting and bias in the sample. The 1979 ISDP sample captured a higher proportion of aggregate wealth and also had a higher proportion of wealthy individuals than the pension survey of the same year. Consequently, the reported inequality based on the ISDP is higher. The top 1.5 percent held 26 percent of total wealth in the ISDP, while the top 0.96 percent owned 16.2 percent in the pension survey. The concentration estimates from the 1984 SIPP and the 1983 SCF provide an indication of the extent of the problem of inadequate coverage in some wealth surveys. Based on the 1984 SIPP file, Lamas and McNeil (1986) estimate that the share of wealth held by the top 1.9 percent was 26 percent, compared to 34.5 percent for the top 1 percent from the unadjusted 1983 SCF data.

Inequality estimates from synthetic databases which combine several sources may also be subject to biases, both from the underlying data sources and the methodology employed. Results from two such databases are reported in Table 4.5. The first are from the 1969 MESP database, created from a synthetic match of Internal Revenue Service tax records to the 1970 census one-in-a-thousand Public Use Sample and the capitalization of selected income flows to corresponding asset types (for example, dividends to stock shares). Asset and liability values were then aligned to the Ruggles and Ruggles (1982) national balance sheet totals for the household sector. The methodology is described in detail in Wolff (1980, 1982, and 1983). Various problems arise from the imputation procedures used. Two are worth noting here. The first is that the tax unit differs from the household unit and the second is that a not insignificant fraction of families in the United States are not subject to federal income tax and thus do not file tax returns. Both problems create biases in the matching procedure. From the MESP database, it was estimated that the share of the top 1 percent of households was 30.8 percent of total household net worth, a figure that was slightly lower than the corresponding estimate of 32.4 percent for 1962.

The second source is Greenwood's synthetic database, based on estate files which were merged with income tax records. In this case, there appear to be some sampling problems. Her estimated aggregate wealth was 74 percent of the balance sheet figure. Her estimates of total financial securities and stocks, assets held largely by the wealthy, were actually higher than the balance sheet estimates, while the total value of real estate, an asset concentrated in the middle class, was only 80 percent of the balance sheet total (see Greenwood 1987, p. 126). Greenwood calculated that the top 1 percent owned 32.6 percent of total wealth in 1973, a share that is probably overestimated as a result of the underestimation of total assets. An alternative estimate of 24.0 percent is given in row 3 of Table 4.5, calculated by dividing Greenwood's estimated wealth of the top 1 percent by the balance sheet total for the household sector.

From these results, it is difficult to draw much in the way of conclusions in regard to time trends. The estimated share of the top wealth holders appears to be more a function of the sampling biases of the data source than of real changes in the economy. However, the data do seem to support the view that there was a decline in wealth inequality during the 1970s in the United States, and a subsequent rise thereafter, during the early 1980s.

4. Cross-Sectional Comparisons

In this section, I consider three related topics. The first part compares estimates of household wealth inequality for a single country at the same time but drawn from different data sources. The comparisons are conducted with data from the United States and France. In the second part, I look at differences in household wealth by age group. As will be discussed below, a considerable amount of theory has been developed around the hypothesis that age is a primary determinant of household wealth levels. In the third part of this section, some cross-national comparisons of household wealth inequality will be presented.

A. Wealth Inequality Estimates from Different Sources

As the discussion of trends in household wealth inequality in the United States is brought up, there often exist considerable discrepancies in estimates of household wealth inequality from different sources. In Table 4.6, I have compiled estimates of the share of the top 1 percent of wealth holders in the United States for 1962 based on estate tax data and household survey data (the SFCC). The concentration estimates for the 1962 SFCC have been adjusted to correspond to the aggregate household balance sheet totals for each asset. The estate data figures are estimates of the share of the top 1 percent of households from Wolff and Marley (1989). The estimated shares of wealth held by the top 1 percent of *individuals* based on estate data are quite close to the shares of wealth held by the top 1 percent of households estimated from the survey data. However, the shares of wealth held by the top 1 percent of *households* estimated from the 1962 SFCC are significantly higher, by about 7 percentage points, than those derived from estate data. One possible reason for this difference is the conservative assumption used in converting the estate data to a household base. If it was instead assumed that all married men in the estate sample of top wealth holders had married women with wealth, the concentration estimates would have been higher, but not enough to account for the difference (see Wolff and Marley 1989 for details). Another possible reason for the discrepancy between the estate and survey estimates is that there is a serious underreporting problem in the estate data. The results in this table indicate the need for further work on the effect of the unit of observation (household versus individual), and on measures of wealth

Table 4.6

A Comparison of Shares of Top Wealthholders Based on 1962 Estate Tax and Household Survey Data for the United States

A. Share of total assets held by top 1 percent of wealth holders

	Estate data		1962 SFCC[a]
	Individuals	Households[b]	Households
Wealth Definition[c]			
W1	28.4%	20.5%	27.8%
W2	30.1	22.1	29.9
W3	28.8	20.9	28.5
W4	22.5	16.1	22.3

B. Share of total net worth held by top 1 percent of wealth holders

	Estate data	1962 SFCC[a]
	Individuals	Households
Wealth Definition[c]		
W1	29.1%	29.7%
W2	31.1	31.8
W3	29.5	27.4
W4	22.4	21.9

Source: Wolff and Marley (1989), Tables 5, 6, 8, and 13.

[a] The results are based on the 1962 SFCC after alignment to the national balance sheet totals.
[b] The results are based on lower bound estimates for W2.
[c] See the notes to Table 4.3 for the definitions of W2 and W4. W1 is the same as W2, except that trusts are valued at their actuarial value, which represents 40 to 60 percent of the total reserves of trusts (see Wolff and Marley for details). W3 is defined as W2 plus the total value of pension reserves, less the cash surrender value of pensions (which is included in W2).

inequality, as well as the need for further reconciliation between estate data estimates and household survey estimates of wealth inequality.

Table 4.7 presents a comparison of estimates of the size distribution of wealth in France based on different estimating techniques. The source for this is the 1987 study of Kessler and Masson. Four different methods have been used over the last ten years in France. The first, based on direct sample surveys, has been carried out for 1973, 1975, 1977, and 1980. Extreme underreporting is evident from these surveys. In the first two, reported survey wealth amounted to only half of the national balance sheet estimate of household wealth. In the latter two surveys, the declared value of corporate stock represented only 15 percent of the total value held by households. Moreover, the relative degree of underreporting

Table 4.7

The Concentration of Wealth in France:
Estimates from Alternative Sources

Source and method	Year	Unit	Type of wealth	Top percent of wealth holders	Share of total wealth	Gini coeffi- cient
I. Sample surveys						
CREP (1975)[a]	1975	households	gross	10.0%	50.2%	0.71
				5.0	30.0	
				1.0	13.0	
CREP (1980)[b]	1980	households	gross	12.0	56.0	0.70
				4.0	29.0	
II. Income capitalization						
Coutiere et al. (1981)[c]	1975	taxpayers	gross	10.0	57.5	0.72
				1.6	26.0	
	1975	households	gross	10.0	54.0	
III. Estate duty method						
Fouquet and Strauss- Kahn (1981)	1977	individuals[d]	net	0.5	13.2	0.81
				1.0	19.1	
				5.0	46.6	
	1977	households[e]	net	0.5	8.8–13.0	
				1.0	12.9–18.7	
				5.0	31.3–45.5	
IV. Annual wealth tax						
Direction de la prévision (1983)[f]	1981	taxpayers	net	0.45	9.9	

Source: Kessler and Masson (1987, Table 7.6).

[a] The CREP 1977 survey led to the same results.

[b] The Gini coefficient for net wealth is 0.72.

[c] The results depend upon the rate of return.

[d] The results depend upon the mortality rates chosen.

[e] The results depend upon assumptions with regard to mating patterns.

[f] This is a minimum estimate based upon declared asset and liability values.

of household assets tends to be a positive function of the level of household wealth. This fact helps explain why household surveys in France tend to understate the concentration of household wealth.

The second method, the income capitalization technique, has been used on income tax data for 1975, and the third, the estate duty method, has been applied to probate records for 1977. However, because of legislation, a large number of inheritances are not recorded in the estate tax sample. The fourth source is from an annual wealth tax that was first imposed in 1981. This tax is levied on all taxpayers whose wealth exceeds 3 million francs, after a 2 million franc deduction for so-called "professional assets." Data are available for the first year of the tax, 1981. Underestimating is believed to be in the order of 15 to 20 percent.

Despite the difference in sources and methods, the results on wealth inequality do not differ that greatly. The Gini coefficient based on household surveys is 0.71 for 1975 and 0.70 for 1980, while that based on income capitalization is 0.72 for 1975. The share of the top 10 percent of households in 1975 is estimated to be 50 percent based on sample survey data and 54 percent based on income capitalization. From sample survey data, the share of the top 1 percent of households in 1975 is estimated to be 13 percent, while from estate tax data, the share of the top percentile in 1977 is estimated to fall between 13 and 19 percent.[13] Finally, the top half percent of households is estimated to hold between 9 and 13 percent of total wealth in 1977 based on estate tax data, whereas the top 0.45 percent of taxpaying units is estimated to own a minimum of 10 percent of total wealth in 1981, on the basis of annual wealth tax data.

B. Age-Wealth Profiles

One of the most heavily researched topics in the field of household wealth is the relation between age and wealth accumulation. This great interest derives from the so-called life cycle model. Since the publication of Modigliani and Brumberg's now seminal paper in 1954, a vast amount of literature, both theoretical and empirical, has accumulated on the life cycle model. In the basic lifecycle model (LCM), as developed by Modigliani and Brumberg, households are assumed to save in order to spread out their consumption uniformly over their lifetime. In particular, since an individual's working life normally extends to only age 65 or so, households will save during their working years for consumption during retirement. This directly implies that household wealth, defined as accumulated savings, will rise with age until retirement and then decline.

In the starkest form of the model, it is assumed that families earn the same amount in each year until retirement, that lifetime earnings are fully consumed over the lifetime, that age of retirement and longevity are known with certainty at the beginning of work life, and that the interest rate is zero. Under a restricted class of utility functions, maximization of lifetime utility leads to a constant annual consumption over the lifetime. The savings pattern that directly follows is a constant savings rate per year until retirement and a constant dissavings rate thereafter. The resulting age-wealth profile is an inverted "V." Net worth rises linearly with age until retirement age and then declines in linear fashion with age. In a later paper, Ando and Modigliani (1963) dropped the assumption of a zero interest rate and, instead, assumed that the return on assets is positive and constant over time. The resulting profile is an inverted "U," with net worth rising with age until around retirement age and declining thereafter. In both cases, the "hump-shaped" profile implies quite directly that wealth declines after retirement, an issue which has generated considerable controversy.[14]

In this survey, I consider raw age-wealth profiles based on U.S. data. These are shown in Table 4.8, based on a variety of U.S. sources over the period from 1962 to 1983. These have not been corrected for the two sources of bias which affect the use of cross-sectional profiles as a test of the longitudinal LCM. First, because real earnings and income typically increase over time, the cross-sectional age-wealth profiles may be hump-shaped even though the longitudinal profiles rise over time (see Shorrocks 1975). Second, as Shorrocks (1987) notes, there is typically a positive correlation between wealth and longevity, so that there is a sample selection bias in the use of cross-sectional profiles as a test of the LCM. In particular, cross-sectional profiles may show an upward trend in wealth, particularly among the older age cohorts, even though the longitudinal profiles are hump-shaped. The two biases are obviously offsetting, but the net effect of the two is not known (though also see Bernheim 1986 for an analysis).

Table 4.8 shows the raw age-wealth profiles for traditional wealth (HDW). The first is based on the 1962 Survey of Financial Characteristics of Consumers (SFCC), which has been adjusted for underreporting and aligned with national balance sheet totals (see Wolff 1987a for details). The first breakdown of mean wealth by age shows a steady increase across the younger age cohorts, a peak of 1.5, the overall mean for the 55–64 age cohort, and a very slight drop for the 65 and over age cohort. A more detailed breakdown shows a peak at 1.7, the overall mean for the 55–59 age cohort, and a steady decline with age thereafter except for a dip for the 60–64 age cohort.[15]

The second set of results is based on the 1969 MESP database, a synthetic dataset constructed by sample matching and aligned with national balance sheet totals (see Wolff 1980, 1982, and 1983 for details). The results show a steady increase of mean wealth from the youngest age cohort to the 55–64 age group and then a very slight increase between the latter and the 65 and over group. Peak wealth occurs at 1.4 the overall mean. The 1973 Greenwood data show a steady increase in mean wealth across age group, with a peak occurring for the 65 and over age group of 1.4 the overall mean. The Greenwood data are based on a synthetic database and exclude consumer durables and household inventories. However, the other components align fairly closely with national balance sheet totals.

The last two sources show fairly pronounced hump-shaped profiles. The first

Table 4.8

Raw Age-Wealth (HDW) Profiles from Various Sources, 1962–83[a]

Age group	1962 SFCC[b]		1969 MESP[c]		1973 Greenwood[d]		1979 ISDP[e]		1983 SCF[f]	
	Mean by age group	Ratio to overall mean	Mean by age group	Ratio to overall mean	Mean by age group	Ratio to overall mean	Mean by age group	Ratio to overall mean	Mean by age group	Ratio to overall mean
Under 25	$4,499	0.13	$17,745	0.39	$9,763	0.26	$8,800	0.14	$18,347	0.14
25–34	14,681	0.44	27,404	0.60	24,096	0.64	24,520	0.39	46,901	0.35
35–44	26,353	0.79	36,688	0.80	36,454	0.97	64,950	1.04	106,035	0.78
45–54	35,191	1.05	48,637	1.06	43,669	1.16	79,120	1.27	229,636	1.70
55–64	50,261	1.50	63,668	1.39	48,068	1.27	105,740	1.69	244,352	1.80
65 and over	49,346	1.48	64,798	1.41	50,855	1.35	79,380	1.27	217,473	1.61
Mean	$33,417	1.00	$45,969	1.00	$37,711	1.00	$62,430	1.00	$135,400	1.00

Memo				
55–59	58,144	1.74	240,908	1.78
60–64	41,806	1.25	247,946	1.83
65–69	55,032	1.65	309,913	2.29
70–74	48,107	1.44	206,044	1.52
75–79	44,711	1.34	168,622	1.25
80 and over	33,802	1.01	126,364	0.93

[a] The statistics are for family or household wealth. Families are classified by age group by age of the head of household in 1962–1979 and by age of respondent in 1983.

[b] *Source:* 1962 Survey of Financial Characteristics of Consumers, adjusted to align with national balance sheet totals. See Wolff (1987b) for details.

[c] *Source:* 1969 MESP file, adjusted to national balance sheet totals. See Wolff (1980,1982,1983) for details.

[d] *Source:* Greenwood (1987). The 1973 data are based on a synthetic database of household balance sheets. The balance sheets exclude consumer durables and household inventories. The other components align fairly closely with national balance sheet totals.

[e] *Source:* Radner and Vaughan (1987). The results are based on the 1979 Income Survey Development Program. The data are not adjusted to national balance sheet totals.

[f] *Source:* 1983 Survey of Consumer Finances, adjusted to align with national balance sheet totals. See Wolff (1987b) for details.

of these is from the 1979 Income Survey Development Program (ISDP) file, which is not aligned to national balance sheets and has substantial underreporting problems. These results show peak wealth occurring for the 55–64 age cohort at 1.7 the overall mean and then a sharp drop for the oldest age cohort at 1.3 the overall mean. The last set of results is based on the 1983 Survey of Consumer Finances, which has been adjusted to align with national balance sheet totals (see Wolff 1987a for details). The first breakdown shows peak wealth occurring for the 55–64 age group, at 1.8 the overall mean, and then a sharp decline to 1.6 the overall mean for the 65 and over group. The more detailed breakdown indicates mean wealth rising steadily with age peaking for the 65–69 age group at 2.3 the overall mean and then falling sharply after thereafter.

Three conclusions can be drawn from the raw age-wealth profiles. First, the more detailed age breakdowns of mean wealth clearly indicate the existence of hump-shaped cross-sectional age-wealth profiles for both the 1962 and 1983 data. This suggests that more aggregated profiles, particularly those with a single age group for families 65 and over, do not provide reliable evidence on the existence of hump-shaped profiles. Second, peak wealth seems to occur for the 65–69 age cohort. This is consistent with earlier tests of the LCM (see Friedman 1982 and Hammermesh 1982, for example). Third, both the aggregated and more detailed age-wealth profiles suggest rather strongly that the cross-sectional age-wealth profiles have become more hump-shaped over the 1962–83 period and with higher mean wealth at the peak.

However, these results based on average wealth profiles by age group should not be construed as incontrovertible evidence in support of the life cycle model. In previous work (Wolff 1981), cross-sectional regressions based on the life cycle model were run using the 1969 MESP database. A typical regression was of the form:

$$HDW_i = \beta_0 + \beta_1 AGE_i + \beta_2 AGE_i^2 + \varepsilon_i$$

where AGE_i is the age of the head of household i and ε is a stochastic error term. Though both age coefficients were statistically significant, this regression explained less than 0.4 percent of the total variation of wealth holdings among households (that is, the R^2 statistic was less than 0.004). The inclusion of a measure of permanent household income did improve the explanatory power of the model, but the R^2 statistic never exceeded 0.02. Indeed, for certain groups, such as nonwhites, rural residents, and those with little education, the goodness of fit was even lower and the coefficients of the regression model were insignificant.

There were three ways by which the goodness of fit of the life cycle model was substantially improved. First, the sample of households was restricted to white, urban, educated families. This increased the R^2 from 0.010 to 0.15. Second, the top five percentiles of the wealth distribution were eliminated from the sample. The R^2 statistic jumped from 0.015 to 0.075. Third, the measure of household wealth was restricted to so-called life cycle wealth, defined as the sum of net equity in owner-occupied housing (the gross value less the mortgage debt), consumer durables, household inventories, cash and demand deposits, and the cash value of life insurance and pensions less consumer debt. When life cycle wealth was regressed on the age variables and lifetime income for educated urban whites, the R^2 increased to 0.159.

Table 4.9, which shows the portfolio composition of wealth by income and wealth class, provides the rationale for these results. Life cycle assets tend to diminish in importance in the household portfolio as income or wealth increase. Except for the first two or three income and wealth classes, the percent of total household wealth held in the form of net equity in owner-occupied housing, consumer durables and household inventories, demand deposits and currency, and life insurance and pension cash surrender value declined with both income and wealth. In contrast, the proportion of total household wealth held in the form of time and savings deposits; bonds, securities, stock, and trust equity; and equity in business and investment real estate increased almost continuously with household income and wealth. For the bottom two wealth classes, life cycle wealth accounted for over 80 percent of total wealth, while for the upper three wealth classes capital wealth comprised over 82 percent of total *HDW*. Thus, in conclusion it appears that the life cycle model is an apt description of the reasons for which the white, urban, educated middle class accumulate housing, durables, and liquid assets. The rich appear to have very different motives for saving and very different sources of saving, while the poor do not earn sufficient income over their lifetime to accumulate much in the way of assets.

C. International Comparisons of Household Wealth Distribution

Due to differences in sources, definitions of household wealth, and accounting conventions, international comparisons of household wealth inequality are rather precarious to make. However, Kessler and Masson (1987) do present some comparative data on wealth concentration for eight industrialized countries. Based on their figures, the share of total wealth of the top 1 percent ranges, in descending order, from 32 percent in the United Kingdom (1974), 28 percent in Belgium (1969) and the Federal Republic of Germany (1973), 25 percent in Denmark (1973) and the United States (1972), 20 percent in Canada (1970), and 19 percent in France (1977) to 16 percent in Sweden (1975).

Based on the more recent estimates, shown in Tables 4.1, 4.2, and 4.3, the disparity in wealth inequality among Sweden, the United Kingdom and the United States is not as great as the Kessler-Masson data would suggest. In 1975 the share of the top 1 percent of wealth holders in the United Kingdom was 24 percent, and that in Sweden was 21 percent. In 1972, the share of the top percentile was 32 percent in the United Kingdom and 29 percent in the United States. Moreover, and more importantly, the disparity in wealth inequality among these countries has declined substantially since the early part of the

Table 4.9

Percentage Composition of Household Wealth by Income and Wealth Class, 1969[a]

	Number of households (in 1,000s)	Mean HDW	Percentage composition							
			Owner-occupied housing (equity)	Durables plus inventories	Demand deposits and currency	Time and savings deposits	Bonds, securities, stock, and trust equity	Equity in business and investment real estate	Insurance and pension cash value	Consumer debt[c]
All	63,457	$45,969	13.1%	14.9%	3.6%	13.1	34.1%	23.4%	3.9%	−6.1%
1. Income classes										
(a) $0–9,999	18,268	5,944	7.3	78.8	7.9	3.5	2.4	1.2	9.6	−10.8
(b) $5,000–7,499	10,393	24,673	15.7	23.4	5.4	14.6	21.9	23.6	4.1	−8.6
(c) $7,500–9,999	10,614	26,346	19.9	26.9	4.6	13.2	20.5	16.9	5.2	−7.3
(d) $10,000–14,999	12,293	36,181	21.0	24.2	4.0	12.1	21.2	17.3	6.6	−6.4
(e) $15,000–19,999	4,406	60,834	17.9	17.5	4.6	14.3	24.8	19.9	7.2	−5.1
(f) $20,000–24,999	1,623	100,188	12.8	11.6	3.1	13.4	34.4	22.1	6.3	−3.7
(g) $25,000–49,999	1,528	179,433	9.6	7.4	2.6	14.4	35.8	30.3	4.6	−4.6
(h) $50,000–99,999	332	549,627	3.5	2.9	1.6	13.9	46.2	37.1	1.6	−6.8
(i) $100,000 or over	162	2,469,210	0.5	2.2	0.8	5.8	81.8	19.5	0.4	−10.8

2. Wealth classes[b]

(a) $0–9,999	18,268	5,944	7.3	78.8	7.9	3.5	2.4	1.2	9.6	–10.8
(b) $10,000–24,999	21,233	16,627	32.8	42.0	4.8	6.4	6.1	5.7	8.3	–6.1
(c) $25,000–49,999	12,000	34,802	29.9	22.6	5.1	12.0	14.4	13.4	6.8	–4.2
(d) $50,000–74,999	4,380	60,926	17.1	12.4	5.3	23.9	16.8	23.0	4.4	–3.0
(e) $75,000–99,999	2,240	85,899	13.9	8.8	4.7	22.0	20.8	28.2	3.5	–1.9
(f) $100,000–249,999	3,693	149,529	7.7	5.6	3.7	16.6	34.0	31.3	2.8	–1.8
(g) $250,000–499,999	788	333,977	4.3	3.3	2.4	11.3	48.0	29.8	2.1	–1.3
(h) $500,000 or over	466	1,768,747	0.7	1.6	1.0	9.2	59.5	28.1	0.5	–0.6

[a] This table is adapted from Wolff (1983, Table 5). All results are based on the 1969 MESP file.
[b] Households with negative net worth are excluded from this part of the table.
[c] This is defined as all household debt except mortgage debt.

century. In 1920, the share of the top percentile was 50 percent in Sweden; in 1922, it was 39 percent in the United States; and in 1923, it was *over 60* percent in Great Britain. Thus, the cross-national data suggest, if anything, a convergence in levels of wealth inequality among industrialized countries over the century.

5. Concluding Remarks

Three findings of particular importance emerge from this survey. First, there was a gradual but persistent decline in the degree of wealth inequality among households from the early part of the twentieth century to the mid-1970s. This observation is based on data for Sweden, the United Kingdom, and the United States, the only countries for which such long time-series information is available. The share of total household wealth held by the top 1 percent of wealth holders declined from 50 percent in 1920 to 21 percent in 1975 in Sweden. The share of the top 1 percent in Great Britain fell from 61 percent in 1923 to 23 percent in 1974. The decline in wealth inequality in the United States was less dramatic. The share of the top 1 percent of individuals fell from a peak of 38 percent in 1922 to 27 percent in 1956, with most of the decline occurring during World War II. The estimates from Smith (1987) show a further decline to 19 percent in 1976. Results from other sources, particularly household surveys, seem to support this finding.[16] It is interesting to note that these three countries differ quite considerably in regard to tax policy, the extent of social transfers, macroeconomic performance, and other social and political institutions. Despite such differences, there appears to be a trend toward convergence in levels of household wealth inequality among industrialized countries.

Second, since the mid-1970s, wealth inequality seems either to have leveled off or to be rising. This result is based on data for the same three countries. In the United Kingdom, the share of the top 1 percent was 23 percent in 1974 and 1983. In Sweden, the share held by the top 1 percent (in market prices) increased from 17 to 19.5 percent. In the United States, the top 1 percent held 19 percent of total wealth in 1976 and 24 percent in 1981. The reasons for this stoppage or possible reversal have not been fully analyzed. However, based on the work of Harbury and Hitchens (1987) for the United Kingdom, Spant (1987) for Sweden, and Wolff and Marley (1989) for the United States, it appears that one important reason for this has been the rapid appreciation of stock prices since the mid-1970s. In any case, these results raise the provocative question of whether this long term historical trend toward increasing equality has been permanently halted or, indeed, reversed.

Third, despite this historical downward trend in inequality, household wealth is still highly concentrated today. In the mid-1970s, the richest 1 percent held a quarter of all household wealth in France and the United States, over 30 percent in the United Kingdom, and about a sixth in Sweden. Indeed, household wealth is considerably more concentrated than household income. Greenwood (1987), for example, calculated that the top 1 percent of wealth holders owned 24 percent of total wealth in the United States in 1973, while the richest 1 percent of families in regard to income received 11 percent of all income.

The studies reviewed in this survey raise several provocative questions and point the way toward future research on the distribution of household wealth. First, what factors are responsible for the sharp decline in wealth inequality observed in Europe and the United States from the early part of this century to the mid-1970s and its potential reversal since then? Are the causes the same in different countries? What role has government policy played in this development? Second, despite the dramatic reduction in wealth inequality, the concentration of household wealth is still very high today, particularly in comparison to income. Third, there appears to be a convergence among industrialized countries in the level of wealth inequality. Does this suggest some "natural" law of development or some remarkable stability in class structure, or do these apparent similarities across countries mask different social forces? Fourth, attempts to account for the high degree of wealth inequality in these countries on the basis of life cycle and other demographic factors have yielded very little. This suggests major modifications in formal models of household wealth accumulation to include more behavioral and institutional factors. Possible items are the distribution of entrepreneurial skills, bequest behavior, government policy variables, and class-specific behavior based on either different motives for saving or liquidity constraints on asset portfolios.

Fifth, more attention should be paid to the reconciliation of household wealth data from different sources, particularly those based on different units of observation. The Wolff-Marley and Kessler-Masson papers provide illustrations of such an effort. Moreover, eclectic approaches which involve combining different parts of the wealth distribution from sources where they are particularly well represented should be explored. Sixth, it is apparent that no single wealth concept can adequately meet all the purposes for which it is used. In regard to savings behavior, is the appropriate concept conventional wealth or financial assets? In regard to welfare measurement, is current wealth or expected lifetime resources a better gauge? From a political economic perspective, is capital wealth or some variant of it the best index of economic and social control? In wealth studies, it seems reasonable to report several wealth measures, which may reflect different motives for saving, different degrees of liquidity or substitutability, or different needs, as, for example, between current consumption and future consumption. In conclusion, I hope that this survey serves to stimulate further research on this topic.

Notes

1. One important topic that will not be dealt with here, except in passing, are behavioral models of household wealth accumulation. For surveys of this topic, see, for example, King (1985), or my 1988 paper.

2. Actually, the projected Medicare and Medicaid payments are so large that in future years they probably cannot be reasonably ignored. Such "medi-wealth" would then have to be added to the household balance sheets.

3. More correctly, the current market value reflects current *expectations* about future income flows. For my purposes here, I shall ignore this distinction.

4. The exceptions are defined contribution pension plans, such as TIAA-CREF, in which benefits depend directly on contributions. The capital value of such a plan would equal the accumulated contributions to date, since increased benefits from future contributions would simply offset the liability of the future contributions.

5. This is very different than for marketable forms of wealth, for which the current market value reflects individuals' *expectations* about the future, whereas for social security and pension wealth, their value depends on the *actual* future macroeconomic conditions.

6. Another possibility is a generational concept of the family. This might be appropriate for very rich families, whose motivation is to increase their wealth holdings over their lifetime in order to pass it on to succeeding generations. See Kessler and Masson (1987) for a discussion of this concept.

7. In the United Kingdom, the threshold is considerably lower, so that the vast majority of estates file tax returns.

8. It should be noted that the earlier data reported by Shorrocks, principally 1923 to 1965, refer to England and Wales only. See Table 4.1.

9. This result is based on a comparison of Lampman's 1953 results (1962) and Schwartz's 1976 and 1981 estimates (1983). In 1953, married women represented 18 percent of the sample. In 1976 they comprised 16.8 percent and in 1981, 18 percent.

10. The parameter g is the expected rate of growth in real social security benefits over time.

11. There was a slight increase in the concentration of total retirement wealth between 1962 and 1983. The Gini coefficient for the sum of pension wealth and social security wealth (for g equal to 0.02) is 0.47 for the 1962 data, compared to 0.50 for the 1983 data (result not shown). Moreover, the magnitude of retirement wealth relative to traditional wealth grew considerably over the period, from 38 percent of W2 in 1962 to 88 percent in 1983. The net effect was that the decline in the Gini coefficient from the addition of retirement wealth was greater in 1983 than in 1962 because of the increased magnitude of retirement wealth relative to traditional wealth.

12. The 1979 ISDP results are from Radner and Vaughan (1987). The 1979 pension survey estimates are from Cartwright and Friedland (1985). The 1962 SFCC and 1983 SCF are from Table 4.4.

13. The top 1 percent of individuals is estimated to hold 19 percent of total wealth in 1977. The range for households is derived from extreme assumptions with regard to mating patterns among individual wealth holders.

14. Subsequent work has concentrated on extending the model by relaxing its various assumptions. There are three directions that are particularly noteworthy: (i) uncertainty, particularly about length of life; (ii) the role of social security and pension wealth; and (iii) the bequest motive. See Wolff (1988) for further discussion.

15. The dip occurs for the cohort which was born around 1900 and which reached the typical age for the beginning of household wealth accumulation at the time of the Great Depression. It is this factor which most likely accounts for the cohort's relatively low wealth holdings in 1962.

16. Actually, Soltow (1971 and 1975) argued that wealth concentration in the United States may have been relatively constant from about the mid-1800s up until the Great Depression. From U.S. census data, he estimated that the top 1 percent of all free males

held 29 percent of total wealth in 1860 and 27 percent in 1870. Gallman (1969), on the basis of a smaller sample of representative communities from the 1860 and 1900 Censuses, estimated that the share of the top 1 percent was 24 percent in 1860 and between 26 and 31 percent in 1900. Lampman (1962), using estate tax data, estimated that the top 1 percent of individuals held 32 percent of total wealth in 1922 and the top 1 percent of families owned between 23 and 26 percent of household wealth. Thus, the decline in wealth inequality was not nearly as dramatic in the United States as it was in Europe. On the other hand, the United States was a more egalitarian society than European nations in the nineteenth and early twentieth centuries.

References

Ando, Alpert, and Franco Modigliani. "The Life Cycle Hypothesis of Saving: Aggregate Implications and Tests." *American Economic Review*, vol. 53 (March 1963), 55–84.

Atkinson, A. B. "The Distribution of Wealth in Britain in the 1960's—the Estate Duty Method Reexamined." In James D. Smith, ed. *The Personal Distribution of Income and Wealth, NBER, Studies in Income and Wealth*, no. 39. New York: Columbia University Press, 1975, 277–319.

Atkinson, A. B., and A. J. Harrison. *Distribution of Personal Wealth in Britain*. Cambridge: Cambridge University Press, 1978.

Avery, Robert B., Gregory E. Elliehausen, and Arthur B. Kennickell. "Measuring Wealth with Survey Data: An Evaluation of the 1983 Survey of Consumer Finances." *Review of Income and Wealth*, Series 34 (December 1988), 339–70.

Bernheim, B. D. "Dissaving after Retirement: Testing the Pure Life Cycle Hypothesis." In Z. Bodie, J. Shoven, and D. Wise, eds. *Issues in Pension Economies*. Chicago: University of Chicago Press, 1986, pp. 237–74.

Cartwright, William S., and Robert B. Friedland. "The President's Commission on Pension Policy Household Survey 1979: Net Wealth Distribution by Type and Age for the United States." *Review of Income and Wealth*, Series 31 (September 1985), 285–308.

Centre de Recherche Économique sûr L'Épargne (CREP). "Les compartements financiers et le patrimoine des ménages." Mimeo, 1975, 1977, 1980.

Coutiere, A., F. Hatem, P. Mantz, and C. Pontagnier. "La concentration du patrimoine des foyers." *Économie et Statistique* (October 1981).

Feldstein, Martin. "Social Security, Induced Retirement, and Aggregate Capital Accumulation." *Journal of Political Economy* 82 (September/October 1974), 905–26.

———. "Social Security and the Distribution of Wealth." *Journal of the American Statistical Association* 71 (December 1976), 800–807.

Friedman, J. "Asset Accumulation and Depletion Among the Elderly." Paper presented at the Brookings Institution Conference on Retirement and Aging, 1982.

Fouquet, Annie, and Dominique Strauss-Kahn. "The Size Distribution of Personal Wealth in France: A First Attempt at the Estate Duty Method." Mimeo, 1981.

Gallman, Robert E. "Trends in the Size Distribution of Wealth in the Nineteenth Century." In Lee Soltow, ed. *Six Papers on the Size Distribution of Wealth and Income*. New York: National Bureau of Economic Research, 1969, pp. 1–25.

Goldsmith, Raymond W. *The National Wealth of the United States in the Postwar Period*. National Bureau of Economic Research. Princeton: Princeton University Press, 1962.

Greenwood, Daphne T. "An Estimation of U.S. Family Wealth and its Distribution from Microdata, 1973." *Review of Income and Wealth*, Series 29 (March 1983), 23–43.

———. "Age, Income, and Household Size: Their Relation to Wealth Distribution in the United States." In E. Wolff, ed. 1987b, pp. 121–40.

Greenwood, Daphne T., and Edward N. Wolff. "Relative Wealth Holdings of Children and the Elderly in the United States, 1962–1983." In John L. Palmer, Timothy Smeeding, and Barbara Boyle Torrey, eds. *The Vulnerable*. Washington, DC: Urban Institute Press, 1988, pp. 123–48.

Hammermesh, D. S., "Consumption During Retirement: The Missing Link in the Life Cycle." National Bureau of Economic Research Working Paper no. 930, 1982.

Harbury, C. D., and D. M. W. N. Hitchens. "The Influence of Relative Prices on the Distribution of Wealth and the Measurement of Inheritance." In E. Wolff, ed. 1987b, pp. 248–75.

Haveman, Robert, Barbara L. Wolfe, Ross E. Finnie, and Edward N. Wolff. "Disparities in Well-Being among U.S. Children over Two Decades: 1962–83." John L. Palmer, Timothy Smeeding, and Barbara Boyle Torrey, eds. *The Vulnerable*. Washington, DC: Urban Institute Press, 1988, pp. 149–70.

Kessler, Denis, and Andre Masson. "Personal Wealth Distribution in France: Cross-Sectional Evidence and Extensions." In E. Wolff, ed., 1987b, pp. 141–76.

King, Mervin. "The Economics of Saving: A Survey of Recent Contributions." In Kenneth J. Arrow, ed. *Frontiers of Economics*. Oxford: Basil Blackwell, 1985.

Lamas, Enrique J., and John M. McNeil. "Factors Associated with Household Net Worth." Paper presented at the American Economic Association Meetings, December 1986.

Lampman, Robert. *The Share of Top Wealth-Holders in National Wealth, 1922–56*. Princeton: Princeton University Press, 1962.

Modigliani, Franco, and R. Brumberg. "Utility Analysis and the Consumption Function: An Interpretation of Cross-Section Data." In Kenneth K. Kurihara, ed. *Post-Keynesian Economics*. New Brunswick, NJ: Rutgers University Press, 1954.

Projector, Dorothy, and Gertrude Weiss. "Survey of Financial Characteristics of Consumers." Federal Reserve Technical Papers, 1966.

Radner, Daniel B., and Denton R. Vaughan. "Wealth, Income, and the Economic Status of Aged Households." In E. Wolff, ed. 1987b, pp. 93–120.

Ruggles, Richard and Nancy Ruggles. "Integrated Economic Accounts for the United States, 1947–1980." *Survey of Current Business*, vol. 62 (May 1982), 1–53.

Schwartz, Marvin. "Trends in Personal Wealth 1976–1981." *Statistics of Income Bulletin*, vol. 3 (Summer 1983), 1–26.

Shorrocks, A. F. "The Age-Wealth Relationship: A Cross-Section and Cohort Analysis." *Review of Economics and Statistics*, vol. 57 (May 1975), 155–63.

———. "U.K. Wealth Distribution: Current Evidence and Future Prospects." In E. Wolff, ed. 1987b, pp. 29–50.

Smith, James D. "Trends in the Concentration of Personal Wealth in the United States 1958–1976." *Review of Income and Wealth*, Series 30 (December 1984), 419–28.

———. "Recent Trends in the Distribution of Wealth in the U.S.: Data, Research Problems, and Prospects." In E. Wolff, ed. 1987b, pp. 72–89.

Soltow, Lee. "Economic Inequality in the United States in the Period from 1860 to 1970." *Journal of Economic History* 31 (December 1971), 822–39.

———. *Men and Wealth in the United States, 1850–1870*. New Haven: Yale University Press, 1975.

Spånt, Roland. "Wealth Distribution in Sweden: 1920–1983." In E. Wolff, ed. 1987b, pp. 51–71.

Stewart, Charles. "Income Capitalization as a Method of Estimating the Distribution of Wealth by Size Group." *Studies in Income and Wealth*, vol. 3. New York: National Bureau of Economic Research, 1939.

Williamson, Jeffrey G., and Peter H. Lindert. "Long-Term Trends in American Wealth Inequality." In James D. Smith, ed. *Modeling the Distribution and Intergenerational*

Transmission of Wealth. Chicago: Chicago University Press, 1980, pp. 9–93.

Wolff, Edward N. "Estimates of the 1969 Size Distribution of Household Wealth in the U.S. from a Synthetic Database." In James D. Smith, ed. *Modeling the Distribution and Intergenerational Transmission of Wealth*. Chicago: Chicago University Press, 1980, pp. 223–63.

———. "The Accumulation of Household Wealth over the Life-Cycle: A Microdata Analysis." *Review of Income and Wealth*, Series 27 (June 1981), 75–96.

———. "Effect of Alternative Imputation Techniques on Estimates of Household Wealth in the U.S. in 1969." In D. Kessler, A. Masson, and D. Strauss-Kahn, eds. *Accumulation et Repartition des Patrimoines*. Paris: Economica, 1982, pp. 147–80.

———. "The Size Distribution of Household Disposable Wealth in the United States." *Review of Income and Wealth*, Series 29 (June 1983), 125–46.

———. [1987a]. "Estimates of Household Wealth Inequality in the U.S., 1962–1983." *Review of Income and Wealth*, Series 33 (September 1987), pp. 231–56.

———, ed. [1987b]. *International Comparisons of the Distribution of Household Wealth*. New York: Oxford University Press, 1987.

———. [1987c]. "The Effects of Pensions and Social Security on the Distribution of Wealth in the U.S." In E. Wolff, ed. 1987b, pp. 208–47.

———. "Social Security, Pensions, and the Life Cycle Accumulation of Wealth: Some Empirical Tests." *Annales d' Économie et de Statistique*, no. 9 (January/March 1988), pp. 199–226.

———. "Methodological Issues in the Estimation of Retirement Wealth." In D. Slottje, ed. *Research in Economic Inequality*, vol. 3, forthcoming.

Wolff, Edward N., and Marcia Marley. "Introduction and Overview." In E. Wolff, ed. 1987b, pp. 1–26.

Wolff, Edward N., and Marcia Marley. "Long-Term Trends in U.S. Wealth Inequality: Methodological Issues and Results." In R. Lipsey and H. Tice, eds. *The Measurement of Saving, Investment, and Wealth*. Studies of Income and Wealth, vol. 52. Chicago: Chicago University Press, 1989.

Wolfson, Michael C. "Lifetime Coverage: The Adequacy of Canada's Retirement Income System." In E. Wolff, ed., 1987b, pp. 179–207.

5

The Definition and Measurement of Poverty

Aldi J. M. Hagenaars

Introduction

> Few aggregate economic indicators are watched as closely as poverty
> statistics, and yet there is probably less professional consensus on the
> measurement of poverty than on any other indicator
>
> —*Duncan, 1987*

In this chapter the various theoretical and methodological problems causing the
lack of consensus on poverty measurement will be analyzed. These problems
both arise at the individual level of identifying a household or person as poor,
and at the aggregate level, in the construction of a summary statistic of poverty
for a certain country or subgroups within that country. Analysis of the theory and
assumptions underlying specific poverty definitions is especially important, as
both the population of poor and the extent of their poverty appear to depend to a
large extent on the definition chosen (Hagenaars and de Vos 1988).

This chapter is divided into two parts, dealing in turn with the identification of
poverty and the aggregation of poverty across individuals.

1. Identification of the Poor

How is poverty to be defined? In order to answer this question we need to
consider what unit of analysis we are interested in (individual, household, family, country), and we have to develop a yardstick that allows us to classify this
unit as poor or nonpoor. It would be even better if the yardstick also gave some
information about the extent of poverty of the unit concerned.

In poverty research, various units of analysis, and various yardsticks have

I thank Lars Osberg and Stephen Jenkins for their valuable comments on an earlier
draft of this chapter.

been used. In this section we will concentrate on the various methods applied to identify poverty at the household level.[1]

The choice of the household as the unit of analysis is based upon the assumption that poverty of household members cannot be considered independently of each other, since they share the products of both market labor and household labor. After having identified a household as poor or nonpoor, the individual household members will be classified in the same category. We hence ignore the possibility that within one household inequality is such that one member should be considered poor, and others nonpoor.[2] Although the identification of the poor is thus based on the household as unit of analysis, the aggregation of poor may still be based on individuals.

Once the unit of analysis is chosen, how is the yardstick of poverty to be developed? Basically, three different concepts are used in the poverty literature in order to define a household as poor or nonpoor:
1. income
2. consumption
3. welfare

1.1. Poverty Definitions, Based on Income

Income, the first concept used to define some household as poor, seems to be the natural choice, as it reflects the budget restrictions within which the household can choose its consumption goods. It is also ideal for a yardstick to the extent that it is measured on a cardinal scale, allowing both the incidence of poverty, and the extent of poverty to be measured and compared over households. If income is accepted as a yardstick, the only problem left is to define the level of income that will distinguish the poor from the nonpoor, for different household types.

This level, commonly referred to as the poverty line, may be defined in various ways, which will be explained below. However, before describing various ways in which a poverty line may be defined in terms of income, we have to specify the income concept to be used. One might decide to use annual cash household income as the indicator for poverty. However, the choice of current, rather than lifetime income, of actual, rather than potential or full income and the choice of cash income, rather than the sum of cash and noncash income may all be questioned. According to the New Consumer Economics, developed by Becker (1965), the basic concept to be used in any one time period should be full income rather than income, where full income is defined as the total amount of money one might earn when all available time is devoted to paid labor (on the assumption that everybody is free to choose between home production, labor and other uses of time). The concept to be used in a life-cycle context should, generalizing the same theory, be "full wealth": the present value of the maximum money income achievable over a lifetime by devoting all time and resources to earning income.[3] This life-time version of the full-income concept allows for the fact that the choice between current income and future income may depend on the household's tastes and preferences: if a person chooses to invest a lot of time in human capital, this current net income may be low, but his full wealth is probably higher than that of a high-school drop-out who just manages to earn a little more than the money provided on a scholarship.

A similar extension should be made to include the value of income in kind, like the value of noncash government services (see, e.g., Smeeding 1977, Moon 1977, but also Rowntree 1901 with respect to home production). As taxes and social security premiums paid do not necessarily equal the value of the services to the household, this requires an additional estimate of the value of noncash income (see Smeeding's chapter in this volume), to be added to full wealth. The sum of all these elements amounts to an indicator of economic status, which may differ widely from current after-tax income.

Garfinkel and Haveman (1977a, 1977b) have described a procedure to estimate the "earnings capacity" of a household, which indicator is closest to this concept of economic status. They point out some of the limitations of such an extended income concept. The underlying assumption of free choice between alternative uses of time may not always be valid, requiring modifications of the indicator in case of, for instance, illness or involuntary unemployment. They also mention the distinction between economic status and utility or welfare: the presence of children, for instance, may convey utility to the parents, which is not included in the measure of economic status. Another example of the difference between the two concepts economic status and utility may be found in the way year-to-year fluctuations in income may be treated. Variability in income may affect utility as a result of risk aversion (Mirer 1974), whereas this may not accurately be reflected by an index of permanent income. If, in spite of these objections, annual cash household income is chosen as the yardstick to be used, one should define a poverty threshold in terms of this income concept.

Such a poverty line may be *relative* or *absolute*. An absolute poverty line does not depend on the income distribution in society, but is chosen to reflect some fixed level of resources needed to sustain life and health. The definition of an absolute poverty line may be based either on some general notion regarding the minimum amount of money needed to make ends meet, like the $1,500 and $3,000 poverty lines used shortly after the declaration of the war on poverty by President Johnson in 1964, or on the results of research on the income level needed to meet basic needs, like food, clothing, housing, etc.[4]

A relative poverty line is directly derived from the income distribution in society, reflecting a definition of poverty as a state of relative, rather than absolute deprivation.

> Poverty is a dynamic, not a static concept. Man is not a Robinson Crusoe living on a desert island. He is a social animal entangled in a web of relation-

ships at work and in family and community which exert complex and changing pressures to which he must respond, as much in his consumption of goods and services as in any other aspect of this behavior. . . .

Our general theory, then, should be that individuals and families whose resources over time fall seriously short of the resources commanded by the average individual or family in the community in which they live, whether that community is a local, national or international one, are in poverty. (Townsend 1962, pp. 219, 225)

One basis for theories on relative deprivation was laid by Runciman (1966), who suggested that somebody is relatively deprived of a certain position, good, or service if:

—he does not have this position (good, service),

—he sees some other person or persons, which may include himself at some previous or expected time, as having this position (good, service),

—he wants this position (good, service),

—he sees it as feasible that he should have this position (good, service). Several aspects of this definition are worth mentioning. Relative deprivation is basically defined as a state of the mind, not necessarily an objective situation. The question whether one feels relatively deprived depends on the people that one knows or looks at as reference persons for one's own behavior. Finally, relative deprivation may depend on one's previous or future position. These factors would imply that relative deprivation is very much an individual, subjective situation.

This is not, however, the way most poverty researchers have interpreted and applied the concept of relative deprivation. Townsend (1979) stresses the importance of the assessment of actual, objective deprivation compared to others as well as subjective deprivation, since some groups in the population (for instance the retired) may be conscious of only small deprivation, but are in fact substantially deprived by objective criteria. Sen (1979) agrees with respect to this objective nature of deprivation; stating that, "the measurement of poverty must be seen as an exercise of description assessing the predicament of people in terms of prevailing standards of necessities. It is primarily a *factual* rather than an ethical exercise when the facts relate to what is regarded as deprivation." In the choice of "prevailing standards of necessities" Sen follows Adam Smith, who wrote that, "Under necessaries, therefore, I comprehend not only those things which nature, but those things which the established rules of decency have rendered necessary to the lowest rank of people" (1776, p. 399). The choice of certain basic needs or necessaries for the purpose of deriving a poverty line will be discussed in the next section.

Some relative poverty lines are defined directly in terms of income, without reference to basic needs. Such a completely relative poverty line based on income has been defined in two different ways. The first is to set the poverty line at a percentage of mean or median income in society (Abel-Smith and Townsend 1965, Fuchs 1967, Rainwater 1969, Rein 1974, Lansley 1980). This definition

Figure 5.1 **The Definition of Aggregate Poverty Indices: Head-count Ratio**

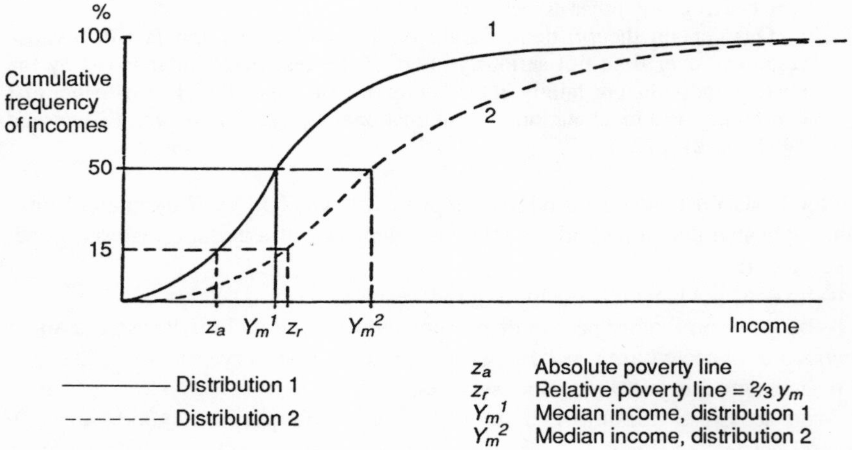

z_a Absolute poverty line
z_r Relative poverty line = $\frac{2}{3} y_m$
Y_m^1 Median income, distribution 1
Y_m^2 Median income, distribution 2

——— Distribution 1
- - - - - Distribution 2

implies that poverty may be reduced if the relative situation of the poor improves. A second relative interpretation of poverty is found by defining the lowest decile or quintile of the income distribution to be poor (Miller and Roby 1970). In this relative type of definition, poverty is to a large extent identified with income inequality, and cannot be solved as long as some inequality remains. Obviously, the choice of a relative or an absolute poverty line has major implications for a social and economic policy needed to reduce poverty: a relative poverty line as a percentage of median income requires reduction of income inequality, whereas an absolute poverty line requires growth for the poor. The difference between the two types of definitions is illustrated in Figure 5.1.

In the change in income distribution from y^1 to y^2 it is assumed that median income has changed, but income inequality has not; this results in a reduction of the percentage of poor according to the absolute definition z_a, but in no change in the percentage of poor according to the relative definition z_r.

Economic growth does not necessarily imply that relative poverty remains unchanged: if median income is increased because of an increase of the income of only the rich, relative poverty will increase as a result of the larger income inequality. Absolute poverty would not change in such a situation.

However the poverty line is defined, the presence of different households, of different size and composition, calls for the use of some equivalence scale, in order to differentiate the poverty line according to household composition. These equivalence scales may be derived in various ways, as explained in the Jenkins's chapter of this book.

The relative and absolute poverty line definitions mentioned above are *objective* definitions in the sense that they give an outsider's view on the money needed in order not to be called poor. A different category of definitions are *subjective*, in the sense that these definitions are based on the opinion of a sample of people in society on the amount of money needed. In a number of Gallup polls people are asked to give the minimum amount necessary to get along for a representative family, e.g., two adults with two children. Rainwater (1974) defined a poverty line for such a representative family by taking the average of all answers given. The resulting poverty line is not *a priori* determined to be absolute or relative, but its nature depends on the opinion of people in society. *A posteriori* Rainwater found the poverty line thus defined to change by the same percentage as mean income; Kilpatrick (1973) found that the poverty line increases by 6 percent when mean income increases by 10 percent.

In a different version of the subjective poverty line definition, people are asked to give the minimum amount needed to get along *for their own household* (Goedhart et al. 1977, Colasanto, Kapteyn, and Van der Gaag 1984, Hagenaars 1986). Instead of taking the average of all answers given, these authors analyze statistically the relationship of answers given and various household characteristics, like household income and family size. The poverty line itself is regarded as the average of all answers of those households who consider themselves to be exactly on the borderline of poor and nonpoor, i.e., the households who, in reply to the question what income they considered to be absolutely necessary, have stated their actual household income. Since households of different size and composition are included in the sample, the poverty line is easily differentiated according to family size. Poverty lines derived in this way are called Leyden poverty lines, after the place of origin of their definition.

We conclude this section on poverty line definitions based on income with a brief summary of the advantages and disadvantages of this approach. Poverty lines based on income are numerous, enabling one to choose a definition reflecting one's view of poverty as either a state of objective absolute deprivation, a state of objective relative deprivation, or a subjective state of deprivation. The poverty lines are easily calculated and differentiated according to household size. A disadvantage is that poverty lines in terms of current cash household income do not take into account permanent income, leisure, household production, and other noncash income, which do influence a household's well-being. The Leyden poverty line might be used to differentiate households according to these factors as well, if relevant information is available in the survey data.

1.2. Poverty Definitions Based on Consumption

Several poverty definitions are directly or indirectly based on the (cost of) consumption of some specific goods. The level of the absolute poverty line in terms of income, for instance, is usually determined by calculation of the minimum amount necessary to meet "basic needs." In definitions of this type, two problems have to be solved:

a. What needs are considered to be basic?
b. How should the cost of the basic needs be calculated?

a. Choice of Basic Needs.

The concept of "basic needs" presupposes that there is a hierarchy of needs, of which only the lower end should concern poverty researchers. Such a hierarchical ordering of needs is mentioned by Marshall (1920). A classification of human motives by Maslow (1954) distinguishes physiological needs (hunger and thirst), safety, belongingness and love, esteem and status, and self-actualization.

The choice of certain needs as "basic" reflects an absolute interpretation of the concept of poverty. Usually only the first two motives, physiological needs and safety, are accepted as subsistence needs, independent of the style of living of other people in society. Poverty is thus defined as lacking the essentials for survival, which is a very absolute definition indeed. Anthropologists like Douglas and Isherwood (1979) doubt whether such a distinction between "goods that sustain life and health and others that service the mind and heart" is valid: social obligations are as basic to mankind as are food and drink. A poignant example of expenditures on services that may be a heavy burden on poor households without improving their own physical well-being is given in Dominique Lapierre's (1986) chronicle of life in a Calcutta slum:

> Wood for a cremation is very expensive. That's why indigents and people without families are thrown into the river without being burned. All together it would cost a hundred and fifty rupees to have the body of our friend vanish into smoke. (p. 174)

Social obligations like this appear to be even more important to the Indians described than food and clothing.

Researchers like Townsend (1979) apply a theory of relative deprivation to the consumption of goods and services, and define somebody to be poor, when his consumption pattern falls short of the general or standard consumption pattern in society. In such a definition, a hierarchy of needs is no longer supposed to be relevant, following Douglas and Isherwood, or it is assumed that the really "basic needs" are met by everybody in society, so that attention may be shifted from absolute to relative poverty.

Sen (1985) strongly objects to the gradual shift in emphasis among researchers from absolute poverty to relative poverty, which ignores what he calls the "irreducible absolutist core" implicit in the concept of poverty. Sen introduces a new concept to define poverty: the "capability to function." Poverty should, according to his view, be absolute in terms of the capability of functioning with respect to nourishment, participation in society, and transport. Because different societies require different functionings, absolute poverty defined in terms of capabilities may still involve some relativity in terms of foods required, but the completely relative poverty line, as presented by Townsend, is rejected in this view.[5] However, operationalizations of Sen's concept of capabilities are not easily found (see de Vos and Hagenaars 1988).

We will therefore restrict our summary to those methods that have been applied in empirical research.

b. Cost of Basic Needs

Once a number of needs are chosen to be "basic" one can calculate the cost of meeting these needs. The starting point is usually the cost of food, for which nutritional experts (the Agricultural Department in the United States) are asked to give an estimate of the intake of calories required to subsist. Townsend (1962), Rein (1974), and Hagenaars (1986) show that the nutritionists frequently disagree about the level of calories needed, depending among other things on level of physical activities, age, sex, occupation, housing, climate, and leisure activities. Hence, the resulting estimates are not as absolute and objective as they are claimed to be.

The dietary allowances are to be transformed into a minimum food basket, of which the cost is calculated. In doing this, one should take account of the customary social consumption. Aside from the cost of food, the other basic needs have to be measured. Rowntree (1901) calculated these other costs of living separately using survey data on the minimum cost required for clothing, fuel, etc. However, the problem of choosing items as "necessary" is so hard as to prevent many other authors from trying. Orshansky (1965), for example, argued that "there is no generally acceptable standard of adequacy for essentials of living except food." She therefore proceeded to use food expenditures only as the basis for a poverty line.

Orshansky used the inverse of an estimate of the average proportion of income spent on food in the United States (⅓), and tripled the food expenditures in order to cover all other items. This poverty line definition, which is at present in use in the United States, would be relative if both costs of food and the average proportion of food expenditures were adapted to reflect general changes in expenditure pattern in society; however, in practice it is absolute, since the food expenditures are only adjusted for price inflation and the proportion of food expenditures to income is not changed over time. The equivalence scale, implicit in this U.S. poverty line, hence depends on the differences in food expenditures over household types. A criticism of this procedure is that the economies of scale for expenditures other than food may be substantially different, which is not taken into account. Economies of scale for housing, for instance, are usually much smaller; single persons spend a larger percentage of their income on housing than families. The present U.S. poverty line may therefore not present an accurate reflection of basic needs for all household types.

A completely relative definition of poverty, based on consumptive behavior is provided by Townsend (1979). Townsend hypothesizes that as resources of a household are diminished there is a point at which a sudden withdrawal occurs from participation in the customs and activities that are usual in the community. This point at which withdrawal escalates disproportionately may be defined as the poverty line. In order to measure this poverty line, some operationalization of "participation in society" is needed. A huge number of indicators, varying from "not having a cooked breakfast most of the days of the week" to "not going for a holiday once a year," are used to develop a deprivation score for each household. This deprivation score is related to household income, in order to find the poverty line, at which deprivation increases disproportionately.

However, both the empirical and the conceptual basis of this poverty line is weak (see Piachaud 1981, Hagenaars 1986). The material provided to show the existence of a kink in the deprivation score at the poverty line is inconclusive. Moreover, the choice of a number of indicators as representative of a general standard of living in society is as problematic in the definition of this relative line as it is in the definition of an absolute line. Consumption patterns may vary with age, family composition, health and a host of other variables, apart from income. By imposing a fixed consumption pattern on households, one may erroneously label households as poor, when they choose to behave differently from the standard for any of these other reasons. In *Poor Britain,* Mack and Lansley (1985) solve some of these problems, by asking households about the reason for their lack of certain goods or participation.

A third category of poverty lines, based on consumption, is the food-ratio method. This method, introduced by Watts (1967) was meant to allow for the comparison of poverty among households of different sizes and composition. A certain food-income ratio is taken to be the poverty threshold: families with an actual food-income ratio higher than this threshold are considered to be poor, whereas families with a lower food-income ratio are nonpoor. The poverty line may be absolute or relative, depending on the updating of the poverty threshold with changing standards of living in society. The advantage of this method, as well as Orshansky's method, is that no choice of basic needs other than food is needed. A disadvantage of the method, however, is that the equivalence scale implied is based on the cost of food only, whereas the economies of scale for, say, housing and clothing may be quite different from the economies of scale for food.

Summarizing, the operationalization of poverty in terms of consumption of certain goods is required for an absolute poverty line in terms of basic needs, or a relative poverty line in terms of lack of participation in society. All poverty lines based on consumption share, however, one basic problem: households may differ in consumption behavior because of differences in health, age, life-style, and a number of variables other than income. Poverty definitions that are based on some standard consumption behavior may not properly take these differences into account.

1.3. Poverty Definitions Based on Welfare

Although many researchers say that, "ideally, the distribution of welfare should be studied instead of the distribution of income" (Thurow 1969, p. 13), few actually use an explicit welfare concept in the derivation of the poverty line.

Obviously, this is due to the fact that it requires knowledge of the relationship between welfare and income (or some broader measure of "command over resources"), knowledge that is impeded by numerous conceptual and measurement problems. Several of the poverty definitions given above are, however, meant to be a proxy for welfare. Garfinkel and Haveman's earnings capacity takes into account home production, leisure, and human capital, as these variables influence the welfare of a household. However, there is still a difference between this indicator of economic status and welfare, as mentioned above. Watts (1968) developed the food-ratio method in order to derive equivalence scales that yield equal welfare for households of different size and composition. This welfare proxy, however, suffers from the assumption of equal economies of scale for food and other expenditures.

A very different approach to welfare measurement that results in subjective poverty definitions has been developed in the so-called Leyden school, or Income Evaluation Theory (Van Praag 1968). In this approach, it is assumed that people are able to evaluate various income levels in terms of welfare, as represented by words like "insufficient," "good," or "very good." By the use of survey questions directed to the relationship between (subjective) welfare and income, one obtains empirical information on the welfare function of income. This information may then be systematically analyzed with respect to differences over households, e.g., with respect to family size, region, etc.

The information on welfare is obtained by direct questioning; a six-level version of this so-called income evaluation questionnaire runs as follows:

> Please try to indicate what you consider to be an appropriate amount of money for each of the following cases.
> Under my (our) conditions I would call an after-tax income per week/month/year (please encircle the appropriate period) of:
> about £— very bad
> about £— bad
> about £— insufficient
> about £— sufficient
> about £— good
> about £— very good

It is assumed that the welfare level associated with "just sufficient" is the same for all households; the differences in the income levels household state are needed to reach this welfare level reflect differences in home production, leisure, social reference group, and household size and composition. These answers are subjective, but they may be "objectified" by analyzing the systematic variation of these answers over household composition, region, employment, etc., and taking the average of all variables that are assumed to be irrelevant. This income evaluation question may be used to define a poverty line, by considering a specific welfare level (e.g., between "sufficient" and "insufficient") to represent the welfare level distinguishing the poor from the nonpoor. The observed relationship between this welfare level and income is then used to define a poverty line in terms of income, such that all people with an income level below that line consider their own income to be insufficient, and people with an income level above that level consider their income to be (more than) sufficient.

A similar (welfare) interpretation may be given to other poverty definitions, based on survey questions on the minimum amount needed "to get along" or words to that effect. "To get along" is a description of a welfare level, and the income level defined by these survey questions is a poverty line defined in terms of this welfare level.

These poverty lines all use empirical subjective survey information as their point of departure. In fact, the subjective element of such poverty line definitions is both their strong and their weak point. If one wants to define poverty as a situation of low welfare, one has to take into account that welfare is a subjective state of mind that may be influenced by psychological and sociological variables as well as by economic factors. The subjective poverty line definitions may take these factors into account. However, acknowledging the basically subjective nature of welfare does not help to solve the problem of defining an objective poverty line, which is the aim of most researchers (and probably all policy makers). As mentioned above, the subjective survey information may be "objectified" to some extent, permitting the derivation of a poverty line that may be used for social policy.

As an objection against poverty lines based on subjective welfare proxies, Sen (1985), argued that the subjective evaluation of a situation is often influenced by the psychological need to minimize the difference between aspirations and reality, by social roles, and by past experience. Hence if a lower poverty line were found for women and the old-aged than for men and the young, respectively, this might reflect social roles and aspirations, rather than actual need. Reflections like these, as well as reluctance to use survey data, with all its associated validation and measurement problems will make some researchers and policy makers resort to the use of a poverty line based on income or consumption, rather than on a subjective welfare measure, in spite of the conceptual advantages of the latter.

Summarizing, although welfare is theoretically the best basis for a poverty line definition, in practice both the measurement problems and the essentially subjective nature of welfare cause a new set of problems. To some extent, however, these latter problems are implicitly present in all poverty line definitions, and only made more explicit in poverty line definitions aiming to be a proxy for welfare. Human behavior, as well as the evaluation of one's situation in terms of welfare or utility, varies because of many reasons, not only because of differences in command over resources. Which of these reasons should be considered relevant for the purpose of a poverty definition? However this question is answered, every selection will result in a difference between the population of poor according to the criteria chosen and the population of poor according to their subjective welfare. In order to analyze this difference, it is therefore always advisable to obtain information on both subjective evaluations and objective conditions of households.

1.4. Does the Choice of Definition Matter?

In the paragraphs above the advantages and disadvantages of a number of poverty definitions are discussed. If, however, the differences between these poverty definitions in practical research are relatively small, this discussion would be only of theoretical value, without much relevance for poverty research or policy. In this section I will therefore review empirical studies in which the composition and size of the population of poor is compared, using different definitions of poverty.

The relevance of the choice of money income versus a more comprehensive measure of economic status is demonstrated in work by Garfinkel and Haveman (1977a, 1977b). They compare the composition of the population of poor (both households and individuals) based on the current income poverty line to the composition of the poor based on their index of "earnings capacity."

According to the current income poverty line, households in which the main breadwinner is black, full-time working, and has a low level of education are underrepresented, as are large families. Older people and farmers, on the other hand, are overrepresented in the population of poor according to the current income poverty line.

Smeeding (1977) shows that the size of the population of poor households shrinks from about 12.8 percent (1972 data) to 6.6 percent when a comprehensive income measure is used, rather than census income. His measure of comprehensive income includes taxes paid, intrahousehold transfers, and the cash equivalent of in-kind transfer benefits, such as food stamps, Medicare, Medicaid, public housing, and rent assistance.

Van Praag, Spit, and Van de Stadt (1982) compare the food ratio poverty line to the subjective income poverty line (Leyden poverty line) with respect to the family size elasticity resulting from these definitions. The food-ratio definition has an elasticity of about 0.62 (the Netherlands, 1975), whereas the elasticity of the Leyden poverty line was estimated to be 0.16.

A recent comparison of family size elasticities according to different methods for ten different countries is presented in Buhmann et al. (1988). They show differences in the order of magnitude between 0.18 and 0.72 for one country (the United States), and 0.12 and 0.84 between countries.

A comparison of the *level* of the Leyden poverty line to the official United States poverty line was presented in Colasanto, Kapteyn, and Van der Gaag (1984), and Danziger et al. (1984). The results of the two studies are contradictory as regards the relative levels of the two poverty lines and the equivalence scale implied, possibly due to a confusion on the part of the respondents whether before-tax or after-tax income was asked for in the income evaluation question.

Hagenaars (1986) compares poverty percentages for eight European countries on the basis of the Leyden poverty line and an absolute poverty line. It appears that the incidence of poverty in these countries varies considerably with the choice of the poverty line, for example between 16 percent and 4 percent for the Netherlands and Belgium.

Finally, Hagenaars and de Vos (1988) compared the size and composition of the population of poor in the Netherlands, using eight different definitions of poverty. The overall percentage of poor varies between 5.7 percent and 23.5 percent. This variation is even larger within specific social subgroups, like the old aged.

The conclusion to be drawn from these studies is that it certainly makes a difference, and sometimes even a large difference, which definition is chosen as the basis of empirical poverty research. In each poverty study the question which poverty concept should be used has to be addressed very carefully, because of both its theoretical and its practical relevance. The choice of definition may depend on the economic situation of the country one is looking at: in a country suffering from a famine, a definition based on "basic needs" is more appropriate than a definition based on relative deprivation. Sen (1985) applies this argument to the Dutch "hunger winter" of 1944: according to a completely relative definition, poverty was not necessarily larger during that winter than in other years, because *everybody* suffered the results of the food shortage. This would ignore, however, the "absolute core" in poverty, which was observed by a large number of people in starvation and under-nourishment. In most Western countries, in generally more prosperous situations, however, a more relative definition of poverty may be needed to take into account changes in the necessities over time and place.

A possible solution of the problem of choosing a poverty line is presented by Shorrocks and Foster (1987) and Atkinson (1987). They suggest that one might try to order groups or countries in terms of poverty over a large range of possible poverty lines. If, even with varying definitions of the poverty line, one country is consistently poorer than another, the ranking of countries may be made without discussing which definition is appropriate. For a given country, at a given moment of time, however, the choice of a definition may still be extremely relevant, especially if one tries to establish a certain minimum social assistance level. In terms of such a minimum income level, the Leyden poverty line may yield the answer to the question what income level is generally accepted as the minimum for that country at that time.

2. The Aggregation of Poverty

Once a certain poverty line for some standard household is defined in terms of a poverty threshold, say z, one may use survey data on household income to

Figure 5.2 **The Definition of a Poverty Line**

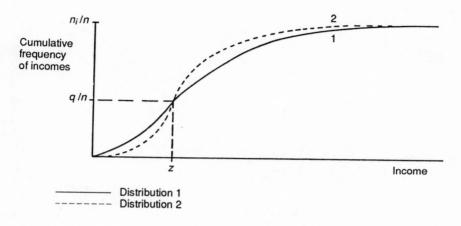

Distribution 1
Distribution 2

measure the extent of poverty. The poverty threshold may be defined in terms of (extended) income, consumption, or welfare, as discussed above; the litera- ture on poverty indices almost exclusively concentrates on poverty lines in terms of income. There are several aspects of "the extent of poverty" that one may be interested in. The first concerns the size of the population of poor, and is traditionally represented by the head-count ratio, or the percentage of the total population with an (extended) income level lower than the poverty line, represented by q/n in Figure 5.2.

This indicator of poverty may be used to measure the percentage of poor *households* or the percentage of poor *persons;* in the latter case the household head-count should be weighted with the number of household members in each family. It is sensitive to the *number* of households or persons who are poor, but is completely insensitive to the extent to which their income falls short of the poverty line; no difference is observed between distributions 1 and 2 in Figure 5.2. The (average) income shortfall is, however, a second aspect of poverty, that one may be interested in. The poverty gap, defined as the average income shortfall of all the poor, is sensitive to this average *extent* of poverty, but is completely insensitive to the *number* of poor. In Figure 5.3 it is seen that two different distributions may have an equal average gap, but com- pletely different poverty percentages.

Sen (1976) was the first to develop one indicator for the extent of aggregate poverty, which combined these two aspects of poverty with a third: the income inequality of the poor (represented by the Gini coefficient of the income distribu- tion of the poor). Sen starts by assuming the product of the head-count ratio and the poverty gap ratio to be a proper index, in case all the incomes of the poor are equal; yielding

Figure 5.3. **The Definition of Aggregate Poverty Indices: Average Poverty Gap**

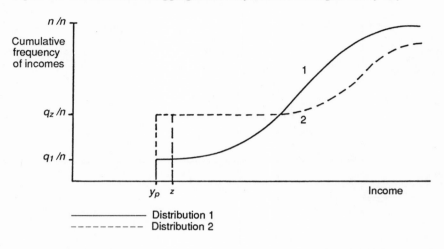

Distribution 1
Distribution 2

$$q/n \left[(z - y_p)/z\right]$$

This product may also be written as

$$1/n \sum_{i=1}^{q} (z - y_i)/z$$

When the incomes of the poor are not equal, they all get the same weight in this poverty index. One might, however, argue that large poverty gaps should get a larger weight in the overall poverty index. In other words:

$$1/n \sum_{i=1}^{q} w_i (z - y_i)/z$$

where w_i is a decreasing function of the income of the poor.

Sen's seminal work has generated an extensive literature on poverty indices combining the relative number of poor, the income shortfall and the income distribution of the poor (see, for example, Foster 1984 and Hagenaars 1986 for surveys). Most of these indicators are derived, like Sen's, from a set of axioms, chosen to represent the *a priori* notions of the researcher on the aggregation of poverty. The best known of these axioms are:

Symmetry Axiom
Poverty depends on the income levels of anonymous persons; if the same distribution of incomes is found, but with other persons, this should not affect poverty.

Monotonicity Axiom
A reduction in income of a person below the poverty line must increase the poverty index.

Transfer Axiom
A pure transfer of income from a person below the poverty line to anyone who is richer must increase the poverty index.

Population Homogenity Axiom
If two or more identical populations are pooled, the poverty index should not change.

Focus Axiom
A change in the income distribution of the nonpoor should not change the poverty index.

Transfer Sensitivity Axiom
The increase of a poverty index as a result of a transfer of a fixed amount of money from a poor person to a richer person should be decreasing in the income of the donor and vice versa.

Subgroup Monotonicity Axiom
The poverty index should increase when poverty in a subgroup increases and vice versa.

Decomposability Axiom
The poverty index should be a weighted average of the poverty indices, applied to specific subgroups within the population (with weights equal to their population share).

Some of these axioms have a straightforward interpretation and justification: comparable to the arguments used in income inequality literature (see the chapter by Stephen Jenkins, this volume). The Symmetry Axiom requires that it not be the case that "some persons are more equal than others." The Monotonicity Axiom states that a poverty index should be sensitive to the increase in poverty of any individual poor person. The Population Homogenity Axiom has empirical relevance when a dataset has to be reweighted in order to be representative of the population. Decomposability has its equivalent in income inequality literature.

Figure 5.4. **Poverty Index, Defined as Welfare Gap**

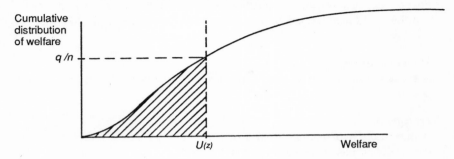

The other axioms are not, however, without problems. The Transfer Axiom basically makes a statement on interpersonal poverty comparison: the increase in poverty of a poor person who loses a certain amount of money is considered to be larger than the decrease in poverty of a person slightly richer who receives this amount of money (resulting in different weights w_i). This comparison may refer to two different welfare functions: the individuals' own welfare functions, or the Social Welfare Function adapted by the researcher. The first interpretation essentially boils down to interpersonal welfare comparison, and might be justified with the acceptance of an interpersonally comparable, concave welfare function of income. A still stronger statement on interpersonal welfare comparison is made when the Transfer Sensitivity Axiom is adopted. The Social Welfare Function interpretation implies an equally strong statement by the researcher on the emphasis that should be given, in the aggregate poverty index, to different degrees of poverty, as represented by the weights w_i.

Interpersonal welfare comparison has always been a problematic issue in economics: the comparability of "welfare" over persons has been regarded as impossible by most economists since the "Ordinalist Revolution." It is clear, however, that any aggregate index of poverty necessarily implies such a comparison. Sen (1976) used the rank order of a poor individual as an indicator of his position in the interpersonal welfare ordering of the poor, avoiding the choice of a specific individual welfare function. The weight w_i is hence chosen to be $(q+1 - I)$, resulting in Gini-type measurement of inequality. Other researchers in this area have usually adopted Sen's approach of weighting income shortfalls, with some modifications.

It is obvious that several of the problems mentioned in the previous section still apply here: is it welfare, or income, that should form the basis of a poverty concept? How should welfare, or income, be compared over households with different size and composition? Does the Transfer Axiom apply to current income, or to an extended income concept? Although these problems appear both in the stage of identification and in the stage of aggregation of the poor, it is rare to find them discussed at both stages, let alone answered consistently.

If it is welfare that one is interested in, the poverty index should not be aimed at weighting and averaging *income* shortfalls, but *welfare* shortfalls. Figure 5.4 illustrates the possibility of measuring average poverty by the average welfare gap. The social welfare functions, described in Jenkins's chapter in the context of income inequality, may usefully be applied to poverty measurement as well: if we define the censored income distribution y^* as the distribution where all $y_i > z$ are put equal to z_i, the Dalton index, applied to poverty measurement, is

$$D_p = 1 - SW(y^*)/SW(z),$$

where y^* is the income distribution censored at the poverty line z, implying

$$y_k^* = y_k \text{ if } y_k < z$$
$$y_k^* = z \text{ if } y_k \geq z$$

For an additive social welfare function this yields:

$$D_p = q/n \sum_{i=1}^{q} [U(z) - U(y_i)] / qU(z)$$

or the product of the head-count ratio and the average welfare shortfalls.

This approach, advocated in Hagenaars (1986), requires the choice of a welfare function.[6] If one is willing to assume this function, inconsistencies between the theory determining the poverty *line* and the poverty *index* are avoided. Such inconsistencies, for instance, arise with the Focus Axiom. This axiom states that the poverty index should not change when the income of the nonpoor changes. If, however, one has decided to adopt a relative poverty definition, the poverty line itself shifts upwards when the income of the total population changes, for instance as a result of a change in the income of the nonpoor. Hence, the Focus Axiom, in its present form, applies to absolute indices of poverty only, or to situations where the poverty line is taken to be exogenous. This contrasts sharply with one of the justifications of Sen for including income inequality among the poor as a relevant aspect of poverty, which is based upon the "relativist" view of poverty, defining deprivation as an essentially relative concept. If poverty is indeed interpreted as relative deprivation, deprivation with respect to more than just all other poor in the society should be studied.

In fact, the use of a theory of relative deprivation in the derivation of a poverty index poses the same problems as described above in the definition of a poverty line: is it subjective, individual deprivation that we are interested in? Or is it an objective state of deprivation? According to the first interpretation,

which follows straightforwardly from Runciman's theory of relative deprivation, a dynamic utility function that includes interdependencies between different individuals would be the appropriate instrument to represent the extent of
welfare (or poverty) of individuals. If an objective state of deprivation is the
basis of one's poverty definition, one may wish to avoid the explicit use of
utility functions.

The axiomatic approach to the construction of a poverty index is not, therefore,
without problems. Moreover, the basic intention of Sen and others, of integrating the
relative number of poor, the average poverty gap, and the income inequality among
the poor into one poverty index, necessarily requires a choice between these three
aspects of poverty since certain income transfers may reduce one and increase another
aspect of poverty. A first example of such a transfer is the situation where a poor
person gives some of his income to someone who is slightly richer.

Consider a population of ten persons, with a poverty line at the level of 1,000,
and the following distribution of income:

$$y_1 = 100$$
$$y_2 = 200$$
$$y_3 = 302$$
$$y_4 = 999$$
$$y_5 = 1,100$$
$$y_6 = 1,200$$
$$y_7 = 1,200$$
$$y_8 = 1,300$$
$$y_9 = 1,500$$
$$y_{10} = 2,000$$

If the person with income y_3 transfers two income units to the person ranking
above him, the transfer axiom requires this transfer to be poverty-increasing. As
a result of the transfer, however, person 4 crosses the poverty line, resulting in a
lower poverty percentage. Which of these two opposite directions do we want
the overall poverty index to go in?

A second example involves a situation where the population of poor is extended by, say, immigration (or birth) of new members of the population. Suppose in the situation described above, two new persons are added to the
population of poor, each with an income equal to the average income of the poor.
The income inequality among the poor decreases as a result of this immigration.
The relative number of poor, on the other hand, increases as a result. Which of
these two effects should dominate in the overall poverty index?

It is clear that no straightforward answers exist to these questions. I would suggest
that the answer depends on the nature of the poverty line, and on the implicit
interpersonal welfare comparison made in each poverty index. The nature of the
poverty line may be completely absolute, resulting in some "hunger line," an income
level below which starvation may occur. With such a poverty line, it is pointless to
discuss the income inequality among the poor, as they are all in a similarly deplorable

situation. In that case, the number of people below the poverty line is the only relevant figure. If the nature of the poverty line is to some extent relative, however, the poverty line is not a sharp cut-off point separating the poor from the nonpoor, but a point on a continuum between very poor and very rich. In that case one may indeed distinguish various degrees of poverty. In doing so, however, an interpersonal comparison of welfare is unavoidable. Almost all poverty indices have been shown (Hagenaars 1986) to be applications of the Dalton (or Atkinson) index of income inequality to poverty measurement.

How this general poverty index is to be operationalized depends on the choice of the social welfare function, and, if applicable, on the choice of individual welfare or utility functions. Again, one may wonder whether the choice of a specific poverty index, given a certain poverty line, makes much difference for empirical research. Thon (1979) has shown that the extent of poverty in four racial groups in Malaysia shows a different ranking for different poverty indices. Hagenaars (1986) also finds slight changes in poverty orderings between eight European countries, when different poverty indicators are used; in her research the choice between a relative or an absolute poverty *line* has, however, a larger impact than the choice of a specific poverty *index*. Although the differences may not be very large for cross-sectional comparison of different countries or different social subgroups, they are quite likely to be substantial when changes over time in the poverty status of one country or subgroup are considered. The choice of a poverty indicator should in such a situation be made with reference to the aims of social policy: if one wishes to reduce the number of people below the poverty line, the head-count ratio is obviously the index to use in order to measure the success of the policy. If one aims at a general alleviation of the extent of poverty of the poor, the poverty gap might be used. If both objectives are aimed at, some social welfare function has to be chosen to obtain the proper mix of these two elements in the poverty index to be used.

Concluding Remarks

In this chapter a review is given of various methods of identifying the poor, and of measuring the extent of their poverty. It is seen that both in the identification and in the aggregation stage, some welfare judgments are made, either explicitly or implicitly. Advantages and disadvantages of various methods are given. Empirical evidence shows that the choice of a specific method is extremely relevant for the size and composition of the resulting population of poor.

Notes

1. I will use the broader term "households" in the remainder of this chapter for all economic units that share their income and home, whether related to each other by marriage or family ties or not. This is not necessarily the definition used by researchers

applying the different definitions, but it allows the basic theoretical issues to de discussed in a general framework.

2. The assumption that the welfare level of different household members cannot be considered independently of each other does not imply that the welfare within a household is necessarily equally distributed. However, data on intrahousehold welfare inequality is as yet so scarce as to make inferences on differences in poverty between household members impossible.

3. For this life-time concept to be valid, it is required that capital markets are perfect. One of the main motivations behind the social security systems in welfare states, however, is to counter the imperfection of these markets; see also the discussion in Paul Cullinan's chapter in this volume.

4. See Hagenaars (1986) for a survey of methods used to arrive at an absolute poverty line.

5. See de Vos and Hagenaars (1988) for a critical review of the definitions of Townsend (1979) and Sen (1985).

6. Equivalent to the income inequality situation, an "Atkinson version" of this index may be defined as

$$A_p = 1 - [y *EDE]/z, \text{ where } SW (y *EDE) = SW (y *)$$

References

Abel-Smith, B., and P. Townsend (1965). *The Poor and the Poorest*. Occasional Papers on Social Administration, no. 17. London: Bell and Sons.

Atkinson, A. B. (1987). "On the Measurement of Poverty." *Econometrica*, vol. 55, 749–64.

Becker, G. S. (1965). "A Theory of the Allocation of Time." *The Economic Journal*, vol. 75, 493–517.

Buhmann, B., L. Rainwater, G. Schmaus, and T. M. Smeeding (1988). "Equivalence Scales, Well-being, Inequality and Poverty: Sensitivity Estimates across Ten Countries Using The Luxembourg Income Study (LIS) Database." *Review of Income and Wealth*, Series 34, no. 2 (June), 115–42.

Colasanto, D., A. Kapteyn, and J. van der Gaag (1984). "Two Subjective Definitions of Poverty; Results from the Wisconsin Basic Needs Study." *Journal of Human Resources*, vol. 19, 127–37.

Danziger, S., J. van der Gaag, M. K. Taussig, and E. Smolensky (1984). "The Direct Measurement of Welfare Levels; How Much Does It Cost to Make Ends Meet?" *Review of Economics and Statistics*, vol. 66, 500–505.

De Vos, K., and A. J. M. Hagenaars (1988). *A Comparison of the Poverty Concepts by Sen and Townsend*. Rotterdam: Erasmus University.

Douglas, M., and B. Isherwood (1979). *The World of Goods*. New York: Basic Books.

Duncan, G. J. (1987). "The Perception of Poverty." Book Review, *Journal of the American Statistical Association*, vol. 82, no. 399, pp. 959–60.

Foster, J. E. (1984). "On Economic Poverty: A Survey of Aggregate Measures." *Advances in Econometrics*, vol. 3, 215–51.

Fuchs, V. (1967). "Redefining Poverty and Redistributing Income." *Public Interest* (Summer), 88–95.

Garfinkel, I., and R. H. Haveman (1977a). "Earning Capacity, Economic Status, and Poverty." *Journal of Human Resources*, vol. 12, 40–70.

———. (1977b). *Earning Capacity, Poverty and Inequality*. New York: Academic Press.

Goedhart, Th., V. Halberstadt, A. Kapteyn, and B. M. S. van Praag (1977). "The Poverty Line: Concept and Measurement." *The Journal of Human Resources*, vol. 12, 503–20.

Hagenaars, A. J. M. (1986). *The Perception of Poverty*. Amsterdam: North Holland Publishing Company.

Hagenaars, A. J. M., and K. de Vos (1987). "The Definition and Measurement of Poverty." *Journal of Human Resources*, vol. 23, 211–21.

Kilpatrick, R. W. (1973). "The Income Elasticity of the Poverty Line." *The Review of Economics and Statistics*, vol. 55, 327–32.

Lansley, S. (1980). "Changes in Inequality and Poverty in the U.K., 1971–1976." *Oxford Economic Papers*, vol. 32, no. 1, 134–51.

Lapierre, D. (1986). *The City of Joy*. London: Arrow Books.

Mack, J. and S. Lansley (1985). *Poor Britain*. London: Allen and Unwin.

Marshall, A. [1890] (1920). *Principles of Economics*, 8th ed. London: Macmillan.

Maslow, A. H. (1954). *Motivation and Personality*. New York: Harper and Row.

Miller, S. M., and P. Roby (1970). *The Future of Inequality*. New York: Basic Books.

Mirer, Th. W. (1977). "Aspects of the Variability of Family Income." In M. L. Moon and E. Smolensky, eds. *Improving Measures of Economic Well-Being*. Madison, WI: Institute for Research on Poverty.

Moon, M. L. (1977). "The Economic Welfare of the Aged and Income Security Programs." In M. L. Moon and E. Smolensky, eds. *Improving Measures of Economic Well-Being*. Madison, WI: Institute for Research on Poverty.

Orshansky, M. (1965). "Counting the Poor: Another Look at the Poverty Profile." *Social Security Bulletin*, vol. 28.

Piachaud, D. (1981). "Peter Townsend and the Holy Grail." *New Society*, vol. 57, 419–21.

Rainwater, L. (1969). "The Lower-Class Culture and Poverty-War Strategy." In D. P. Moynihan, ed. *On Understanding Poverty*. New York: Basic Books.

———. (1974). *What Money Buys: Inequality and the Social Meanings of Income*. New York: Basic Books.

Rein, M. (1974). "Problems and the Definition and Measurement of Poverty." In P. Townsend, ed. *The Concept of Poverty*. London: Heinemann.

Rowntree, B. S. (1901). *Poverty: A Study of Town Life*. London: MacMillan.

Runciman, W. G. (1966). *Relative Deprivation and Social Justice*. London: Routledge & Kegan Paul.

Sen, A. K. (1976). "Poverty: An Ordinal Approach to Measurement." *Econometrica*, vol. 44, 219–31.

———. (1979). "Issues in the Measurement of Poverty." *Scandinavian Journal of Economics*, vol. 81, pp. 285–307.

———. (1983). "Poor, Relatively Speaking." Oxford Economic Papers, vol. 35, 153–70.

———. (1985). *Commodities and Capabilities*. Amsterdam: North Holland Publishing Company.

Shorrocks, A. F. and J. E. Foster (1987). "Transfer Sensitive Inequality Measures." *Review of Economic Studies*, vol. 54, 485–97.

Smeeding, T. M. (1977). "The Economic Well-Being of Low Income Households, Implications for Income Inequality and Poverty." In M. Moon and E. Smolensky, eds. *Improving Measures of Economic Well-Being*. Madison, WI: Institute for Research on Poverty.

Smith, A. [1776] (1979). *The Wealth of Nations*. Harmondsworth, U.K.: Penguin Books.

Thon, D. (1979). "On Measuring Poverty." *Review of Income and Wealth*, vol. 25, 429–39.

Thurow, L. C. (1969). *Poverty and Discrimination.* Washington, DC: The Brookings Institution.

Townsend, P. (1962). "The Meaning of Poverty." *British Journal of Sociology*, vol. 13, 210–27.

————. (1979). *Poverty in the United Kingdom.* Harmondsworth, U.K.: Penguin Books.

Van Praag, B. M. S. (1968). *Individual Welfare Functions and Consumer Behavior.* Amsterdam: North Holland Publishing Company.

Van Praag, B. M. S., Th. Goedhart, and A. Kapteyn (1980). "The Poverty Line: A Pilot Survey in Europe." *The Review of Economics and Statistics*, vol. 62, 461–65.

Van Praag, B. M. S., J. S. Spit, and H. Van de Stadt (1982). "A Comparison between the Foodratio Poverty Line and the Leyden Poverty Line." *Review of Economics and Statistics*, vol. 64, no. 4, pp. 691–94.

Watts, H. W. (1968). "An Economic Definition of Poverty." In D. P. Moynihan, *On Understanding Poverty.* New York: Basic Books, 316–29.

————. (1967). "The Iso-Prop Index: An Approach to the Determination of Differential Poverty Income Thresholds." *The Journal of Human Resources*, vol. 2, 3–18.

6

Short- and Long-Term Poverty in the United States: Measuring the American "Underclass"

Patricia Ruggles

Over the past two decades, a substantial amount of research has been undertaken on the size and characteristics of the poverty population in the United States. This research has ranged from highly impressionistic accounts of the lives of the poor to sophisticated statistical analyses of the incidence and duration of persistent poverty. Much of this research has focused on very basic issues, such as the relative size of the long-term poor population compared to the group that is seen to be poor at a given point in time. Most of our official statistics on poverty focus on this latter group—those who are poor in a given year on the basis of their annual income in that year. However, recent research has been particularly concerned with the identification of factors that may cause families and individuals to become persistently poor, and with the design of strategies that might help limit the size of this group in the future.

Many writers on long-term poverty have discussed its relationship to issues of class and culture, and have proposed in particular that a subset of the long-term poor may in fact constitute a separate culture within the larger society, which may be characterized as an "underclass." Much of the literature on this underclass of the permanently poor has focused on relatively anecdotal accounts of their lives, however, which can result in impressionistic and conflicting analyses of the causes of this type of long-term poverty. Although case histories and journalistic approaches can be helpful in understanding the dimensions of the problem, they do little to help us assess the relative importance of various factors in explaining poverty over the long run. Therefore, this article summarizes briefly the arguments made by some of the best-known authors of these pieces, but focuses on the more empirically oriented literature in this area.

Among authors with a more measurement-oriented approach, two general trends can be identified. Writers in the first group, including for example Frank Levy, Martha Hill, Greg Duncan, and Mary Jo Bane and David Ellwood, have generally concentrated on those who are persistently poor over some specified period of time. This focus has the advantage of being relatively easy to translate into population measures, since specific criteria for membership in the group can be set, and counts of the number of persons meeting these criteria can then be undertaken. Within the overall group of persistently poor, further distinctions have sometimes been made. For example, some analysts have examined only the nonelderly persistently poor, under the assumption that the causes and possible cures for persistent poverty are typically rather different for the young and the old.

A second group of writers in this area, whose work generally follows in the tradition of William Julius Wilson, have concentrated not so much on the characteristics of individuals who are in poverty, but rather on the characteristics of localities associated with the underclass (see for example Wilson 1987). In general, this approach posits a causative link between the characteristics of neighborhoods (e.g., poor housing, low employment opportunities) and the behaviors of the individuals that inhabit them. Analysts with this outlook use the idea that, to the extent that "underclassness" is a cultural phenomenon, it may be most practical and perhaps most meaningful to identify first the cultures or neighborhoods in which it occurs, and then to consider the association between the neighborhood and individual characteristics and behaviors. This approach, exemplified by the work of Ricketts and Sawhill (1988) and Ricketts and Mincy (1988), focuses on behavioral deviancy rather than on poverty per se, and is therefore somewhat outside the scope of this article. Nevertheless, it is worth noting that the specific deviant behaviors chosen—out-of-wedlock childbirths, high rates of unemployment or of nonlabor-force–participation, high rates of school drop-out, and so forth—are both much more likely to occur among the long-term poor (and to be a factor in maintaining long-term poverty) and less likely to be considered deviant when they occur among those with adequate financial resources. (Movie stars who have children without being married, for example, are now generally considered entirely unremarkable.)

Because the focus of these studies is on the neighborhood (generally measured in terms of Census tracts) rather than on the individual, it is difficult to compare estimates of the size of the underclass derived from these studies with those from studies that consider mainly poverty as measured at the individual or family level. Neighborhood-based studies typically include all residents of the neighborhoods in question in their underclass definitions, although generally fewer than half would qualify as poor under our official poverty guidelines, and a smaller percentage would be long-term poor. On the other hand, such studies exclude long-term poor living in less deprived areas. Neither definition is inherently more valid. For some policy purposes (designing housing and employment policies, for example) neighborhood-based estimates may be particularly helpful, while for others (considering the need for long-term income support) estimates based on the individual's personal resources may be more useful. In any case, the remainder of this article focuses on estimates of the latter type.

The primary aim of this paper, then, is to summarize what is known about the number and characteristics of the long-term poor, to contrast them with those who are poor for shorter periods, and to consider whether in fact they can be said to make up an underclass. The analysis presented here, therefore, starts with an examination of the poverty population, the short-term poor, and the persistently poor. Next, the paper considers the relationship between persistent poverty and the underclass, and discusses the extent to which the long-term poor may or may not be part of such a class. Finally, the policy implications of these findings and of findings on the duration of poverty in general are discussed.

In examining these issues, this paper relies heavily on several important empirically oriented studies that have examined long-term poverty. These studies are summarized and discussed, and, where they disagree, attempts have been made to reconcile their results (or where that is not possible, to explore the sources of their disagreement). Although, like most of the empirically oriented writers whose work is reviewed here, this paper concentrates almost exclusively on the economic and demographic characteristics of the poor (and particularly, the persistently poor), this does not indicate that other factors such as attitudes, cultural factors, and so forth are considered to be unimportant. It is simply that such factors cannot generally be measured, particularly on a population-wide basis, using available data. These factors are discussed briefly in the concluding section of this paper, however, which assesses the state of our knowledge concerning the determinants of long-term poverty and points out some of the remaining areas in which more could potentially be learned.

The next section of this chapter, then, reviews the early literature on the poverty population and the underclass, and discusses attempts to define and measure these groups. The following section briefly presents some historical statistics on the composition of the poverty population as a whole, and contrasts the characteristics of the short and the longer term poor.

The middle section contains a review of the empirical literature relating to the long-term poor, concentrating on those authors that have attempted to produce a comprehensive measure of the size of the persistently poor population. The specific definitions used by each major author are discussed briefly, and data sources, methods, and results are compared. This section ends with a discussion of the implications of these findings for current estimates of the size of the persistently poor population as a whole. The following section goes on to explore further distinctions within this group—the proportions who are elderly, who are children, who are disabled, and so forth. Again, the findings of different studies in this area are compared, and their implications are assessed for the overall composition of the persistently poor, and for the proportion of this group that could reasonably be considered underclass. The further implications of these findings for theories concerning the origin and growth of the underclass and for potential strategies to reduce that growth are briefly discussed. Finally, as noted above, the concluding section summarizes the state of our knowledge in this area, and outlines some additional possibilities for further exploration.

Defining and Measuring the Poverty Population
and the Underclass: The Early Literature

Much of the early literature on poverty and the underclass in America relied primarily on case studies, which were used to argue that at least some of the poor were different from the rest of American society in some fairly fundamental ways. Writers such as Michael Harrington (1962), Oscar Lewis (1966), and Edward Banfield (1970) argued that many of the poor were trapped in a "culture of poverty" that was transmitted from generation to generation, making it difficult for individuals brought up within that culture to take advantage of any opportunities for betterment that did arise. This theory dominated the policy debate in the poverty area during the 1960s and early 1970s, and is still very influential, in various somewhat modified forms. Although in general it has been subject to few broad empirical tests, this theory underlies most intuitive notions of the underclass that are in use today, and for that reason a brief review of its history is appropriate here.

The Underclass and the "Culture of Poverty"

In order for an underclass to come into being and to persist over time, it is necessary that at least some of the poor experience some sort of barrier to economic advancement, whether this barrier is externally imposed or is related to their own particular characteristics. In the absence of such barriers, virtually all poverty would presumably be transitory in nature. The writers mentioned above all saw the culture of poverty as posing such a barrier, and thus leading to a permanent and self-perpetuating underclass within American society. These writers differed considerably as to exactly what the components of this culture of poverty were thought to be, however, and even as to what proportion of the poor were thought to be affected.

Harrington, for example, applies the concept of a culture of poverty rather loosely, using it simply to argue that the poor as a whole have fewer opportunities for advancement, and are less able to take advantage of those opportunities, than is the case for middle-class or wealthy Americans. His analysis has more to do with the impacts of class stratification on opportunities, as he perceives them, than with any specific theories as to the motivation or attitudes of the poor themselves. He argues, in fact, that no matter how highly motivated they are, most of the poor cannot succeed. To the extent that the transitionally or temporarily poor exist at all they are presumably excluded from Harrington's discussion, but he does not explicitly recognize the existence of this population.

Lewis, on the other hand, is careful to distinguish between the poor as a whole and those who are trapped in the culture of poverty. Lewis guesses that this latter group accounts for perhaps 20 percent of the poverty population as a whole, or between 6 million and 10 million people. He outlines a set of specific characteristics having to do with lifestyles and with values that he believes are transmitted within this culture, and which together act to reduce the likelihood that an individual from this culture will enter the mainstream of American society.

Although the specific characteristics included or excluded vary from writer to writer, most recent work on the underclass as such follows in the tradition started by Lewis. The notion that there exists a culture in the anthropological sense which defines a subset of the poor has been widely disputed, but less rigorously defined versions of Lewis' thesis are still common. A variety of writers, from Kenneth Auletta (1982) to Charles Murray (1984), have implicitly assumed that specific subpopulations of relatively long-term poor can be identified within the poverty population, and that these subpopulations share certain characteristics which make it unlikely that they will break out of the cycle of poverty on their own. While these authors have very different perspectives on the origins of these subpopulations and on the impacts and potential impacts of various antipoverty strategies, they nonetheless share the belief that there are specific, nonincome-related factors pertaining to at least some of the poor that make them fundamentally different from other Americans, and that these factors are largely responsible for their continued long-term poverty.

Empirical Approaches to Defining and Measuring the Underclass

Part of the explanation for the generally anecdotal or case-study approach used by early writers on poverty and the underclass has to do with the fact that representative data on the characteristics of the poor, and especially of the persistently poor, have become available only relatively recently. The official definition of poverty used for most government-published statistics today was developed in 1965, and representative cross-sectional data on the characteristics of the poverty population were also largely unavailable before the mid-1960s.[1]

Data on the duration of poverty have been even harder to find; the major longitudinal data base used to study transitions in and out of poverty, the University of Michigan's Panel Study of Income Dynamics (PSID), started tracing its panel of 5,000 families in 1968 (collecting information in that year on 1967 incomes). The first longitudinal studies using these data did not appear until the early 1970s (see Morgan et al. 1974) and the first study to address the issue of the underclass explicitly by analyzing the probability of remaining poor over a specified period of time appeared in 1977 (Levy 1977). Since then, a number of additional studies have examined the persistently poor, and have considered the extent to which their characteristics are in fact significantly different from those of the poverty population as a whole.

Before turning to a detailed discussion of those studies, however, it may be helpful to set the context by discussing the changes in the overall poverty population that have occurred since the mid-1960s. Examination of these data may help us to consider, for example, the extent to which the size and other characteristics of the poverty population have in fact changed over time, whether as the result of policy initiatives aimed at this group or because of other changes in the structure of the economy and of the population as a whole. To the extent that some subgroups within the population have become less likely to be poor at all, they may also be less likely to be among the persistently poor from whom the underclass are presumably largely drawn. Conversely, those whose representation among the poor as a whole has grown may make up a growing proportion of the long-term poor.

Composition of the Poverty Population, 1967–85

Several important trends have affected the composition of the poverty population over the past twenty years, as Table 6.1 illustrates.[2] The overall percentage of the population that was poor was remarkably similar in 1967 (the first year for which comprehensive cross-sectional data are available) and in 1985, at about 14 percent. This similarity masks a number of ups and downs in the overall poverty rate that have occurred over this period, however.

The poverty rate for the population as a whole fell dramatically during the decade of the 1960s, from over 22 percent in 1960 to about 12 percent in 1969. The 14 percent figure seen in 1967, then, represents a brief resting place in this longer downward trend. Poverty rates for the population as a whole reached their lowest point in 1973, at just over 11 percent. The recession of the mid-1970s sparked a brief rise in poverty rates, which peaked at 12.3 percent in 1975. Poverty rates then fell again through 1978, reaching a low of 11.4 percent, before being pushed up again by the recession of the early 1980s, eventually reaching another peak of 15.2 percent in 1983. The 14 percent poverty rate seen for 1985, then, again represents a brief period of improvement following a recession.

In addition to the overall trends in the poverty level that took place over this period, some important shifts also occurred in the structure of poverty—that is, in the profiles of those likely to have been poor at different points during the period as a whole. These shifts can be best observed by comparing cross-sectional data on the composition of the poverty population from different years during the period. In the interests of simplicity of presentation, three sample years have been chosen as the focus of much of the following discussion: 1967, 1976, and 1985. Although this focus may obscure some intermediate shifts in composition, these years do illustrate the major trends occurring over the period as a whole. The first and last of these years have almost the same overall poverty rate, allowing a very direct comparison of compositional variables. The overall poverty rate in 1976 was somewhat lower, at 11.8 percent, but unemployment rates in that year and in 1985 were very similar, and the two years represent approximately the same point in the recovery from a recession. These parallels are particularly helpful in comparing aspects of poverty that may be related to employment and to labor force participation.

Table 6.1

Composition of the Poverty Population: 1967, 1976, and 1985
(numbers in thousands; persons as of March of the following year)

Poverty group	1967 Total number[a]	1967 Percent of the poverty population	1967 Poverty rate	1976 Total number[a]	1976 Percent of the poverty population	1976 Poverty rate	1985 Total number[a]	1985 Percent of the poverty population	1985 Poverty rate
All persons in poverty	27,769	100	14.2	24,975	100	11.8	33,064	100	14.0
By age									
Persons 65 and over	5,388 (9.3)	19.4	29.5	3,313 (10.4)	13.3	15.0	3,456 (11.6)	10.5	12.6
Related children under age 18[b]	11,427 (35.8)	41.2	16.3	10,081 (30.1)	40.4	15.8	12,483 (26.3)	37.8	20.1
By family type									
Persons in families with female householders	6,898 (9.0)	24.8	38.8	9,029 (11.4)	36.2	37.3	11,600 (13.1)	35.1	37.6
Persons in all other families	15,873 (84.5)	57.2	9.6	10,063 (78.5)	40.3	6.4	14,129 (73.7)	42.7	8.2
Unrelated individuals	4,998 (6.6)	18.0	38.1	5,344 (10.1)	21.4	24.9	6,725 (13.2)	20.3	21.5
By race									
White	18,983 (88.2)	68.4	11.0	16,713 (86.8)	66.9	9.1	22,860 (84.9)	69.1	11.4
Black	8,486 (11.0)	30.6	39.3	7,595 (11.5)	30.4	31.1	8,926 (12.1)	27.0	31.3

Source: Computed from Current Population Survey for years indicated.
[a] Share of each demographic group as a percentage of the total population of the United States shown in parentheses.
[b] Includes children in families only.

Long Run Shifts in the Composition of Poverty

Probably the most striking trend in the composition of the poverty population seen since 1967 has been the decline in the proportion of the poor who are elderly—a change that has come about almost entirely as the result of increased income support for the elderly population. In 1967, almost 30 percent of the elderly had below-poverty incomes, but this proportion had declined to less than 13 percent by 1985. Interestingly, most of this decline in poverty rates for the elderly occurred during the first half of this period; by 1976, the poverty rate for persons aged 65 and over had fallen to about 15 percent. Because the elderly are coming to account for a growing proportion of the population as a whole, the share of the total poverty population that is elderly has not declined as much as has the poverty rate for this group. Nevertheless, in 1967 almost 20 percent of those in poverty were aged 65 or older, compared to a bit over 10 percent in 1985.

If, as indicated above, the proportion of elderly in poverty has declined substantially without a comparable decline in poverty rates as a whole, some other group or groups must have replaced the elderly in the poverty population. Contrary to what might be expected, the group experiencing this growth in their share of the poverty population does not appear to include the very young. Children do not account for any larger share of this population now than they did in 1967 or 1976—over this period, their share has actually declined very slightly, from about 41 percent to about 38 percent. However, poverty rates for children—the proportion of all children who are in poverty—*have* risen significantly, especially in the last few years, going from about 16 percent in both 1967 and 1976 to about 20 percent in 1985. The fact that this rise has not resulted in an increase in children's share of the total poverty population is again attributable to basic demographic changes in the population as a whole: children simply account for a smaller share of the total population than they did in either 1967 or 1976. Over the 1967 through 1985 period as a whole, related children under 18 years old have declined from almost 36 percent of the total population of the United States to about 26 percent.

Overall poverty rates have remained high in spite of the decline in poverty seen for the elderly, largely as a result of increases in the number of nonelderly families in poverty, and this increase has been greatest among persons in female-headed families, as Table 6.1 demonstrates.[3] Again, it is interesting to note that poverty rates for those in such families have not risen significantly. Although close to 38 percent of this population was in poverty in 1985, this represented a slight decline from the rate seen in 1967. Rather, it is the almost 50 percent increase in the relative size of this group in the population as a whole over this period that accounts for its rise as a proportion of the poverty population.

In summary, then, shifts in the composition of the poverty population over the past twenty years have largely been driven by the same demographic factors that have affected the population as a whole. The major exception to this pattern has been the dramatic decline in poverty rates for the elderly, which has decreased the proportion of the poor over age 65 even while the elderly's share of the total population has grown. (The decline in the proportion of unrelated individuals in poverty seen in Table 6.1 is largely a result of this same phenomenon, since a very large proportion of these individuals are elderly.)

Most of the nonelderly, however, are approximately as likely to be in poverty now as they were in 1967. The one group that constitutes a partial exception to this, children under age 18, have seen an increase in their poverty rates over the past five years or so. As discussed above, however, this increase has not contributed to a growth in the share of the poverty population accounted for by children, nor has it involved an increase in the poverty rate for female-headed families. Rather, it results from two factors: an increase in the proportion of children who live in female-headed families, and a rise in poverty rates for children in families with married-couple or male heads. (In 1979, for example, immediately before the start of the most recent recession, approximately 5.4 percent of the children in such families were poor, compared to about 7 percent in 1985.) This latter rise can be attributed largely to the lingering effects of the recession, which have included relatively high rates of unemployment continuing even as the economy's productive capacity has made some recovery.

Impacts of the Recession on the Composition of Poverty

Table 6.2, which shows the distribution of all poor households by the work status of the household head, illustrates the impacts of the recession in more detail.[4] As this table shows, the proportion of poor households in which the head would normally have been expected to work was fairly stable up through 1979, at about 37 or 38 percent of the poverty population. Between 1979 and 1984, however, the proportion of poor who could have worked jumped to 47 percent. About one third of these potential workers did not work at all in 1984. These nonworkers accounted for approximately 15 percent of all poor households in 1984, up from less than 12 percent in 1979 and only about 8 percent in 1967. In addition, even among those who did work the proportion who worked only part of the year—47 weeks or less—was also up in 1984, at almost 17 percent of the poverty population compared to 14 percent in 1979 and 9 percent in 1967. Presumably, this high proportion of potential workers who did not work can be at least partially accounted for by the high unemployment rates resulting from the recession.

To some extent, then, it would appear that this recent shift in the composition of poverty may be temporary, in that if unemployment rates return to the levels seen in the 1960s or even the late 1970s many of the currently unemployed in the "expected to work" category may return to the work force, thus escaping poverty. Other trends, such as the increase in the proportion who are disabled or who are women with very young children, also appear to be moderating. Neither of these groups has increased substantially, as a proportion of all poor household heads, since 1979, although both went up quite a bit between 1967 and 1979.

Table 6.2

Percentage Distribution of Poor Households by Work Status of Head, Selected Years, 1967–84

	1967	1971	1979	1984
Poor households	100.0	100.0	100.0	100.0
Head not expected to work	62.9	62.5	61.5	53.0
Elderly	40.4	34.7	27.6	20.1
Women, child under 6	7.0	9.8	12.6	12.8
Student	5.5	6.5	7.7	7.7
Disabled	10.0	11.5	13.6	12.3
Head expected to work	37.1	37.5	38.5	47.0
Weeks worked:				
0	8.3	10.1	11.8	15.1
1 to 47	8.8	12.2	14.0	16.8
48 to 52	20.0	15.2	12.9	15.1
Household poverty rate	17.1	15.0	13.1	15.2
Unemployment rate	3.8	5.6	5.8	7.7

Sources: Danziger and Gottschalk (1986, p. 18). Computed from March 1968, 1972, 1980, and 1985 Current Population Survey data tapes.
Note: Columns may not add to subtotals because of rounding.

Annual Versus Subannual Poverty Measures

The figures shown so far have all been drawn from the official poverty statistics, and have therefore been based on the official U.S. definition of poverty. As is discussed elsewhere in this volume, that official definition involves the comparison of a family's annual cash income to an annual income threshold that varies with family size and composition. Analysts—especially those with an interest in long-term poverty—have tended to think of this poverty population as fairly stable within a year; annual income is thought of as a fairly good measure of total resources at a point in time. In fact, however, several recent studies have shown that there is a substantial amount of turnover within the poverty population during a given calendar year. Using calendar year 1984 data from the Survey of Income and Program Participation (SIPP), for example, Roberton Williams has found that, although about 11 percent of the population observed in that survey were poor on the basis of their annual incomes, only about 5 percent were poor for all 12 months of 1984.[5] Even more surprisingly, about 26 percent of the population were poor in at least one month. These data imply that spells of very low income are actually quite common in the population as a whole.

Recent work of mine confirms this implication. Using SIPP data, I found that only about one-fourth of those with a spell of poverty over the 16 month period from September 1983 through the end of 1984 had annual incomes below the poverty level, although almost three fourths had incomes below 200 percent of the poverty line, and almost 90 percent were below 300 percent of poverty. In 1984, 300 percent of poverty was approximately equivalent to the median family-income level. Thus, while most of those with subannual spells of poverty would not appear in our official poverty statistics, the majority have fairly low annual incomes, and they probably do not have substantial resources upon which to draw during poverty spells. These short spells may therefore represent periods of substantial hardship even though they are typically not represented in the official statistics.[6]

Not only are there many more short spells of poverty than might be expected on the basis of annual income data, but an analysis of the durations of poverty spells as measured in months reveals that in fact spells lasting more than a year are quite atypical. Table 6.3 shows the percentage of poverty entrants remaining in poverty after selected numbers of months, by family type.[7] As can be seen, less than 12 percent of all entrants remain in poverty for twelve or more months.

Both the probability of entering into poverty and the duration of poverty spells varies across demographic groups in expected ways. Whites are less likely to enter poverty and have shorter spells if they do enter than do non-whites; persons in female-headed families are more likely than the average to enter and experience longer spells when they do. People in families with elderly members are less likely to enter poverty, but if they do enter they typically remain poor longer. Persons in families with children have the opposite pattern; they are a bit more likely to enter poverty than the average, but they also leave more quickly. Perhaps the most striking thing about the figures shown in this table, however, is that even the groups most likely to experience long poverty spells—people in families with female heads and with elderly members—are still relatively unlikely to experience continuous spells of poverty of twelve months or more. In all, about 80 percent of people who start a poverty spell, even in these groups, leave poverty within a year.

The final column of Table 6.3 shows the distribution of spell lengths for those with annual incomes below the relevant annual poverty thresholds. As discussed above, this group accounts for only about one-fourth of all those with a month or more in poverty. Spell durations are noticeably longer for this group than for the population as a whole, but even among this group continuous poverty spells lasting a year or more are relatively rare: over 70 percent of all entrants with below-poverty level annual incomes have left poverty within the year. Although some of these exits may of course be followed by relatively rapid reentries (overall, about 15 percent of entrants reenter within the sixteen month period), presumably most of the long-term underclass would be drawn from the 30 percent of the annual-poor population that is also continuously poor.

Table 6.3

Percentage of Entrants into Poverty Remaining at Selected Months, by Characteristics of Entrant

	All entrants	Race		In a family with:			With annual income below annual poverty threshold
		White	Nonwhite	Children	Female head	Elderly	
Number of cases with a poverty entry	11,070	8,700	2,370	6,909	3,405	1,688	2,713
Percentage with a poverty entry	18.6	17.4	24.9	20.0	24.5	16.7	24.5
Percentage of entrants remaining after							
4 months	45.8	44.0	53.5	43.1	51.6	63.9	71.6
8 months	20.0	18.7	25.8	17.8	26.9	28.6	48.5
12 months	11.5	10.8	14.8	9.2	18.4	20.2	29.9

Source: Computed from a 16 month sample from the 1984 panel of the Survey of Income and Program Participation. See Ruggles (1988) for details.

The Composition and Duration of Poverty and Its Relationship to the Underclass

What does all this information about the composition and short-term duration of poverty tell us about the existence, size, or growth patterns of the underclass? The answer to this question of course depends to some extent on the concept of the underclass being considered. Although, as discussed earlier, this concept tends not to be well defined, most writers in the culture of poverty tradition appear to be considering a subset of the poverty population that typically has features such as high rates of female headship, low labor force attachment, and sometimes membership in a minority race, urban residence, or both. Such persons are characterized as being particularly likely to be persistently poor and to become welfare-dependent. Although presumably some underclass members become elderly in time, and age alone may not suffice to remove them from the underclass, the elderly as a group are generally not included in such broad characterizations of the underclass.

The evidence on population patterns within the poverty population that might relate to the size and growth of the underclass, then, is somewhat mixed. On the one hand, even though nonwhites and those in families with underclass characteristics such as female heads are more likely to be continuously poor than are members of the population at large, continuous poverty lasting a year or more is relatively rare even in these groups. Further, although the proportion of the poor living in female-headed households has increased since 1967, it has not risen any faster than the proportion among nonpoor households, and in fact it has not increased at all since the mid-1970s. In fact, female-headed households are just about as likely to be poor now as in 1967. Additionally, poverty rates for blacks, while still much higher than those for whites, have fallen somewhat over the past twenty years, and blacks now account for a smaller proportion of the total poverty population than they did in 1967 (see Table 6.1). These data would appear to indicate that even these groups, while relatively likely to be poor, are not very likely to be continuously poor, and the part of the poverty population with these characteristics is not currently increasing relative to the population as a whole.

The evidence on labor force attachment, on the other hand, is less encouraging. It appears from Table 6.2 that an increasing proportion of the poor are persons who presumably could work but who either are not doing so, or, if they are, are not earning enough to take them out of poverty. As discussed above, some of this shift is almost certainly recession related, and may prove to be temporary if unemployment rates fall. For example, poverty rates for families headed by married couples—a group that normally exhibits a very high degree of labor force attachment—rose from 5.3 percent in 1979 to 6.9 percent in 1984. Presumably, this rise was related to the increase over the same period in unemployment rates of married men with present spouses, from 2.8 percent to 4.3 percent. It is reasonable to expect that if employment opportunities were to increase, such men would generally reenter the work force, and for the most part are not in any danger of falling instead into a permanent or semipermanent underclass of the unemployed or marginally employed.

Other segments of the labor force, however, had much higher base rates of unemployment before the recession, and also experienced dramatic increases over the 1979 to 1984 period. For black males as a whole, unemployment rates went from 11.4 percent in 1979 to 16.4 percent in 1984. As a result of these high unemployment rates (and possibly also of other factors such as an increase in the number of potential workers who have dropped out of the labor force because of inability to find an acceptable job) there was a substantial decrease in the proportion of black males and of black teenage females who were employed over this period, as Table 6.4 demonstrates. Between 1979 and the bottom of the recession in 1982–83, employment of black male teenagers declined by almost 30 percent, compared to a fall of about 16 percent for white males in the same age group. Employment declines experienced by blacks were in general almost twice as large, in percentage terms, as those experienced by whites of the same age and sex (the one exception being adult females, who experienced relatively steady levels of employment regardless of race). And, for teenagers in particular, these declines were experienced in spite of employment rates that were much lower than those of their white counterparts to begin with. These very low employment rates could be a factor in inducing many such teenagers to give up the search for work altogether, turning to other sources of income, which may include either illegal activities or welfare. Although empirical evidence on this point is limited, one version of the "culture of poverty" hypothesis would hold that if such alternatives become well-established sources of support at an early age, this may lead to continued marginal labor force attachment throughout life.

It is worth noting, however, that although employment rates for blacks generally remain well below those of comparable whites, there has been a sharp upturn in employment, especially for black teenagers, over the past two years. The increase in employment seen for this group has substantially outpaced the improvements in overall employment seen for white teenagers, allowing blacks to gain somewhat in total employment compared to whites of the same age and sex. Further, almost two thirds of adult black males are employed, and about 75 percent are in the labor force—compared to about 79 percent of adult white males. These data support the evidence for the rarity of continuous poverty for nonwhites as a whole seen in Table 6.3, and indicate that the vast majority of blacks do manage to establish a satisfactory degree of labor force attachment in adulthood, in spite of the difficulties faced by black teenagers in finding jobs.

In general, then, it appears from the cross-sectional data that most of the changes seen since the late 1970s in the size and composition of the population exhibiting the underclass characteristics may well have been related to the recession of the early 1980s, rather than to any underlying major shifts in behavior or mores. Whether these changes will disappear as unemployment rates fall may be

Table 6.4

Civilian Employment/Population Ratio, 1979–84

	Total	White Males 16–19	White Males 20+	White Females 16–19	White Females 20+	Black Males 16–19	Black Males 20+	Black Females 16–19	Black Females 20+
1979	59.9	55.7	77.3	49.4	47.3	28.7	69.1	22.4	49.3
1980	59.2	53.4	75.6	47.9	47.8	27.0	65.8	21.0	49.1
1981	59.0	51.3	75.1	46.2	48.5	24.6	64.5	19.7	48.5
1982	57.8	47.0	73.0	44.6	48.4	20.3	61.4	17.7	47.5
1983	57.9	47.4	72.6	44.5	48.9	20.4	61.6	17.0	47.4
1984	59.5	49.1	74.3	47.0	50.0	23.9	64.1	20.1	49.8
1985	60.1	49.9	74.3	47.1	51.0	26.3	64.6	23.1	50.9

Source: Economic Report of the President, U.S. Government Printing Office, Washington, DC, 1986, Table B–37, p. 295.

more debatable, but early indications look fairly positive. Unemployment rates for black male teenagers have already fallen to about 41 percent in 1985 from their peak of almost 49 percent in 1982, for example, and poverty rates actually fell more for blacks and for female-headed families between 1984 and 1985 than they did for whites or for married-couple families. As discussed above, however, these cross-sectional data cannot tell us whether these changes affect only a part of the poverty population, leaving behind a core of persistently or permanently poor who are not likely to be helped by the recovery, and whose numbers may even be growing over time. The next two sections therefore review the available evidence relating to the existence, size and characteristics of this persistently poor group.

Evidence on the Persistence of Poverty: How Many Are Persistently Poor?

Although writers on the underclass have disagreed as to the specific features that qualify one for membership in this group, virtually all have included persistent low-income status (at least as pertains to reported or legal income) as an important defining characteristic. Indeed, for many writers the "underclass" and the "persistently poor" are almost interchangeable concepts. Statistics on the poverty population as a whole help us to track changes in the low-income population over time, but as noted earlier we cannot tell from these cross-sectional data whether this population contains the same particular individuals from year to year, or whether it consists of many more individuals, each of whom spends only a relatively short period of time living in poverty. (The data on within-year turnover in the poverty population seen above appear to be generally more consistent with the second hypothesis.) Clearly, these two possibilities have quite different implications for any notion of the underclass, as well as for the policies that might be designed to alleviate the problems of poverty.[8]

As Frank Levy pointed out in his 1977 paper on the size of the underclass, most writers of the 1960s implicitly assumed that the bulk of those in poverty were poor over the long run. It seems to have been widely assumed that most of those in poverty typically remained poor from year to year, with minor fluctuations at the margins of the poverty population resulting from changing economic conditions (Levy 1977, pp. 5–6). If the poverty population was in fact basically static over time, then cross-sectional statistics of the type cited earlier could be used to form a fairly accurate picture of its long-run characteristics.

To the extent that significant numbers of individuals move in and out of the poverty population over the fairly short run, however, the characteristics of the long-term poor may start to diverge from those of the poverty population as a whole. Both Morgan et al. (1974) and Levy, using data from the PSID, found that there were in fact significant numbers of people leaving and entering the poverty population each year. Levy went on to estimate the probability of remaining poor for a cohort of persons who were poor in 1967, and came to the conclusion that fewer than half could be considered "permanently poor." These findings raised the possibility that the long-run poor might in fact be significantly different from the poverty population as a whole, as it was known from cross-sectional data.

Early analyses of the PSID such as Morgan et al. (1974), Levy (1977), and Coe (1978) have sparked a whole series of investigations into the numbers and characteristics of the persistently poor. To a major extent, the findings of these studies have depended on the specific definitions of persistent poverty and the particular measurement methodologies used. The next three subsections therefore review the findings of a broad selection of these studies, with an emphasis on the definitional and methodological approaches of each and their implications for the resulting estimates.

Definitional Issues in Measuring the Number of Persistently Poor

Over the past ten years, a fairly large number of writers have explored the numbers and characteristics of the persistently poor in the United States. Those that have attempted to produce estimates of the total numbers of such permanently or persistently poor persons have almost all relied on the PSID. The PSID has a number of advantages for such studies; it is the only nationally representative survey that follows a panel of the same individuals on a year by year basis over a long period of years—in some sense, it tracks income and poverty status over a period of years in much the same way that the SIPP data presented earlier do over a period of months. Clearly, for the purpose of studying the persistence of poverty, a sample that follows specific individuals through a long period of time is necessary. The major drawback of the PSID is its relatively small sample size—the panel as a whole consisted of 5,000 families first interviewed in 1968, and there has been some attrition since then. This sample is divided into a subsample of 2,000 that focuses particularly on the low-income population, and one of 3,000 that is nationally representative. For most analytic purposes, these samples must be combined to achieve a sufficiently large number of cases for analysis.

As Table 6.5 demonstrates, it has been possible for researchers in this area to produce, even using a common data base, a wide range of estimates of the number of persistently poor. To some extent, of course, the estimated number of long-term poor depends on the year being considered. Presumably, as both the U.S. population as a whole and the poverty population have expanded, the number of persistently poor has also gone up. Even if all estimates are standardized to a single year, however, the range is still large. For example, if all the estimates in Table 6.5 were standardized to 1978 (the last year of PSID data typically available for use in these studies) the range would still be from about 3 million to about 20 million persons, or from about 12 percent to about 80 percent of the number appearing poor in 1978 on a cross-sectional basis.

Table 6.5

Estimated Size of the Underclass: Review of Several Studies

Author	Date	Definition of underclass or *permanent poor*	Estimate of size
Lewis (1966)	None	"Culture of Poverty"	6 million to 10 million persons; 20 percent of poor on annual basis.
Levy (1977)	PSID 1967–73	In poverty (census poverty thresholds) at least 5 years between 1967 and 1973	10 million to 11 million persons; 40 to 45 percent of poor on an annual basis (base is 1967 poverty population).
Coe (1978)	PSID 1967–75	In poverty (census poverty thresholds) every year from 1967 through 1975	3 million persons; 12 percent of the annual poverty population (1.1 percent of the U.S. population). (Base is 1976 poverty population.)
Rainwater (1982)	PSID 1967–76	Always in poverty (relative income definition) over various accounting periods, 1967–76	1. Annual accounting period: 11 million persons—5.2 percent of U.S. population (45 percent of CPS-based poverty population, 1976 base). 2. Three year accounting period: 20 million persons—9.4 percent of U.S. population.
Hill (1981)	PSID 1969–78	In poverty (census poverty thresholds) at least 8 out of 10 years, 1969–78; also in poverty (same definition) every year from 1969 through 1978	1. 8 out of 10 years: approximately 6 million persons—2.6 percent of U.S. population (20 to 25 percent of annual poverty population—1978 base).

Study	Data	Definition	Findings
			2. Every year for 10 years: approximately 1.6 million persons—0.7 percent of the U.S. population (about 6 percent of annual poverty population, 1978 base).
Bane and Ellwood (1983)	PSID 1969–78	Spell of poverty lasting more than 8 years; census poverty thresholds times 1.25. Nonelderly only	3.5 million to 12.5 million (1978 base) depending on definition. 1. 16.7 percent of nonelderly beginning spells of poverty will experience spells of poverty that will last more than 8 years. 2. In any given year, 59.6 percent of nonelderly poverty population (5.6 percent of total U.S. population) are in the midst of a spell of poverty lasting more than 8 years.
Duncan et al. (1984)	PSID 1969–78	In poverty (census poverty thresholds) 8 or more years	5 million to 6 million persons (1978 base); 2.2 percent or 2.6 percent of total U.S. population (depending on whether person or household weights are used); 20 percent to 25 percent of annual poverty population.
Bane and Ellwood (1986)	PSID 1970–82	Spell of poverty lasting more than 9 years; census poverty thresholds times 1.25. Nonelderly only	1. 12 percent of nonelderly beginning spells of poverty will experience spells lasting more than 9 years (13.1 percent are beginning spells of more than 8 years). 2. 51.5 percent of nonelderly poverty population are in the midst of a spell of poverty lasting more than 9 years (53.8 percent are in spells lasting more than 8 years).

Even a cursory inspection of Table 6.5 makes it clear that most of these differences in the estimated incidence of long-term poverty can be accounted for as resulting from differences in the definitions of poverty used and in the specific populations being measured. Most of the writers included in the table have used census poverty thresholds to determine who is or is not in poverty at a given point in time, although one writer, Lee Rainwater, uses a relative poverty measure—50 percent of the median income.[9] In addition, another pair of authors, Mary Jo Bane and David Ellwood, use 125 percent of the census threshold as their poverty threshold, in an attempt to compensate for the fact that a larger proportion of total income is reported on the PSID than on the Bureau of the Census's Current Population Survey (CPS).[10]

The number of years over which one must be poor in order to qualify as "permanently" or "persistently" poor varies even more across authors. At one extreme, Richard Coe requires members of his permanently poor group to be poor in every year over a nine year period. Not surprisingly, this results in a relatively small estimate of the permanently poor population—about 12 percent of the poverty population as a whole, or about 3 million people in 1976.

Most of the other authors allow those with some short intervals out of poverty to be considered poor if they are poor most of the time; Levy, for example, requires poverty in five out of seven years, while both Hill, and Duncan et al. consider those who are poor in at least eight out of ten years to be among the long-term poor. Bane and Ellwood consider those poor for more than eight years to be permanently poor, but unlike the other authors they examine only the nonelderly poor. Rainwater examines a variety of different definitions of the long-term poor, including several based on income accounting periods of different lengths. His one-year accounting period corresponds to conventional annual income measures, while the three-year period, which involves comparing total income over three years to a poverty standard equal to three times his one-year standard, allows some fluctuations in income as long as the average remains low. A comparison of Rainwater's results for the one-year accounting period to Coe's "poor in every year" statistics, which refer to almost the same set of years, indicates how generous Rainwater's relative poverty standard is compared to the CPS poverty thresholds, since aside from the poverty threshold used these two measures are almost identical. According to Rainwater's definition, about 11 million persons in 1976 would have been always poor over the preceding ten years, compared to Coe's estimate of about 3 million.

The Impact of Methodological Differences on Estimates of the Persistently Poor

Finally, in addition to definitional differences, methodological differences also account for some substantial variations in the estimates. Generally, three different measures of the base population are used as a basis of comparison in these examinations of the long-term poor. The most common approach, used by Hill (1981), and Duncan et al. (1984), and implicitly, by those who use an "always poor" definition, is also in some ways the simplest. Under this approach, the base population consists of all those present throughout the observation period, and the "persistently poor" are those who are poor for some specified proportion of those years, whenever such years may fall.

While this approach has some intuitive appeal, particularly for studying the characteristics of those who are among the long-term poor, it does not provide a very good estimate of the size of the persistently poor population (and may in fact result in some distortions of reported distributions of characteristics as well). The major problem is that some of those who are not poor for some specified number of years during the observation period—for example, eight (to use the number chosen by Duncan et al.)—are in fact in the midst of spells of poverty that have been going on or will go on for a total of eight or more years, although unfortunately some of these years happen to fall outside the period for which data were collected. Thus, the true number of individuals in the sample who were actually poor for at least eight out of ten years (at least some of which fell during the sample period) cannot be estimated using these data, since those years of poverty falling outside the sample period are not observed.

This type of problem, in which complete observations on some sample items (in this case, spells of poverty) cannot be obtained because the sample is incomplete at one or both ends, is generally known as sample censoring. Statistics derived from such a censored sample cannot be used either to predict what proportion of any given year's poverty population will be persistently poor in the future, or to estimate what proportion of those poor at a given point in time are in the midst of long spells of poverty, because the information on the individual spells observed in the sample is not complete, leading us to underestimate the average length of the observed spells. As a result, the implications of measures based on samples of this type for the probability of becoming or remaining persistently poor are rather hard to interpret. Possible approaches that would avoid at least some of the sample censoring problems experienced by Hill and by Duncan et al., such as those used by Levy and, most notably, by Bane and Ellwood, produce statistics whose implications are at least somewhat clearer.

Levy, for example, uses what is essentially a cohort approach. He estimates the probability that those who were poor in 1967 will continue to be poor in at least five of the next seven years. Although he is not able to take into account the number of years those in poverty have already been poor, Levy's estimate does have the advantage of being usable to predict what proportion of those who are poor at a given point in time will continue to be poor for a specified number of years into the future. In other words, while Levy does not entirely solve the problems of censoring that affect the estimates produced by Hill and by Duncan et al., his estimates can at least be readily interpreted in policy terms. Using Levy's technique it is possible, for example, to generalize that of those found to be poor on a cross-sectional basis in a given year, a certain percentage (according to Levy, 40 to 45 percent) will continue to be permanently poor, under his definition. Since policy options can only affect the future poor, this group within the poverty population as a whole is likely to be of particular interest: they represent those who, without intervention, are likely to remain poor, and therefore those for whom interventions of some type are most likely to be necessary. Levy's estimate may still be an underestimate of the persistently poor as a proportion of all who are poor in a given year, since presumably some longer-term poor will be ending long spells of poverty during the early years of his cohort analysis, and so will not be picked up as members of his permanently poor population.[11]

A third approach to measuring the proportion of those in annual poverty who are persistently poor is that taken by Mary Jo Bane and David Ellwood. Unlike the other authors discussed here, Bane and Ellwood have made an explicit effort to adjust their estimates of this population for biases related to sample censoring. As discussed above, biases of this type lower most other estimates of the proportion of the poverty population that is persistently poor.

Bane and Ellwood adjust for this problem by examining the distribution of completed spells of poverty (i.e., spells of poverty for which both a beginning point and an end point are known) that can be observed over the years of PSID data that they had available—nine years of usable data in their 1983 paper, and twelve years in the revised version that appeared in 1986. On the basis of this examination, they calculate the conditional probability of leaving poverty after having been poor for a given number of years, finding that although there is a declining probability of leaving poverty with each additional year of poverty experienced, this decline appears to tail off after six to eight years. As a result, a fairly steady proportion of the poor population is estimated to leave poverty each year after that point. This finding is then used to predict what the distribution of completed spells of poverty would look like for those poor at a given point in time during the observation period, if all these spells could be observed in their entirety. A constant probability of leaving poverty, based in the 1983 analysis on the average probability seen for spells of six to eight years, is assumed for spells of nine to thirty years. (All remaining spells of poverty are assumed to end after thirty years.) The resulting distribution of estimated completed spells indicates that as many as 60 percent of those poor at a given point in time may be in the midst of spells that will last for a total of more than eight years. The 1986 analysis generally uses the same methodology but has a longer sample period and therefore more observed spells lasting at least nine years; in this paper about 52 percent of all persons in poverty are estimated to be in spells of more than nine years, and about 54 percent in spells of eight or more years.

Bane and Ellwood's innovative approach is a substantial improvement on measures that ignore the problems of sample censoring altogether. Some cautions, mostly having to do with data limitations, should be observed in interpreting these results, however. The PSID is a relatively small sample, and even using Bane and Ellwood's fairly generous poverty thresholds, the number of persons experiencing durations of poverty of seven or eight years within a nine year period is fairly small. Sample sizes in the 1986 paper are somewhat larger, since a longer observation period is available, but still tend to be low. Understandably, year to year fluctuations in estimated probabilities of leaving poverty are quite large for these relatively long spells, and the standard errors associated with these estimates also tend to increase as sample sizes fall. Thus, while the use of an average exit probability in estimating the incidence of extended spells of poverty (nine years and more) is justifiable given the alternatives, its accuracy cannot easily be assessed.

Unfortunately, estimates of the numbers and duration of longer spells are fairly sensitive to the particular exit probability chosen for these longer spells. For example, reworking Bane and Ellwood's 1983 estimates with an estimated exit probability for spells of nine through twenty-nine years equal to the probability seen for six-year spells (15 percent) would lower the estimated persistently poor population at a given point in time by about 10 percent, while the use of the probability seen for seven-year spells (6 percent) would raise it by an amount almost as large. These estimates imply a rather wide confidence interval around Bane and Ellwood's estimate of about 60 percent. Indeed, the 1986 study, which uses the same assumptions as the 1983 study for years ten through thirty, and reworks the estimates for the earlier years based on observations covering a slightly different timespan, comes up with overall estimates that are significantly lower. According to the later study, about 54 percent of those poor at a point in time are in the midst of a spell of poverty lasting more than eight years.

Bane and Ellwood's estimation methodology has been discussed in relatively great detail here because it implies a somewhat different conception of the persistently poor than is seen in the other studies, with rather different implications for the total size of this population. In addition to the estimation techniques outlined above, however, the Bane and Ellwood study differs from the others included here in several other important ways that should be borne in mind in assessing their results. First, because persons who die are eliminated retrospectively from the PSID, an adequate sample of completed spell data could not be assembled for the elderly, and so Bane and Ellwood's estimates are confined to the nonelderly. As other studies have indicated (and as is discussed in more detail in the next section) the elderly almost certainly account for a substantial proportion of the persistently poor population, and their probabilities of leaving poverty may be quite different from those seen for the nonelderly. For this reason, caution should be used in applying Bane and Ellwood's findings to the derivation of estimates of the numbers of long-term poor within the poverty population as a whole.

Second, Bane and Ellwood's estimates pool data across all the available years of the PSID, assuming that there are no important systematic variations in the average numbers or duration of poverty spells over time. This steady state assumption is necessary, in that unless data from different years can be somehow combined, sample sizes for completed spells will be too small to be analyzed.[12] Nevertheless, such pooling may obscure important changes that in fact do take place over time. For example, both poverty rates and unemployment rates were much higher in the last two or three years of the 1970 through 1982 period than they had been in most of the rest of the period, and the relatively large numbers of new entrants into the poverty population seen in those years could have substantially increased the incidence of relatively short observed spells. (Indeed, this may be one explanation for the differences seen between the 1986 estimates, which include the years 1979–82, and the 1983 estimates, which use data only through 1978.)

Longer term demographic shifts in the poverty population may also bias completed spell estimates, if they cause shifts in the probable duration of poverty spells. To the extent that young children and their mothers are coming to represent a rising proportion of those becoming poor, for example, average spell durations may be lengthening, since according to Bane and Ellwood children born into poverty will on average experience spells of poverty that are almost twice as long as the average for all persons beginning a spell of poverty. Given the sample size problems in the PSID, it will almost certainly be necessary to continue to use pooled data in order to make estimates of the distribution of completed spells, but possibly some adjustments could be made on a post hoc basis to take into account major observed trends in poverty rates, employment, and the demographic composition of the poverty population.[13]

The final caution with regard to the Bane and Ellwood estimates is that they are generally unable to link up multiple spells of poverty experienced by the same individual, so that single spells of poverty are typically treated as independent events. Unlike the Hill estimates and those of Duncan et al., which treat all persons who are poor for the minimum number of years as persistently poor, whether or not these years of poverty are continuous, Bane and Ellwood's analysis is confined to continuous spells of poverty. Some allowance, however, was made by Bane and Ellwood for brief interruptions in spells: a spell was considered continuous even if it was interrupted by a one-year spell out of poverty, if the increase in income experienced was less than one half the poverty standard. This adjustment reduced total spells of poverty among the ever-poor by about one fourth. Because the observation period is relatively short, the number of transitions in and out of poverty that could be observed is fairly limited. As a result, this adjustment probably captures the majority of multiple-spell cases occurring within the observation period, reducing the bias associated with the use of single spells.

The Persistently Poor and the Underclass: What Do These Estimates Mean?

In summary, the major differences seen in the estimates presented in Table 6.5 can for the most part be attributed to methodological differences in their preparation. Any of the approaches used are potentially appropriate for specific policy or analytic purposes. Estimates such as those of Hill or Duncan et al., however, which count only those appearing poor over a given number of years, without correction for biases resulting from sample censoring, are generally less helpful in considering the proportion of those poor at a point in time who might qualify as persistently poor, since as discussed above they will tend to underestimate the relative size of the persistently poor population.

Cohort-based estimates like Levy's, on the other hand, are potentially useful for policy purposes even though they do not fully adjust for sample censoring, since they can be used to consider what proportion of the currently poor population will continue to be poor over some specified period of time. In practical terms, since our cross-sectional data do not typically contain any information on the amount of time the poor have already been poor, information on total spell lengths is less useful for prediction purposes than are estimates applying to specific poverty cohorts. For many policy purposes, as well, the most relevant question is how many people are likely to continue to be poor, rather than how many will eventually experience total spells of some specified length (including time already poor).

In terms of an analysis of the underclass, however, estimates like Bane and Ellwood's, which take into account the total amount of time that those who are poor at a given point in time will eventually spend in poverty, are probably the most useful. For this purpose, the aim is generally to consider how many people spend a relatively large part of their lives being poor and what their characteristics are. While it is clear from these analyses that the details of the definitions and the methodologies used can significantly affect our answers to the first question, in very broad terms the answer seems to be that about half of the nonelderly who appear to be poor at a given point in time are in fact members of this persistently poor population.

That still leaves the question, however, of how exactly persistent poverty relates to a notion of the "underclass." While persistent poverty is a component of most underclass definitions, most writers in this area seem to have in mind a somewhat narrower categorization. As discussed in the introductory section of this paper, characteristics such as female headship, out-of-wedlock births, low labor force attachment, and membership in a minority population are often mentioned in this context. What proportion of the persistently poor population also shares such characteristics, and how does the composition of this population compare to the poverty population as a whole? The next section of this paper examines these questions.

Characteristics of the Persistently Poor Population:
Who Are the Persistently Poor?

As seen in the last section, our best guess based on the evidence of the PSID is that something like 40 percent of those poor at a point in time will continue to be poor for some years to come (using Levy's estimates) and, according to Bane and Ellwood, perhaps half or a bit more of the nonelderly poor are in the midst of longer-term spells of poverty, including the years that they have already been poor. Does that mean that all of these people can also be considered members of the underclass? Clearly, at least some are in groups that we don't normally think of in this context: the retired elderly, some disabled persons, even a few who are long-term low-wage earners. Table 6.6, which presents a variety of estimates relating to the composition of the persistently poor population, illustrates the range of characteristics associated with this group.

Definitional and Methodological Issues

Examination of Table 6.6 makes it clear that definitional and methodological issues are important in considering the composition of the persistently poor population, as well as in estimating its size. The estimates seen in Table 6.6 do not in general vary quite as much as do the size estimates considered in the last section. Indeed, if persistent poverty is a steady state, as Bane and Ellwood assume, then new entrants and exiters should share very similar characteristics. In such a case, a sample of those appearing persistently poor over a given span of years would differ in composition from a completed spell distribution only to the extent that those in different demographic groups have different average durations of time in poverty. Since all those in this sample already have long spells of poverty, remaining variations in duration, while they undoubtedly exist, may be relatively small. In any case, since Bane and Ellwood's methodology does not allow them to estimate completed spell lengths for specific individuals having uncompleted spells of poverty in their PSID sample, the demographic characteristics associated with such a completed spell distribution cannot be examined directly.[14]

Characteristics of the Persistently Poor

A comparison of Table 6.6 with earlier tables that showed the point-in-time composition of the poverty population, such as Table 6.1, indicates that there are some significant differences between the persistently poor, however measured, and the population that is poor on an annual basis. First, it is clear that the persistently poor are considerably more likely to be elderly than are those in the annual poverty population as a whole. To some extent, this may result from the fact that the persistently poor population, at least as measured by these studies, is biased toward those present in the samples in relatively early years, since they have more chances to have relatively long observed spells. As pointed out earlier, poverty rates for the elderly have fallen dramatically over this period. Levy's study, which examines the 1967 poverty cohort, finds a percentage of elderly persons fairly comparable to the annual statistics for that year: 22.6 percent versus 19.4 percent. Nevertheless, all of these studies find higher percentages of

Table 6.6

Estimates of the Demographic Composition of the Persistently Poor Population, from Various Studies[a]

Percentage in household with head who is	Levy (1977)	Coe (1978)	Rainwater[b] (1981)	Hill (1981) (poor 8 of 10 years)	Hill (1981) (poor in every year)	Duncan et al. (1984)
Elderly: age 65 or over	22.6%	22.1%	36.1%	32.4%	26.4%	33%
Disabled						
All		35.9		38.5	32.3	39
Nonelderly	14.2					
Female						
All		73.9		60.9	81.1	61
Nonelderly	26.4[c]			43.4	58.9	44
Unmarried with children		56.2		37.2	48.6	
Black		77.0	32.8[d]	61.8	60.8	62
Employed at least 1500 hours		13.6[e]		16.0	9.2	

[a] For definitions of persistently poor population used in each study, see Table 6.4.
[b] Percentages refer to all adults, not household heads as for other studies.
[c] Nondisabled nonelderly only.
[d] Minority—includes both blacks and hispanics.
[e] In 1975 (final year of panel examined by Coe).

elderly among the persistently poor than among the poverty population as a whole.

It is further worth noting that the less stringent the poverty definition used, in terms of either continuousness of poverty or the level of the poverty threshold used, the higher the proportion of the persistently poor population that is likely to be over 65. For example, Hill's "poor in every year" measure results in a persistently poor population that is about 26 percent elderly, while her "poor 8 out of 10 years" measure finds more than 32 percent who are elderly. Rainwater's definition, which is the least stringent of those considered in terms of the dollar value of the poverty thresholds used, also finds the highest percentage of elderly—about 36 percent. This generally supports the view, also supported in the cross-sectional data, that while the elderly are no longer typically among the poorest of the poor, they are relatively likely to be in the "near poor" category.

The disabled are a second group not generally included in characterizations of the underclass who are nonetheless heavily represented among the persistently poor. These studies fairly consistently find 35 to 40 percent of the persistently poor to be in households headed by disabled persons, compared to 10 to 14 percent of the annual poverty population. Some of this difference may result from overlaps between the disabled and elderly populations in the studies by Coe, by Hill and by Duncan et al. Nevertheless, it seems clear that the persistently poor are significantly more likely to be disabled than are the temporarily poor. Even Levy's results, which exclude the elderly disabled, find more than 40 percent more disabled among the persistently poor in the 1967 cohort than in the 1967 poverty population as a whole. Levy's estimates are still much lower than those of the other authors, but some of this difference is probably accounted for by differences in the span of years examined. Since disabled persons now account for a larger proportion of those poor on a cross-sectional basis than they did in 1967, it seems likely that they also account for a larger proportion of the persistently poor. Again, while this group may in fact be much more likely than the nondisabled to suffer persistent poverty, and in that sense may form part of a semipermanent underclass, it does not seem very likely that their low income status is related to some sort of "culture of poverty."

In all, then, even allowing for some possible overlaps between the elderly and disabled populations as measured in some of these studies, it would appear that perhaps half of the persistently poor are in demographic groups that are not generally considered to be among the underclass. The poverty experienced by the elderly and the disabled appears to result from physical factors that limit their labor force participation, rather than from either lack of opportunity of the type postulated by Harrington or from cultural or attitudinal factors as proposed by Lewis. Although those with some common underclass characteristics such as minority racial status and female household headship are more likely to experience both disability and poverty in old age, the relationships among these characteristics are quite complex and it is not clear how or in what direction any causative link between these factors may operate. Since the considerable majority of both the poor elderly and the disabled are clearly not underclass members by most definitions, and it is relatively unlikely that any policy initiatives designed to aid the underclass would also serve those in these groups, it seems reasonable to exclude these groups as a whole from any potential underclass measure.

But what of the remainder of those among the persistently poor—are their characteristics more like those traditionally associated with the underclass? As Table 6.6 indicates, although there is some disagreement as to specific magnitudes, almost all the authors examined here find that households headed by those with "underclass" characteristics are substantially more likely to be among the persistently poor than among those poor on a cross-sectional basis. For example, estimates of the persistently poor who are in female-headed households range from the 61 percent found by Duncan et al. to the 81 percent found using Hill's "poor in every year" definition. Either measure is substantially higher than the 25 to 35 percent found for the poverty population as a whole. Blacks are also considerably overrepresented among the persistently poor—60 percent or more of this group are black, compared to 30 percent or less of the annual poverty population. And something like 40 to 50 percent of the persistently poor are in households headed by an unmarried person with children. Further, the situation for these groups is just the opposite of that for the elderly: in these cases, the more stringent the definition of persistent poverty, the higher the proportion that have these characteristics. Again, this supports the view gained from the cross-sectional data that the poorest of the poor are also the most likely to be black and in female-headed families.

Finally, the view that the persistently poor are likely to have a relatively low level of labor force attachment is also supported by these data. According to these estimates, something like 10 to 15 percent of the persistently poor were in families whose heads were employed for at least 1,500 hours in the first (or in Coe's case, last) year of their observed poverty spell. In contrast, in 1976 for example about 20 percent of family heads poor on an annual basis worked full-time for forty or more weeks, and another 4 percent worked part-time for at least forty weeks. As might be expected, for the employed, like the elderly, tighter definitions of "persistently poor" tend to lead to smaller estimates of their share of this population.

Conclusions: Implications of this Literature for Estimates of the Size and Nature of the Underclass

What can we conclude, then, about the size and nature of the underclass, based on the evidence presented in this paper? Who are the persistently poor, and to what extent do they overlap with one or more population groups that might be considered underclass?

Our reading of this evidence implies that, while it would be a mistake to assume that all persistently poor persons were also members of some more narrowly defined underclass, there is a sizable proportion of this group—perhaps half—who have characteristics typically associated with the underclass. Further, the proportion in this category seems to rise as the definition of the term "persistently poor" becomes more stringent. Of course, more stringent definitions of persistent poverty also tend to lead to smaller estimates of the size of the persistently poor population as a whole, as was demonstrated in Table 6.5.

Putting together our estimates of the total proportion of the poor who are persistently poor (probably about half) and our estimates of the proportion of the persistently poor who are neither elderly nor disabled (also about half) it becomes possible to conclude that something like one fourth of those who are poor on an annual basis are candidates for being considered as members of the underclass. It should be emphasized that this is only a very rough estimate, which may be affected by a number of other factors. For example, the size of the poverty population as a whole may fluctuate substantially more with recessions and similar economic events than does the size of the underclass, which could change the relative sizes of the two populations. Nevertheless, applying this very rough estimate to the 1985 poverty population, these findings would imply that currently over 8 million people, or about 3.5 percent of the U.S. population as a whole, are potentially members of this underclass. If this underclass estimate were to be further narrowed—for example, confined to those living in urban areas—the estimate as a whole would shrink even further. Hill estimates that about 21 percent of the persistently poor are in urban areas; even if that included the entire nonelderly, non-disabled portion of the sample, which is highly unlikely, then limiting consideration to the urban underclass would reduce the maximum possible size of this group to about 3.5 million persons, or about 1.5 percent of the U.S. population. If the underclass made up the same proportion of the persistently poor in urban areas as in the population as a whole, the urban underclass estimate would be even smaller—under 2 million persons, or less than 1 percent of the population as a whole.

These numbers, having been arrived at through the process of elimination described above, say very little about the causes of persistent poverty for this group, or about the factors that keep them poor over relatively long periods of time. Further, although this group has in broad outline the "underclass" characteristics identified by other writers in this area, the data do not entirely support the view that this group is part of a self-perpetuating culture whose members remain in or near poverty over most or all of their lives. For one thing, Bane and Ellwood's findings make it clear that at least through nine years of observed poverty spells there is some continuing attrition each year, and it seems reasonable to assume, as they do, that such attrition would continue into the future. If this is the case, the number of persons experiencing lifetime spells of poverty, or even spells lasting twenty or thirty years, would be very small indeed. Using

Bane and Ellwood's assumptions, for example, we would find that by year 30 only 1.5 percent of the original poverty population was still experiencing a continuous spell of poverty (even allowing for brief gaps in continuity).

The view that for most people even relatively long-term poverty does not translate into lifetime poverty is supported by the characteristics data seen earlier. As those data make clear, a very large proportion—probably 80 percent or more—of the nonelderly and nondisabled persistent poor are in households headed by an unmarried person with children. This is inherently an unstable state, in that children grow up and leave home at some point. Of course, some of these children may go on to establish poor households of their own, while some of the parents may go on to become poor grandparents with children and finally poor elderly. However, both Bane and Ellwood and various other PSID based studies such as Greg Duncan's—see Duncan, Coe, and Hill (1984)—indicate that some fairly substantial proportion of such households do manage to leave poverty as the result of events such as remarriage of the family head, entry of the head into employment, and entry of the children into employment. All of these events increase in likelihood as the age of the youngest child in the household rises. The cross-sectional data on poverty also indicate that in fact there are very few middle aged nondisabled persons in poverty—which implies that even those who are poor through their twenties and even early thirties are likely to escape poverty at some point, although they may fall back into poverty as they enter old age.

Evidence on the intergenerational transmission of poverty indicates that in general, while those born into poverty are substantially more likely to be poor in adulthood and to have poor children themselves than are those born nonpoor, the vast majority of those born poor are not in fact poor as adults. The literature relating to this issue cannot be explored in detail in this paper, but is reviewed in more detail in Corcoran et al. (1985) and in Sawhill (1988). As they discuss, findings from the PSID indicate that although there is a measurable correlation between parents' and children's poverty statuses, only one in five persons poor as children goes on to become a poor adult.

In summary, then, a narrow view of the underclass as a group trapped in a culture that leads to lifetime or near lifetime poverty simply is not supported by the available data. The number of persons with underclass characteristics such as persistent poverty that is not explained by disability status or by old age appears to be relatively small—in the range of 3 to 4 percent of the total population in 1985, for example. If other characteristics such as urban residence are added to the underclass definition, and "persistent" is extended to mean not just eight or nine years of poverty but twenty or thirty years, the number of persons meeting such an underclass definition becomes very small indeed—in fact, well under one percent of the total population.

Nevertheless, although the underclass in the sense used by Lewis or even by Charles Murray is probably extremely small, it is very clear from the evidence presented in these data that even within the poverty population as a whole there are some groups that are at a special disadvantage. Members of black female-headed families, especially those with children, are much more likely than other people both to be poor and to be persistently poor. While it is probably not the case that most members of such families actually spend an entire lifetime in poverty and then go on to transmit poverty to their children, it is clear that in a broader sense many such families spend many years at a time struggling with inadequate resources. While, as outlined in the first section of this paper, there is little evidence that this group is growing as a proportion of the population over time, there is equally little indication of any very rapid decline in its numbers. For whatever reasons, this group does appear to be much more likely than the average to become poor, and to have a much harder time leaving poverty once they have entered. Consequently, even if they do not constitute an underclass in the sense suggested by Lewis, they may be a group for whom special targeted antipoverty programs may be both appropriate and necessary, if progress against long-term poverty in general is to be made.

Beyond this point, however, a larger and more general conclusion can be drawn from the data on long-term poverty presented here, namely, that the only groups who are exempt from long-term poverty in the United States are those who are able to participate in the paid labor market over most of their lives. Persistent poverty is *not* just a phenomenon of the underclass of those so disadvantaged or so disaffected that they cannot or will not find work. Rather, it affects *all* the major population groups with members who cannot depend on earnings, including the elderly and the disabled. Although our income support and social insurance programs target these groups specifically, and overall spending levels are much higher for them, on a per capita basis, than for the nondisabled working age population, we have not managed to eliminate significant long-term poverty in these groups. To some extent, this may result from the fact that our social insurance programs are typically tied to past work history, so that those with past spells of unemployment or persistent low wages are likely to be entitled to only relatively low benefits once they reach retirement age or become disabled. Others in these groups may have had low wages due to persistent ill health, or may have exhausted their savings in paying for medical expenses. Whatever the specific reasons behind these figures, however, the relative prevalence of long-term poverty for these groups, as for the underclass, indicates a need to reassess the design and effectiveness of our income support system as a whole.

Notes

1. The official poverty statistics are calculated by comparing annual family incomes to a series of poverty thresholds graduated by family size. This methodology was developed by Mollie Orshansky in 1965, and the thresholds are updated each year to reflect changes in prices. For details on these thresholds and the calculation methods used under the official definition see

U.S. Bureau of the Census (1988, Appendix A). For a discussion of the development of the official measure and an assessment of its strengths and weaknesses see Watts (1985).

2. Statistics shown in Table 6.1 are based on the government's official poverty measure, which compares annual income to a series of poverty thresholds that vary by family size, as discussed below (see U. S. Bureau of the Census 1988 for more details). Although the level of poverty in any given year is somewhat sensitive to the specifics of the definition used, the trend in poverty over time is fairly insensitive, as long as the measure involved is of the same general type (e.g., some set of "absolute" poverty thresholds based on the costs of a specific market basket of goods). Thus, although the official measure has some drawbacks as an absolute measure of poverty, discussed in other chapters of this volume, its use to consider trends in poverty across time is less problematic. It should be noted, however, that the use of a relative poverty measure—for example, some stated percentage of the median income—would give a different long-term trend in poverty levels, which would appear to decline less over the 1970s, and to be higher today. The improvement in the relative position of the elderly would also be smaller, but most other compositional trends would remain. See Fuchs (1967) and Lampman (1971) for discussions of the advantages and drawbacks of this type of measure.

3. Persons in all female-headed families, whether with or without children, are considered together in Table 6.1. The increase in the proportion of the poverty population accounted for by this group is in fact entirely accounted for by growth in the numbers of female-headed families *with* children who are in poverty. This group accounted for about 25 percent of all families in poverty in 1967, but for more than 43 percent in 1985. (In contrast, the proportion of the poverty population accounted for by female-headed families without children fell from about 6 percent to about 5 percent over the same period.)

4. Table 6.2, and much of its discussion, are based on materials presented in Danziger and Gottschalk (1986).

5. Monthly poverty is defined here as monthly income below one-twelfth of the appropriate annual income threshold (adjusted for family size and composition). Because the SIPP collects data at more frequent intervals than the Current Population Survey (CPS), which is the survey used to compute the official poverty statistics, and because its major focus is on programs serving the low income population, the SIPP finds more income for this population, which results in an annual poverty rate below the official rate (which was about 14 percent in 1984). See Williams (1986) for more discussion.

6. Some analysts might argue that these short spells of poverty are not very important indicators of hardship, if individuals have assets or access to credit that can tide them over these periods. Forthcoming work by Ruggles and Williams, however, indicates that asset ownership is in fact relatively rare in this population, and the inclusion of assets would have only a small impact on short-term poverty rates (Ruggles and Williams 1989). Similarly, access to credit tends to be very limited for those with no assets, low current incomes, and annual incomes near the poverty line.

7. The estimates shown in Table 6.3 are computed using life table methods, and so are adjusted for sample censoring (percentages shown are for cases remaining in the sample at the selected month). See Ruggles (1988) for details.

8. It is worth noting that some individuals that many would consider underclass—the homeless, persons engaged in certain types of criminal activities, persons who are in and out of institutions of various types—may not make it into our surveys at all, and when they do then any income they have is quite likely to be misreported. Indeed, to the extent that the underclass are less likely to have fixed addresses than the rest of the population, they are likely to be underrepresented in sample surveys in general. These points should be considered in assessing the findings associated with both cross-sectional and longitudinal surveys of the poverty population.

9. Further, since the PSID collects only annual income data, all of these poverty measures are based on annual income only, and thus overstate the average duration of poverty relative to a measure based on monthly income, like the SIPP estimates discussed above.

10. Because of the income reporting differences mentioned above (and possibly, because of sampling differences as well) poverty rates computed without correction from the PSID will be significantly lower than those computed from the CPS (in fact, generally comparable to the SIPP poverty rates reported above). (See Minarik 1975 for details on poverty measurement in the PSID.) Bane and Ellwood state that the use of the 125 percent threshold causes rates computed from the PSID to align more closely with the CPS. Use of this threshold also increases the size of the sample of poor households, making more detailed analyses possible.

11. In addition, Levy's estimate pertains to the 1967 cohort, and, given the changes both in economic circumstances and in transfer programs serving the poor that have occurred since then, it may no longer be an appropriate basis for generalizing about the long-term poor. Levy's technique is not difficult to apply, however, and this estimate is one that could be updated usefully with relatively little effort.

12. The steady state assumption, or some variation on it, is also necessary to allow the calculation of a distribution of completed spells of poverty based on Bane and Ellwood's estimated probabilities of leaving poverty.

13. One way to adjust for such shifts would be to use a hazard model to calculate the probability of remaining poor over time for those within specific demographic groups, as Bane and Ellwood briefly suggest at the end of their 1986 article. The PSID sample may be too small to allow such a strategy to be used effectively, particularly if time-related trends such as unemployment rates are also incorporated into the model.

14. Bane and Ellwood do examine the demographic and economic events associated with observed spell openings and closings. While interesting, these data are not directly comparable either with the compositional statistics presented in Table 6.6, or with Bane and Ellwood's own estimates of the proportion of the point-in-time poverty population that is persistently poor, since of course many more openings and closings are observed for those with short poverty spells than for long ones. Since these estimates cannot be weighted by spell length (using available data) for example, they are not useful for answering questions like, "What proportion of the currently poor population will eventually leave poverty as the result of changes in family composition?" However they do provide an interesting profile of the overall distribution of spell beginnings and endings.

References

Auletta, Ken. *The Underclass*. New York: Random House, 1982.

Bane, Mary Jo, and David T. Ellwood. "Slipping Into and Out of Poverty: The Dynamics of Spells." *The Journal of Human Resources*, vol. 21 (Winter 1986), no. 1:1–23.

———. "Slipping Into and Out of Poverty: The Dynamics of Spells." Working Paper 1199. Cambridge, MA: National Bureau of Economic Research, 1983.

Banfield, Edward C. *The Unheavenly City: The Nature and Future of Our Urban Crisis*. Boston: Little, Brown, 1970.

Coe, Richard. "Dependency and Poverty in the Short and Long Run." In *Five Thousand American Families: Patterns of Economic Progress*, vol. 6, ed. Greg J. Duncan and James N. Morgan. Ann Arbor, MI: Institute for Social Research, 1978, pp. 273–96.

Corcoran, Mary, Greg J. Duncan, Gerald Gurin, and Patricia Gurin. "Myth and Reality: The Causes and Persistence of Poverty." *Journal of Policy Analysis and Management*, vol. 4 (1985), no. 4:516–36.

Danziger, Sheldon, and Peter Gottschalk. "Work, Poverty, and the Working Poor: A Multi-faceted Problem." *Monthly Labor Review*, vol. 109 (1986), no. 9:17–21.

Duncan, Greg J., Richard D. Coe, and Martha S. Hill. "The Dynamics of Poverty." In *Years of Poverty, Years of Plenty.* Ann Arbor, MI: Institute for Social Research, 1984, pp. 33–70.

Economic Report of the President. U.S. Government Printing Office, Washington, DC, 1986, Table B–37, p. 295.

Fuchs, Victor. "Redefining Poverty and Redistributing Income." *The Public Interest* (Summer 1967), no. 8:88–95.

Harrington, Michael. *The Other America: Poverty in the United States.* New York: Macmillan, 1962.

Hill, Martha S. "Some Dynamic Aspects of Poverty." In *Five Thousand American Families: Patterns of Economic Progress,* vol. 9, ed. Martha S. Hill, Daniel H. Hill, and James N. Morgan. Ann Arbor, MI: Institute for Social Research, 1981, pp. 93–120.

Lampman, Robert J. *Ends and Means of Reducing Income Poverty.* Chicago: Markham, 1971.

Levy, Frank. "How Big Is the American Underclass?" Working Paper 0090–1. Washington, DC: The Urban Institute, 1977.

Lewis, Oscar. *La Vida.* New York: Random House, 1966.

Minarik, Joseph J. "New Evidence on the Poverty Count." In *The American Statistical Association, Proceedings of the Social Statistics Section,* 1975, pp. 544–59.

Morgan, James N., Katherine Dickinson, Jonathan Dickinson, Jacob Benus, and Greg J. Duncan. *Five Thousand American Families: Patterns of Economic Progress,* vol. 1. Ann Arbor, MI: Institute for Social Research, 1974.

Murray, Charles. "According to Age: Longitudinal Profiles of AFDC Recipients and the Poor by Age Group." With Deborah Laren. Prepared for the Working Seminar on the Family and American Welfare Policy. Washington, DC: American Enterprise Institute for Public Policy Research, September 1986.

———. *Losing Ground: American Social Policy, 1950–1980.* New York: Basic Books, 1984.

O'Neill, June A., Douglas A. Wolf, Laurie J. Bassi, and Michael T. Hannan. "An Analysis of Time on Welfare." Project Report. Washington, DC: The Urban Institute, June 1984.

Rainwater, Lee. "Persistent and Transitory Poverty: A New Look." Working Paper 70. Cambridge, MA: Joint Center for Urban Studies, 1982.

Reischauer, Robert D. "Policy Response to the Underclass Problem," a comment on "The Underclass—Will It Always Be With Us?" by Richard P. Nathan. Prepared for a Symposium at the New School for Social Research. Washington, DC: The Brookings Institution, November 1986.

Ricketts, Erol R. and Ronald Mincy. "Growth of the Underclass: 1970–1980." Washington, DC: The Urban Institute, February 1988.

Ricketts, Erol R. and Isabel V. Sawhill. "Defining and Measuring the Underclass." *Journal of Policy Analysis Management,* 7.7 (Winter 1988), 2:316–25.

Ruggles, Patricia. "Short-Term Poverty as Observed in the SIPP." Urban Institute Research Paper, August 1988.

Ruggles, Patricia and Roberton Williams. "Longitudinal Measures of Poverty." *The Review of Income and Wealth,* Series 35, no. 3 (September 1989).

Sawhill, Isabel V. "Poverty in the U.S.: Why Is It So Persistent?" *The Journal of Economic Literature,* vol. 26 (September 1988), No. 3:1073–1119.

U.S. Bureau of the Census. *Poverty in the United States: 1986.* Current Population Reports, Series P–60, no. 160. Washington, DC: U.S. Government Printing Office.

Watts, Harold W. "Have Our Measures of Poverty Become Poorer?" Presented at the American Statistical Association in Las Vegas, Nevada, August 1985.

Williams, Roberton. "Poverty Rates and Program Participation in the SIPP and the CPS." Presented at the Annual Meetings of the American Statistical Association, August 1986.

Wilson, William Julius. *The Truly Disadvantaged: The Inner City, the Underclass, and Public Policy.* Chicago: University of Chicago Press, 1987.

7

Social Security and Income Redistribution

Paul R. Cullinan

> We can never insure one hundred percent of the population against one hundred percent of the hazards and vicissitudes of life, but we have tried to frame a law that will give some measure of protection . . . against poverty-ridden old age.
>
> —*President Franklin Delano Roosevelt*
> (*upon signing the Social Security Act of 1935*)

Most discussions of economic inequality focus on the distribution of annual income or wealth. While useful for many purposes, such analyses fail to recognize the extent to which individuals and families change their positions in the income distribution over time. To some extent, this ever-changing composition of different economic strata reflects the relatively predictable impact of age. Workers typically expect income to rise as they move from early adult life into middle age and to decline with retirement in old age.

The life-cycle theory of consumption suggests that individuals attempt to smooth out consumption by redistributing economic resources from periods of relatively high income to spells of low income. The principal mechanisms for these redistributions over the life cycle are the family, Social Security, and private pensions. This chapter focuses on the role of Social Security in affecting the distribution of income over one's lifetime as well as in the general population at a given point in time.

Sections 1 and 2 of this chapter briefly review the life-cycle theory of consumption and the development and rationale for Social Security in the United States. Sections 3 and 4 discuss the potential impacts of Social Security on savings and labor supply decisions and examine the redistributive effects of this institution both across and within generations. Section 5 focuses on the effects of

Any opinions expressed in this paper are solely the responsibility of the author, and do not represent the views of the Congressional Budget Office.

Social Security benefits on elderly incomes by demographic group both in terms of their antipoverty effects and in the degree to which different groups depend on these benefits. The final section summarizes the chapter and briefly mentions other aspects of the Social Security program which provide value to participants but do not directly affect the income distribution.

1. What Is the Life-cycle Theory and What Are Its Implications for the Income Distribution?

Although the life-cycle theory of consumption (LTC) as we currently know it has its genesis in the work of Modigliani and others (Modigliani and Brumberg 1954; Ando and Modigliani 1963), its concepts have long historical roots. Whereas savings—that is, deferred consumption—is often regarded in the economics literature as the rational response to sufficiently high interest rates, precautionary behavior, bequest motives, and other factors provide additional, and at least empirically more powerful explanations for observed savings behavior. From the Old Testament, where Joseph and his sons faced seven bountiful years followed by seven lean ones, to *Poor Richard's Almanac*, with its precept that a penny saved is a penny earned, the notion of self-insurance against the potential shortfall in economic resources has been ingrained as prudent behavior. In addition to saving to protect against adverse economic events (the precautionary motive), other savings flow from the desire of some members of society to provide their offspring with a more comfortable standard of living than they could achieve on their own (the bequest motive). Some analysts also attribute significant savings to the tendency of individuals to set savings "rules" for themselves. The life-cycle model expands these roles of savings to deal with predictable fluctuations in income, primarily the transition from work to retirement.

Under the LTC, individuals understand that, on average, there are relatively predictable patterns of income growth over their adult years, and that it may be desirable to establish a lifetime consumption plan that moderates changes in consumption to offset anticipated increases and decreases in income. In the United States, analysis of both cross-sectional and longitudinal data indicates that individuals and households can expect rising incomes over most of their working lives, and diminished income during and after the period in which they reduce and terminate their attachment to the labor market. On the other hand, consumption data present evidence that consumption is less volatile. Individuals are generally net borrowers during the early years of their adult lives (often to fund investments in human capital and home ownership), and net savers over most of their remaining working lives while they are paying off their home mortgages and investing in their pension rights (see Figure 7.1). The LTC predicts that these consuming units would maintain their preretirement levels of consumption into old age.

The recent literature on the elderly appears to offer mixed signals on the LTC prediction for the consumption and savings behavior of the elderly. Empirical work in this area typically has found little support for the hypothesis that the

Figure 7.1. **Income and Consumption over the Life Cycle**

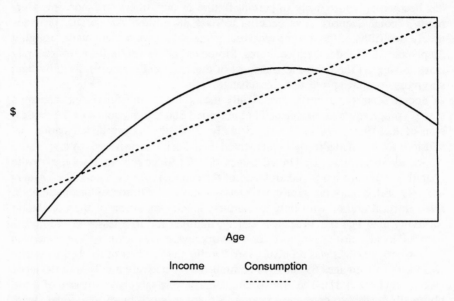

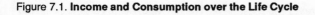

elderly maintain preretirement consumption levels by drawing down their assets, or by dissaving, although some recent work in this area (Bernheim 1987; Hurd 1987) finds that the elderly, particularly after several years of retirement, do dissave. Other studies continue to support the notion that the rate of dissavings among the elderly is consistent with a bequest motive.

In any case, the life-cycle perspective suggests that relatively low annual income may not be an appropriate indicator of economic well-being for some groups of the population. For example, should a student in an M.B.A. program be considered poor? If so, how can one explain the access such an individual has to educational and auto loans? Obviously, lenders have ascertained that the income potential for such a student is more than sufficient to ensure repayment of the loans. The LTC also implies that wealth should be considered as well as income in assessing economic well-being. Assets may have been accumulated specifically to offset a predictable shortfall in income. The millionaire investment banker who retires to paint in a beach-side resort community could have virtually no income, but survives in comfort by divesting his assets.

2. Why Does Social Security Exist?

If individuals are rational and behave according to the LTC, why is there a need for Social Security? There are a multitude of reasons—political, social, and economic—for the creation, nurturing, and continuation of the Social Security system in the United States. Whatever the reason for its existence, however, the program has become an enormously important fixture in the American landscape. Currently, Social Security pays benefits to over 38 million Americans, provides nearly two-fifths of the income received by the elderly, and accounts for roughly 20 percent of all federal expenditures. Moreover, about 130 million workers pay taxes to support the program, and most of these currently receive disability and survivors insurance protection in exchange.

Social Security, or more specifically the Old Age and Survivors Insurance (OASI) program,[1] was established in the United States in the midst of the depression of the 1930s. By that time, virtually all of the industrialized nations of Western Europe had already implemented their Social Security systems.

Social Security in the United States developed largely in response to the changing nature of the population and of the economy. In the late 1800s, America was still largely an agrarian society—almost two-thirds of the population lived in rural areas—with only a relatively small proportion of the population surviving until age 65. In such a society, families and to a lesser extent neighbors and local charities provided for nonworking elderly members. Retirement as we currently know it was relatively rare. During the last half of the 1800s, nearly two-thirds of men ages 65 and over continued to be actively involved in the labor force (Graebner 1981). The nonworking elderly were largely comprised of those physically unable to continue working. Moreover, since these individuals were part of a relatively small population group—those ages 65 and over constituted less than 4 percent of the total in 1890—the burden of supporting this nonworking group was relatively isolated.

By 1930, however, much had changed. Fifteen million more Americans lived in urban settings than in rural areas, labor force participation rates for aged men had dropped by one-sixth, and the elderly's share of the population had risen to over 5 percent. Moreover, with improvements in life expectancy, many more Americans could foresee a significant probability that they would survive until old age. Such a society, with its more mobile work force and a decreasing propensity to live in extended families, meant that the traditional approaches for ensuring economic support for the aged had become outmoded.

Although private life insurance and private savings did (and still do) offer alternative mechanisms for achieving income security in old age, increasing attention was being paid to a federal role in this area.[2] In the midst of the Great Depression, the prospect for many elderly was for continued reliance on public relief. Indeed, many at the time foresaw generations of working Americans who would be dependent on such aid as a result of the financial losses of the 1930s and the outlook that widespread unemployment and underemployment would persist indefinitely. Establishment of a contributory social insurance program designed to spread the burdens of an elderly dependent population over a much larger work force was a natural outgrowth of these concerns. Such a program could provide a mechanism for different generations to share both the risks and returns inherent in a market-based economy. The rapid economic expansion in the postwar period permitted increased transfers to those cohorts burdened most heavily by the economic costs of the depression, while at the same time easing the burden of higher payroll taxes on the working population.

In addition to the redistributional objectives, the Great Depression highlighted how even prudent individuals, through no fault of their own, could find themselves economically disadvantaged as a result of the failures of financial institutions and a widespread economic collapse. Most workers who could choose to save significant portions of their incomes for retirement purposes could not accumulate enough assets to permit portfolio diversification. Thus, even relatively random events—for example, embezzlement or mismanagement—could wipe out retirement savings. Moreover, self-insurance for retirement through private savings generally would not provide sufficient margins to compensate for a prematurely shortened work life caused by disability or widespread unemployment. In addition, the higher levels of price inflation experienced in the past twenty years have emphasized the value of the price-indexed benefits provided by Social Security since 1975.

Another market failure addressed by a compulsory social insurance program is the problem of adverse selection. Private or voluntary insurance arrangements face significant difficulties in annuity markets because purchasers are self-selected and they are likely to be those most likely to receive favorable treatment. For example, individuals most likely to purchase a life annuity are those who believe themselves to be relatively long lived. An actuarially fair premium for the population at risk will attract these individuals, and those with shorter expected lifetimes will choose not to participate. Thus, the suppliers of such annuities would always find these offerings unprofitable.

Another common justification for the federal role in providing retirement income is the need to compensate for the presumed myopic behavior of many workers. Under this view, paternalism is a major reason for social insurance programs, as the average worker is assumed to be too shortsighted to save for events such as unemployment, disability, and retirement. A compulsory program such as Social Security may evolve in part from the recognition that group behavior may be required to overcome such myopia. Moreover, while many workers may make some efforts to accumulate savings for these risks, they may not fully perceive the amount of resources required to meet consumption needs during these periods. Finally, a compulsory program is required under this perspective to ensure that the problem of free-ridership (why should I defer consumption to provide for my own retirement because the society will not allow me to starve) would be minimized.

In 1934, President Franklin Delano Roosevelt established the Committee on Economic Security (CES) to examine the need for federal involvement and to propose programmatic solutions. The CES issued its report in January 1935 and concluded that federal legislation was required which would establish a social insurance system that would incorporate unemployment insurance and old-age insurance benefits. Moreover, income support programs for the aged, blind, and disabled, and also unmarried mothers with dependent children were incorporated into the CES legislative agenda, which was enacted in August 1935.

Original Act. The basic principles of the Social Security program enacted in 1935 were:

• the system was to be self-financed through a payroll tax levied equally on employees and employers;

• benefits were to be related to lifetime contributions;

• lower wage workers were to receive relatively higher benefits compared to their covered wages than were higher wage employees;

• tax payments would be segregated into a government trust fund, invested in interest-bearing government securities, and benefits would be paid from the assets of the trust fund; and

• reserves in the trust fund would be sufficiently high to generate significant interest earnings to help support benefit payments, but the system was not to be fully funded.

However, even before the first benefits were paid, the system was modified to include provisions for the survivors of insured workers. Moreover, the benefit formula was changed so that payments would be based on average monthly earnings in covered employment rather than lifetime earnings. These changes were enacted as part of the 1939 Amendments and were designed to provide more sizable monthly benefit amounts. Because workers reaching age sixty-five in 1942 under the 1935 Act would have received quite meager benefits, as their accumulated payroll taxes would have only covered earnings for the 1937–41 period, this change raised the relative importance of Social Security's role in ensuring adequate incomes, in comparison with its pure insurance function where benefits are tied to contributions. In addition to this programmatic concern, Roosevelt Administration economists argued that the rapid accumulation of payroll taxes was acting as a drag on the overall economy, which had fallen back into a deep recession in 1937. Increased Social Security payments represented one means through which a stimulus could be injected into a lagging economy. In accordance with that objective, the first payments were made in 1940 rather than 1942.

Social Security developments, 1940–88. Since 1939, the program itself has been amended frequently to expand coverage, to provide new benefits, and to update benefit levels in line with rising wages and prices. In 1956,· disability benefits were created for those at least fifty years old, and that age requirement was eliminated in 1960. Reduced old-age benefits were extended to women sixty-two to sixty-four years of age in 1956 and to men in 1961. Under the 1965 Amendments, benefits were provided to the children of retired, disabled, and deceased workers, while the offspring were under twenty-two and in postsecondary school. These student benefits were later eliminated under legislation enacted in 1981.

Table 7.1

Percentage of Work Force Covered, Average Retired Worker Benefit, Average Wages, Selected Years 1940–87

Year	Percent of labor force covered	Average benefit	Average benefit (in 1987$)	Average wages	Average wages (in 1987$)
1940	55	22.60	183.17	1,195	9,685
1950	61	43.86	207.06	2,544	12,010
1960	86	74.04	284.14	4,007	15,378
1970	90	118.10	350.49	6,186	18,358
1980	91	341.40	468.60	12,513	17,175
1987	93	512.65	512.65	17,857	17,857

Sources: U.S. Department of Health and Human Services, *Social Security Bulletin, Annual Statistical Supplement, 1987*. Earnings for 1987 are taken from the 1988 Report of the Trustees of the Federal Old-Age and Survivors Insurance and Disability Insurance Trust Funds. Average earnings in 1940 are drawn from Kollman and Koitz (1988).

As a result primarily of the 1950, 1954, and 1983 amendments, coverage of the private sector work force is virtually complete and nearly all federal workers will be covered by 2020. The only remaining component of the work force that under current law would not be covered by the twenty-first century are employees of certain state and local governmental units. In 1988, nearly 95 percent of the labor force is covered under Social Security.

Over time, average benefits have grown much faster than either wages or prices. The average monthly payment to a retired worker rose by 180 percent from 1940 to 1987, as measured in 1987 dollars. Part of the increase reflects wage growth over the period, but more importantly legislative initiatives enhanced the adequacy of benefits. In particular, benefit levels were increased very rapidly in the 1965–72 period—cumulatively, 72 percent—relative either to prices (35 percent increase) or to average wages (53 percent). Beginning in 1975, benefits were automatically indexed for inflation. Coincidentally, the United States entered a period where inflation surged, so that prices rose more rapidly than average wages (see Table 7.1).

In 1987, Social Security paid about $204 billion in benefits to about 38 million recipients, over 70 percent of whom are at least sixty-five years old. Revenues for the program flow primarily from payroll taxes levied equally on employers and employees, with each paying (in 1987) at a rate of 5.7 percent of

Figure 7.2. **Social Security Benefit Formula
for Those Becoming Eligible for Benefits in 1990**

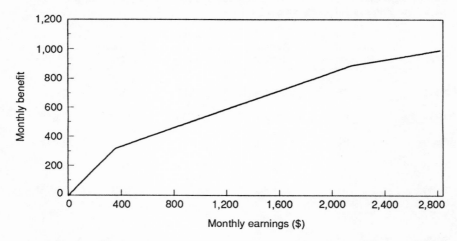

wages up to a maximum taxable earnings level of $43,800. Revenues from these taxes amounted to over $222 billion in 1987.[3]

Benefits. Benefits are currently computed based on an average indexed monthly earnings (AIME) measure which accounts for wages in covered employment during most of a person's adult life. After 1990, the number of years of earnings—including years with no covered wages, counted as years of zero earnings—in the averaging process will be 35 for persons becoming eligible for old-age benefits. Wages are indexed up to the year during which the worker turns age sixty, so that wages earned at earlier ages are treated as if they were earned in that year. The AIME is then plugged into a three-bracket benefit formula—in 1990, the formula is 90 percent of the first $356 of the AIME, 32 percent of the next $1,789, and 15 percent of AIME above $2,145—that has its bend points, $356 and $2,145, also increased every year for the growth in average wages (see Figure 7.2).

The purpose of this form of indexing is to provide benefits over time that replace a similar proportion of preretirement earnings for workers in comparable positions in the earnings distribution. For the average earner retiring at age sixty-five, this replacement rate is about 41 percent. Individuals with higher average earnings would have lower replacement rates, while those with lesser earnings would have higher rates. Benefits paid to individuals who begin receiving benefits before the normal retirement age (NRA) are reduced, and those awarded to persons delaying the receipt of benefits after the NRA are increased. Although the current NRA is sixty-five, the 1983 Amendments raised it in two stages, so that for those reaching age sixty-two early in the twenty-first century the NRA will be sixty-six, and for those reaching age sixty-two in the year 2022 or after the NRA will be sixty-seven.

Table 7.2

Social Security Taxes

Year	Number of taxpayers (in millions)	OASDI tax rate (employee share)	Maximum taxable wage	OASDI taxes paid by avg. earner (current $)	OASDI taxes paid by avg. earner (1988$)
1950	48.3	1.5	3,000	38.16	187.57
1955	65.2	2.0	4,200	66.02	291.74
1960	72.5	3.0	4,800	120.22	480.32
1965	80.7	3.625	4,800	168.88	633.33
1970	93.1	4.2	7,800	259.82	791.73
1975	100.2	4.95	14,100	427.23	939.24
1980	113.0	5.08	25,900	635.68	912.80
1985	121.8	5.7	39,600	958.88	1,054.68
1987	128.0	5.7	43,800	1,017.85	1,059.68

Source: U.S. Department of Health and Human Services, *Social Security Bulletin, Annual Statistical Supplement, 1987.*

Since 1950, Social Security benefits have become increasingly important. During the period, benefit payments for the average beneficiary grew by 248 percent (in 1987 dollars), and total benefits rose from less than 0.5 percent of GNP in 1950 to 4.4 percent in 1987. The proportion of the elderly receiving benefits grew from 45 percent in 1960 to about 93 percent in 1987. Closely paralleling these trends was the fall in the poverty rate for the aged, which in 1987 stood at about one-third of its 1959 level. Despite an 80 percent increase in the number of aged over the past thirty years, the number of aged poor fell by more than one-third. In 1986, Social Security benefits provided about 40 percent of all money income received by the elderly. Further, almost three-fifths of the aged relied on Social Security for more than 50 percent of their income, and about two-fifths would be poor if only non–Social Security income were considered.

Revenues. On the tax side, OASDI tax rates rose from 3.0 percent—the combined employer-employee rate—of covered wages in 1950, to 11.4 percent by 1987, and 12.12 percent in 1988 (see Table 7.2). Combined with the increase in the contribution base (from $3,000 in 1950 to $43,800 in 1987), the maximum

Table 7.3

**Major Characteristics of Social Security Financing, Selected Years
1940–2060**

Year	Trust fund assets as percent of		Program costs as percent of GNP	Worker-beneficiary ratio
	annual outlays	GNP		
1940	2,781	2	b	b
1960	186	4	2.3	5.1
1980	25	1	4.4	3.2
2000	285	14	4.5	3.2
2020	497	29	5.0	2.4
2040	162	9	6.5	1.9
2060	a	a	6.5	1.8

*Sources: 1988 Annual Report of the Board of Trustees of the Federal Old Age and Survivors'
Insurance and Disability Insurance Trust Funds.* U.S. Office of Management and Budget.
Historical Tables, Budget of the United States Government, Fiscal Year 1989.
a. Fund depleted in 2048.
b. Less than 0.5 percent.

tax paid directly by a worker rose by 55-fold—about 1,175 percent in real
terms—over the 1950–87 period, reaching nearly $2,727 in 1987. Increasing
reliance on the payroll tax has resulted in roughly one-third of all families with
Social Security taxpayers owing more in OASDI taxes than in federal income
taxes (see Table 7.2).

Financing. The funding basis of the program has largely come full circle.
Amendments in 1950 moved the program toward a pay-as-you-go system where
annual income and outgo were designed to be in approximate balance. Amendments in 1977 and 1983 restored partial advanced funding, at least until the
retirement of the post–World War II baby boom is nearly complete. Consequently, Social Security payroll taxes are expected to exceed program outlays for
at least the next twenty-five years. Other income to the trust funds including
interest, proceeds from the income taxation of benefits, and several minor
sources of general revenue transfer, bolsters the cashflow of the OASDI trust
funds so that, under the middle path assumptions used by the Social Security
Administration, trust fund reserves would continue to grow until about
2030. Under these projections, the trust funds would then be depleted by 2048
(see Table 7.3).

The changing demographics of the American population have serious implications for the current structure of Social Security financing. In 1950, there were roughly 16.5 workers for every beneficiary; by 1980, this ratio had reached 3.2:1. With the retirement of the post–World War II baby boom and the lower fertility rates beginning in the 1970s, the ratio of workers to beneficiaries is expected to fall to about 1.9 in 2040 and 1.8 by 2060. With its heavy reliance on a payroll tax for its financing, these ratios imply that payroll tax rates will have to rise significantly from the levels established under current law if benefit provisions remain unchanged.

On the other hand, the costs of the Social Security program may be better illustrated by the proportion of the nation's resources that are redistributed under the system. As a share of the Gross National Product (GNP), Social Security costs rose by about 2.1 percentage points from 1960 to 1980, but are projected to remain about 4.5 percent through 2010 and then rise again with the retirement of the baby boom after that time. By 2040, the program is projected to cost about 6.5 percent of GNP, nearly 2 percentage points higher than the levels currently being experienced. The increase in the portion of the GNP going to pay Social Security costs is somewhat less than that which occurred between 1960 and the present, and comparable to the increase in defense spending during the 1979 to 1986 period.

3. Potential Economic Effects of Social Security

Concern about the impact of Social Security on the economy has been expressed throughout the program's history. Early advocates of the program saw the provision of old-age benefits as a method for drawing older workers out of the labor market in order to increase opportunities for younger ones. Detractors viewed the program as reducing incentives for private savings, thereby retarding the growth in the capital stock. More recently, the potential adverse effects of increased payroll taxes on wages, prices, and employment have also concerned policy makers.[4]

3.1. Savings and the Capital Stock

Social Security may, through its effects on national savings, influence the size of the capital stock. In turn, changes in the capital stock may affect labor incomes as well. How is it that Social Security could affect savings and what is the likely effect?

Under a pay-as-you-go Social Security financing mechanism, current tax receipts from today's workers would provide the funds for the benefits received by the retired population. Taxes on the working population reduce its disposable income which in turn should reduce both the consumption and the savings of the families with workers. Benefits are paid to aged nonworking persons who are often assumed to have a higher propensity to consume their incomes than do younger families, because their incomes are lower. Should these assumptions prove correct, a pay-as-you-go system would increase consumption and reduce savings.

More important to the argument that Social Security affects savings are the potential effects that the assurance of retirement income through Social Security could have on workers' private retirement savings. If benefits for each individual were actuarially fair—that is, the discounted present value of contributions equalled the discounted present value of future benefits—then the Social Security system would be assumed to have no effect on aggregate savings, if the contributions were invested in a reserve fund. Assuming that the payroll tax rate did not exceed the rate of retirement savings that would have occurred in the absence of the program, savings through this publicly managed retirement system would simply replace private savings for the same purpose.[5] The system itself would have no effect on total consumption or its distribution over the life cycle under the full-funding alternative.

If, on the other hand, the system is operated on a pay-as-you-go basis, even an actuarially fair system would be expected to reduce aggregate savings. After all, the funding practice does not affect consumption patterns—so long as the tax rate does not exceed the private savings rate—because the provision of actuarially fair benefits assures that the resources available for individual consumption at any point in time is unaffected. But under a pay-as-you-go system, benefits to current retirees are paid out of the tax receipts from current workers. Thus, while consumption is maintained, aggregate savings is not.

When benefits exceed contributions, as has been the case for all cohorts of beneficiaries to date under the U.S. Social Security program, the excess benefits may be considered by participants to be a supplement to their wealth and increase lifetime consumption possibilities. Under this circumstance, one would expect the wealth effect would lead individuals to spread the additional consumption throughout their lives, resulting in relatively more consumption and less savings during their working years. As a result, the life-cycle theory would predict that historically the U.S. Social Security program has reduced aggregate savings, both because of its pay-as-you-go financing basis and because payments to beneficiaries have far exceeded their contributions plus interest.

On the other hand, the provision of age-related benefits may encourage individuals to retire earlier than they otherwise would have planned. To the degree that individuals save to supplement their retirement benefits from Social Security, a shorter working life and a longer period of expected retirement should cause workers to save at higher rates during their working years. Consequently, the provision of these benefits may stimulate private savings through its retirement age effects.

Another argument presented by Robert Barro (1974) is that Social Security should have little effect on either savings or capital formation, since individuals adjust their intrafamily, intergenerational transfers to offset the characteristics of Social Security. Under the Barro hypothesis, while the provision of Social Security benefits to the retired population increases its economic position, it worsens that of subsequent generations through the additional tax liabilities the program entails. However, in this model, the recipient population is altruistic and transfers assets to its offspring in order to help offset future tax liabilities.

As a result, the net effect of Social Security on aggregate savings cannot be determined a priori, and empirical research is necessary to ascertain the magnitude and the direction of the effects. To date, research in the area has been inconclusive. Martin Feldstein's work (1974, 1982) provides evidence that the growth in Social Security has correlated well with reductions in private savings, and hence, the capital stock. His 1982 study suggests that Social Security depressed private savings in 1971 by 34 percent and that "each dollar of Social Security tax corresponds to a $0.92 reduction in private savings" (p. 636). Economists in the Social Security Administration attempted to replicate the Feldstein analysis using various specifications, including altering the time period, the variables, and the construction of the Social Security wealth variable which is fundamental to the Feldstein argument (Leimer and Lesnoy 1982). Their analysis found that minor variations in the specification of the model resulted in large changes in the estimated effects on savings, with some plausible equations and variable constructions yielding decreases in the savings rate, while other specifications increased it. Some estimates based only on the postwar period actually implied that Social Security increased savings. While the most plausible specifications (according to Leimer and Lesnoy), lent weight to the hypothesis that Social Security has no effect on savings, the authors, given the wide range of the results, were unwilling to conclude that there were no effects.

3.2. Labor Supply

The tax and benefit provisions of the Social Security system are often hypothesized to affect labor supply decisions, particularly at older ages. If viewed within the context of the life-cycle model, Social Security with its age-related benefits encourages individuals to concentrate their work effort at younger ages. Under this model, total lifetime hours of work could increase, decrease or remain about the same, either with a Social Security system or without one. In contrast, those who consider the current program to be a tax-transfer system (Pechman, Aaron, and Taussig 1968), in which workers view the payroll tax as a tax rather than as a vehicle through which rights to future benefits are derived, would tend to assume that lifetime work would decrease somewhat.

The empirical literature tends to support the assertion that the Social Security benefits have reduced the work effort of the elderly. Table 7.4 illustrates the historical labor force participation rates of older workers. Much of the decline in these rates appears to correspond with the increased eligibility for and generosity

Table 7.4

Labor Force Participation Rates by Age, 1950–86

	Males			Females		
Year	45–54	55–64	65+	45–54	55–64	65+
1950	95.8	89.9	45.8	37.9	27.0	9.7
1960	95.7	86.8	33.1	49.9	37.2	10.8
1970	94.3	83.0	26.8	54.4	43.0	9.7
1980	91.2	72.1	19.0	59.9	41.3	8.1
1986	91.0	67.3	16.0	65.9	42.3	7.4

Source: U.S. Department of Labor, Handbook of Labor Statistics, pp. 18–19; U.S. Department of Commerce, Statistical Abstract of the United States, 1988, p. 366.

of Social Security benefits. Simple correlations would appear to lend strong support to the assumption that Social Security has depressed the labor supply of older workers. Recent literature in the area suggests that the effects are more complicated and less significant than the declines in participation rates imply (Danziger, Haveman, and Plotnick 1981). Other factors such as the growth in private pensions and the increasing affluence of older Americans would also be expected to lead these workers to choose increasing amounts of leisure in their "golden years." As an upper limit, Danziger, Haveman, and Plotnick suggest that one-half of the decline in the labor force participation rates of older men since 1950 could be attributed to Social Security.

Little research has been directed at the impact of the Old Age and Survivors' Insurance (OASI) portion of Social Security on the labor market activities of younger workers. In 1978, Burkhauser and Turner examined the average work week for prime-age males from 1929 to 1971 to address the question of whether Social Security had an effect on workers at younger ages. They found that, after accounting for other factors such as rising real wages, unemployment, and family size, Social Security appeared to increase the average work week by about two hours. As in the Social Security/savings debate, however, they discovered that the results were quite sensitive to the specification, particularly with respect to the estimating period.

During the past fifteen years, the labor supply effects of the Social Security Disability Insurance (DI) program have received considerable attention.[6] Because the determination of disability under the program relates both to medical condition and to labor market participation, many economists have hypothesized that the program encourages persons with health impairments to withdraw from the labor force and to apply for disability benefits. National surveys indicate that a substantial number of persons reporting severe health limitations continue to work, thus providing a significant pool of workers who might be attracted to leave the labor force in exchange for disability benefits. Using time-series data as well as data from the National Longitudinal Survey of Older Males, Parsons (1980) estimated that the increased availability and generosity of DI benefits was strongly associated with the decline in the labor force participation rate of men age 45 and older over the 1957–77 period. For every 10 percent increase in the ratio of DI benefits to wages, Parsons found a 6 percent increase in nonparticipation in the labor force. Subsequent research by Haveman and Wolfe (1984) also found that DI benefits had significantly reduced the work effort of men in this age group, but their research indicated an effect about one-third as large as Parsons.

4. Distribution of Benefits across and within Generations

In recent years, substantial attention has been paid to the growing concerns that issues of intergenerational equity have largely been ignored in the consideration of the appropriate balance of tax and spending policies of the federal government. One focus of this attention has been the funding practices of the Social Security system, which until recently could be characterized as fundamentally a pay-as-you-go system.

4.1. Implications of the Funding Mechanism on the Distribution of Benefits across Generations

As with other Social Security systems and many private pensions, benefits received by participants during the start-up phase of the program have been large relative to their own contributions. In part, although not entirely, this is a characteristic of social insurance programs that are funded on a pay-as-you-go basis. To some extent, this may simply reflect the fact that Social Security was a transfer system designed to replace and/or to supplement the intergenerational transfers which existed when the program first began to pay benefits.

One measure of this relative degree of generosity accorded generations of recipients during the start-up phase of Social Security is the length of time it took the average recipient to be paid back his and his employers' contributions, evaluated using a realistic interest rate. One study indicates that for unmarried average earners retiring at age sixty-five in 1960, this payback period was about 1.6 years (Myers and Schobel 1983). By 1987, this span had lengthened to 9.8 years, and it is expected to extend to 19.5 years for retirees in the year 2020 (U.S. Congress 1987).

Several economists have approached this question from a different perspective: what portion of benefits received correspond to the payments that would be derived from a private insurance annuity, and what share could be defined as benefits corresponding to a "welfare" component (Burkhauser and Warlick 1981; Boskin, Avrin, and Cone 1983; Boskin 1986). The welfare component

Table 7.5

Average Monthly Benefits for Retirees Age 65 in 1988 with Different Earnings

	Average monthly benefit		Replacement rate	
Earnings level	Worker only	Worker and spouse	Worker only	Worker and spouse
Minimum wage	$412	$ 618	71%	106%
Average wage	$626	$ 939	42%	62%
Maximum wage	$838	$1,257	23%	34%

Notes: Replacement rates equal twelve times the monthly benefit divided by the previous year's earnings. These are $6,968, $17,857, and $43,800 for minimum wage, average wage, and maximum wage, respectively. The maximum wage is the annual earnings limit from which Social Security taxes are withheld.

corresponds to the excess of benefits above that which would have been received under an actuarially fair insurance program. According to Boskin (1986), the estimated share of the benefits represented by this excess has fallen from 89 percent for persons age seventy-two and over in 1984, to less than 20 percent for workers entering the labor force today.

4.2. Distribution of Benefits within Generations

Besides questions of intergenerational equity, the current structure of the Social Security system in the United States results in significant disparities within generations. The major elements contributing to these disparities are the benefit formula, which is weighted toward lower wage workers and the payment of benefits to the related family members of insured beneficiaries.

The weighted benefit formula provides a mechanism through which a given amount of Social Security benefits may be redistributed from recipients with relatively high average lifetime earnings to those with relatively low earnings. Table 7.5 displays the average monthly benefits payable to retirees aged sixty-five in 1988 with different hypothetical earnings histories.

Combined with a benefit formula weighted to provide relatively greater benefits to low-wage workers, the payment of benefits to the dependents and survivors of workers can cause greater benefits to be paid to married workers than to single workers with identical earnings records. Thus, the current system would seem to redistribute from unmarried workers to those who are married.

The U.S. Social Security program as currently structured can also cause married couples with the same total combined earnings, but with different shares of the total earned by the different spouses, to have very different benefits. Over the past fifteen years, these disparities have received considerable attention with the rapid rise in market work among married women, but legislative solutions have not been enacted.[7]

Under current law, spouses, divorced spouses, and surviving spouses are eligible to receive Social Security benefits based on their relationship to a worker who has earned insured status for benefits. For instance, someone aged sixty-five or older who is married to a retired beneficiary—or is divorced but had been married for at least ten years—is eligible to receive a payment equaling 50 percent of the retired worker's basic benefit. Surviving spouses are generally eligible to receive a monthly benefit equal to that which would have been received by the decedent were he or she still alive. The provision of spouse's benefits under the 1939 amendments was designed to improve the adequacy of benefits received by couples.

Many persons receive benefits based, at least in part, on the earnings of their spouse or deceased spouse. For persons eligible for both a spouse's benefit and a benefit as a worker based on their own earnings record, the actual benefits paid equal the higher benefit: the one received as a spouse or the payment received by the worker. Thus, for the lower-paid worker in a married couple, the eventual Social Security payment which that worker would receive in old age is often the same as that which they would have received if they had never worked. Because the low-earning spouse is most commonly the wife, this treatment is often viewed as an unfair treatment of women under the Social Security system in the United States.

As illustrated in Table 7.6, different distributions of earnings between two spouses can lead to a wide range of benefits, even when total earnings are the same. In the case where both members are living, the one couple where only one spouse worked has total benefits that are 20 percent higher than the family with two earners. The differences affecting survivors are even greater. The surviving spouse who earned one-half of the family's total wages could expect to receive less than two-thirds of the benefits that would be paid to the survivor of a one-earner couple with the same earnings.

While most analysts agree that the current benefit structure results in some unfavorable outcomes with respect to the distribution of benefit payments, particularly with regard to working women, there is much disagreement over the advisability and feasibility of various proposed remedies. One approach, referred to as earnings-sharing, would eliminate the payment of spouse's benefits and would allow couples to split the combined earnings equally, with each spouse receiving a worker's benefit from the resulting earnings record. One major drawback with this approach is that many couples and some surviving spouses would receive lower benefits than under current law. Even with a lengthy phase-in period, the switch-over to an earnings-sharing system still adversely affects a

Table 7.6

Comparisons of Total Benefits for Couples with Different Shares of Total Earnings

	Monthly earnings	Benefits
Couple 1		
Spouse 1	$1,800	$ 719
Spouse 2	0	$ 359
Total	$1,800	$ 1,078
Couple 2		
Spouse 1	$ 900	$ 450
Spouse 2	$ 900	$ 450
Total	$1,800	$ 900

		Benefits for survivor		
	Average earnings	As worker	As survivor	Amount paid	% of couples benefit
Couple 1					
Decedent	$1,800				
Survivor	$ 0	$ 0	$719	$719	67%
Couple 2					
Decedent	$1,500				
Survivor	$ 300	$258	$642	$642	67%
Couple 3					
Decedent	$1,000				
Survivor	$ 800	$418	$482	$482	54%
Couple 4					
Decedent	$ 900				
Survivor	$ 900	$450	$450	$450	50%

Source: U.S. Department of Health and Human Services, *Report on Earnings Sharing Implementation Study*, January 1985, pp. 6–11.

significant fraction of women, even many who are already working. Because elderly widows have poverty rates substantially above the rate for the elderly population as a whole, any reduction in benefits for that group has provoked significant adverse political reactions. Providing some minimum benefit guaran-

Table 7.7

Average Household Income by Age of Head, 1975 and 1985 (in 1985 dollars)

Age of head of household	1975	1985
15–24	$17,969	$17,708
25–34	$27,904	$27,904
35–44	$34,165	$35,606
45–54	$36,448	$38,316
55–64	$29,667	$32,045
65+	$16,118	$18,800
Total	$27,544	$29,066

Source: U.S. Department of Commerce, *Money Income of Households, Families and Persons in the United States: 1975* and *1985*.

tees based upon current law would deal with some of these adverse and sometimes unanticipated effects, but would generally be quite expensive. Other proposals such as a double-decker or two-tier approach, where a proportional earnings-based benefit would be paid on top of a flat benefit amount—which could either be means tested or not—suffer from similar problems related to a transition period and its associated costs.

5. Income Distribution over the Life Cycle

As described above, the common perception is that a person can expect to experience rising incomes during much of his working life, but income will decline in later years, and be substantially lower after retirement. This pattern is clearly demonstrated by the figures in Table 7.7. Household money income in 1985 was observed to grow with the age of the household head until about the age fifty, after which time income falls. The decline is particularly striking after age sixty-five.

Labor market activities clearly contribute to the observed pattern of income over the age distribution. In 1985, earnings were observed to peak at about ages forty-five to fifty and to decline significantly after that age. Although part of this decline appears to occur because of reduced work effort, a similar pattern exists for full-time, full-year earners (see Table 7.8).

Closer examination of the data indicates that the earnings patterns vary significantly by a person's educational attainment. As would be anticipated, lesser educated workers enter the labor market earlier and experience slower earnings growth than do those with more education. Full-time workers with

Table 7.8

Average Earnings for Those with Earnings in 1985, by Sex and Age

Age	All Workers			Fulltime Full-Year Workers		
	Total	Male	Female	Total	Male	Female
18–24	$ 7,504	$ 8,485	$ 6,436	$13,241	$14,300	$11,925
25–34	$17,098	$20,547	$12,785	$21,632	$24,067	$17,701
35–44	$21,533	$28,146	$13,579	$26,708	$31,565	$18,526
45–54	$22,042	$29,203	$13,144	$26,970	$32,379	$17,696
55–64	$20,011	$26,164	$11,802	$25,485	$30,247	$16,636
65+	$10,282	$12,708	$ 6,420	$22,389	$25,349	$15,144

Source: U.S. Department of Commerce, *Money Income of Households, Families and Persons in the United States: 1985.*

only elementary school educations had their highest earnings between the ages of forty and forty-four, whereas those with college degrees enjoyed their peak earnings in their early fifties.

These data from a single year, however, may provide a misleading picture of the true patterns of income and earnings over the life cycle. To a large extent, productivity improvements affecting workers over their lifetimes may be expected to result in higher real earnings in 1990 for persons ages forty-five to fifty-four in 1985 than observations based on the earnings distribution in a single year would suggest. Longitudinal data—that is, observations over a number of years on the same person—indicate that earnings do not fall off as rapidly with age as the cross-section data would lead one to believe.

Research by Ruggles and Ruggles (1974) documents rising earnings through much later ages than single-period analyses would indicate. Using Social Security Administration earnings records, these economists demonstrated that, for virtually every cohort of workers born from 1904 to 1940, average earnings during the 1957–69 period rose for each year of life, at least until age sixty. They concluded that these patterns existed regardless of race or sex.

Some recent analysis of income data provides similar information on income over the lifetime. Controlling for family size and consumption needs, Ross, Danziger, and Smolensky (1987a, 1987b) found that, in families with working adults, family income continued to rise with age. Incomes fell with retirement, however. Thus, much of the observed decline in family income as individuals age results not from falling wage rates, but rather from withdrawal from the labor force. The authors conclude that much of the observed changes in income of older Americans can be explained by the changing composition of the older cohorts, which increasingly include relatively fewer workers.

Figure 7.3. **Earnings Patterns of Four Birth Cohorts, 1957–69**   (1957 dollars)

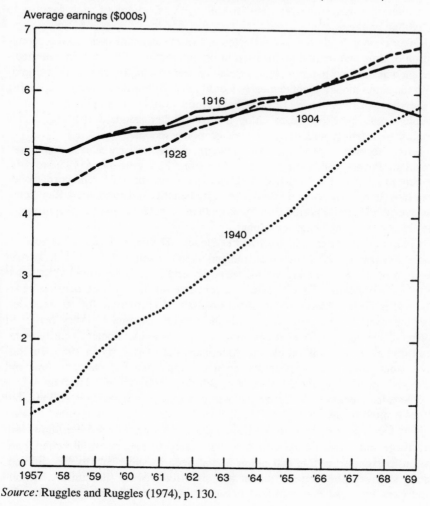

Average earnings ($000s)

Source: Ruggles and Ruggles (1974), p. 130.

One problem with analyzing the income distribution either in cross-section or over time is that measured income reflects choices individuals and households make in response to the institutions affecting them. Annual wages, while measured before individual tax payments, already incorporate any backward shifting of the Social Security and Unemployment Insurance payroll taxes paid by employers, as well as other mandatory labor-related costs such as workers' compensation. Consequently, wages reported in sample surveys or on income tax records measure neither total payments to labor nor the after-tax returns to the worker. Further complicating analyses of the income distribution are fringe benefits, such as employer-provided pensions and health insurance, for which there are little data relating either employer costs or employee valuations of such benefits to individual workers.

Other economic choices not reflected in income statistics concern the combination of time and market goods used in the production of household commodities such as meal preparation, house cleaning, and yard maintenance. Households with the same money income clearly would have different economic well-being if they have different levels of household production. For example, a one-earner couple would be expected to enjoy a much higher standard-of-living than a single-parent family with the same level of money income.

Social Security's effectiveness in reducing elderly poverty rates is easily documented. Poverty rates for the aged fell from 35.2 percent in 1959 to 24.6 percent in 1970, and in 1986 had tumbled to 12.4 percent. This trend corresponds very closely with increases in Social Security benefits and recipiency. Real benefits over the 1959–86 period rose by more than 75 percent, and the proportion of the elderly receiving benefits doubled.

Comparisons of pre- and posttransfer income. The dependency of the aged on Social Security benefits and other transfers is illustrated in Table 7.9. Less than one-half of all aged persons would escape poverty if transfers were not included in their cash income. That is, earnings, property income, private pension benefits, and interest, which provide about one-half of all income for the aged, are distributed across the population such that fewer than one of every two aged persons have nontransfer incomes above the poverty line. Social Security benefits lifted about 8.2 million elderly Americans out of poverty in 1986. In contrast, other public transfer programs such as Supplemental Security Income and veterans' pensions reduce the number of elderly poor by about 0.3 million.

The effectiveness of Social Security in reducing poverty rates is striking, but is not limited to the elderly. In 1986, Social Security benefits resulted in 12.9 million fewer poor persons in the United States, of whom over 4.0 million were under age sixty-five. Despite the fact that nearly 80 percent of all benefits are paid to persons sixty-five and older, Social Security payments to the disabled, young survivors, and retirees under age sixty-five reduce the number of non-aged poor by more than two and one-half times the effects of other transfer programs.

Effects within the aged population. Although Social Security was never intended to provide the sole source of income to the elderly, more than three-fifths of all aged persons rely on the program for at least one-half of their money income. Perhaps even more telling, for almost one-third of the aged population, Social Security benefits account for at least 80 percent of their incomes; for about 14 percent, these benefits are reported to be the sole income source. As would be expected, the relative importance of Social Security as an income source falls as income rises: 95 percent of beneficiaries under $5,000 of total income receive most of their income from Social Security,

Table 7.9

Antipoverty Effectiveness of Cash and Noncash Transfers for Individuals in Units with All Members 65 or Older, Selected Years

	1980	1983	1986
	Number of poor individuals (in thousands)		
Cash income before transfers	10,821	10,843	11,550
Plus social insurance (other than Social Security)	10,650	10,654	11,334
Plus Social Security	3,441	3,231	3,176
Plus means-tested cash transfers	3,133	2,928	2,874
	Poverty rate (in percent)		
Cash income before transfers	60.1	56.2	55.8
Plus social insurance (other than Social Security)	59.1	55.3	54.7
Plus Social Security	19.1	16.8	15.3
Plus means-tested cash transfers	17.4	15.2	13.9

Source: U.S. House of Representatives, *Background Material and Data on Programs within the Jurisdiction of the Committee on Ways and Means,* 1988, Table 11, pp. 730–31.
Note: Poverty rates differ from published rates for all elderly because data in this table exclude those aged living with other non-aged individuals.

whereas the comparable figure for recipients with an income of at least $20,000 is 12 percent.

It is not surprising that significant variation exists among the elderly as to their degree of dependence on Social Security. Earnings and private pensions provide significantly greater incomes to the ''young old'' than to more elderly persons, who rely more heavily on Social Security and asset income (see Table 7.10). For Social Security recipients ages sixty-five to seventy-four, over one-half derive at least 50 percent of their income from this source; for one in five, Social Security provided over 90 percent of their reported income. In contrast, 70 percent of beneficiaries at least seventy-five years old received the majority of their income from Social Security and one-third reported that at least 90 percent of their income was in the form of their Social Security benefits.

Reliance on Social Security and other transfer payments also varies by both marital status and race. In one of every two married couples receiving Social Security benefits, these benefits provided at least 50 percent of the family's income; the comparable share for unmarried aged beneficiaries is 70 percent.

Table 7.10

Social Security as a Proportion of Total Income for Age Units 65 or Older, 1986

Type of Unit	Percent of income							
	1–19	20–39	40–59	60–79	80+	50+	90+	100
Age of head of household								
65 to 74	12	22	21	17	27	55	20	13
75+	6	15	19	18	42	70	33	19
Total	9	19	20	18	34	62	26	15
Marital status								
Married	14	25	23	18	20	50	14	8
Unmaried	6	15	18	17	43	70	34	21
Total	9	19	20	18	34	62	26	15
Race								
White	10	20	21	18	32	60	24	14
Black	5	12	15	19	48	77	42	31
Hispanic	6	11	19	18	46	75	40	31
Total	9	19	20	18	34	62	26	15

Source: U.S. Department of Health and Human Services, *Income of the Population 55 and Older, 1986.*

Moreover, the unmarried are much more likely than are married couples to depend on Social Security for at least 90 percent of their income (34 percent compared with 14 percent). Black and Hispanic Americans also rely much more heavily on Social Security than do white Americans. While over 40 percent of nonwhite beneficiaries depend almost entirely on Social Security for their income (i.e., at least 90 percent of their income), this is true for fewer than one in every four white beneficiary units.

Although unmarried male and female beneficiaries receive comparable shares of their total incomes from Social Security, this measure of dependence can be quite misleading because the average incomes of the two sexes differs dramatically. In 1986, unmarried female beneficiaries aged sixty-five and over had median family incomes of $9,590 compared with $11,680 for their male counterparts—or about 82 percent. The relative incomes of female beneficiaries drops significantly with age, from about 90 percent of the incomes of male beneficiaries aged sixty-five to sixty-nine to about 75 percent for those over eighty. Families with unmarried females aged sixty-five to sixty-nine reported a median income of $11,210, whereas those with a female member at least 80 years old had a median income of $8,970.

6. Concluding Remarks

As a mechanism for transferring current resources from the working population to the aged and disabled population, there are few observers who would question the power and effectiveness of the U.S. Social Security program. Social Security has a marked effect on reducing elderly poverty rates and on increasing the per capita income of the elderly to be comparable to the nonelderly. The ultimate effect of Social Security as an income transfer device is open to question, however. While intensively studied over the past fifteen years, the effects of Social Security's tax and benefit provisions have yet to be conclusively determined. To the extent that individuals—and the institutions they create—react to offset the impact of Social Security in its redistributive effects, the income redistributive power of the program may be more imagined than real.

Under any scenario, however, the Social Security program has enormous support from both the public and, not surprisingly, the politicians. Over 15 percent of all Americans currently receive benefits under the program, and this proportion is projected to reach one-quarter in 50 years. Moreover, nonaged Americans receive indirect benefits from not having to provide as many resources to their aged and disabled relatives, as would be necessary if Social Security did not exist. Financing the program through an earmarked payroll tax has led to the widespread notion that Social Security benefits are an "earned right" guaranteed as part of a social contract.

Although not generous by international standards, the U.S. Social Security program's heavy dependence on payroll tax revenues implies that the resources of the program will be strained in the twenty-first century. As a result, financing alternatives—increased payroll tax rates or general revenues—and benefit changes will have to be evaluated. Given the size of the Social Security system, the potential economic effects of these alternatives will have to be closely scrutinized.

Notes

1. The Social Security Act also includes the legislative authorizations for Medicare, Medicaid, Unemployment Insurance, Aid to Families with Dependent Children, Supplemental Security Income, foster care and adoption assistance, and social services. Although some analysts would consider some or all of these programs to be included under the Social Security umbrella as well, this chapter focuses on the term's narrower, and more common, usage in the United States.

2. Many rationales have been suggested for the federal provision of old-age insurance programs. See Manser (1982) for a more extensive discussion.

3. Social Security payroll tax rates rose to 6.06 percent in 1988, and a scheduled increase in 1990 will bring the tax rate up to 6.2 percent. In addition to the Social Security payroll tax, workers and employers are each required to pay 1.45 percent of covered wages to the Hospital Insurance (Medicare Part A) program.

4. See Aaron (1982) and Boskin (1986) for more extensive discussions of Social Security's impact on the economy.

5. An additional constraint is that the interest rate earned equals the growth rate of earnings.

6. See Leonard (1985) for an excellent review of the literature in this area.

7. See U.S. Congress (1985) and Congressional Budget Office (1986) for analyses of various earnings-sharing plans and other options designed to improve the benefits of older women.

References

Aaron, Henry J. *Economic Effects of Social Security*. Washington, DC: The Brookings Institution, 1982.

Achenbaum, W. Andrew. *Social Security: Visions and Revisions*. Cambridge: Cambridge University Press, 1986.

Ando, Albert, and Franco Modigliani. "The Life-Cycle Hypothesis of Savings: Aggregate Implications and Tests." *American Economic Review*, vol. 53 (March 1963), 55–84.

Barro, Robert J. "Are Government Bonds Net Wealth?" *Journal of Political Economy*, vol. 82 (November/December 1974), 1095–117.

Bernheim, Douglas. "Dissaving After Retirement: Testing the Pure Life Cycle Hypothesis." In Zvi Bodie et al., eds. *Issues in Pension Economics*. Chicago: The University of Chicago Press, 1987.

Boskin, Michael J. *Too Many Promises: The Uncertain Future of Social Security*. Homewood, IL: Dow Jones-Irwin, 1986.

Boskin, Michael J., Marcy Avrin, and Kenneth Cone. "Modelling Alternative Solutions to the Long-Run Social Security Funding Problem." In Martin Feldstein, ed. *Behavioral Simulation Methods in Tax Policy*. Chicago: The University of Chicago Press, 1983.

Burkhauser, Richard V., and John A. Turner. "A Time-Series Analysis of Social Security and Its Effect on the Market Work of Men at Younger Ages." *Journal of Political Economy*, vol. 86 (August 1978), 701–15.

Burkhauser, Richard V., and Jennifer Warlick. "Disentangling the Annuity from the Redistributive Aspects of Social Security." *Review of Income and Wealth*, vol. 27 (April 1981), 401–21.

Congressional Budget Office. *Earnings Sharing Options for the Social Security System*. Washington, DC: U.S. Government Printing Office, 1986.

Danziger, Sheldon, Robert Haveman, and Robert Plotnick. "How Income Transfers Affect Work, Savings and the Income Distribution: A Critical Review." *Journal of Economic Literature*, vol. 19 (September 1981), 975–1028.

Feldstein, Martin S. "Social Security, Induced Retirement, and Aggregate Capital Accumulation." *Journal of Political Economy*, vol. 82 (September/October 1974), 905–26.

Feldstein, Martin S. "Social Security and Private Savings: Reply." *Journal of Political Economy*, vol. 90 (June 1982), 630–42.

Graebner, William. *A History of Retirement*. New Haven: Yale University Press, 1980.

Haveman, Robert, and Barbara Wolfe. "The Decline in Labor Force Participation: Comment." *Journal of Political Economy*, vol. 92 (June 1984), 532–41.

Hurd, Michael D. "Savings of the Elderly and Desired Bequests." *American Economic Review*, vol. 77 (June 1987), 298–312.

Kollman, Geoffrey, and David Koitz. "How Long Does It Take for New Retirees to Recover the Value of Their Social Security Taxes?" *Congressional Research Service Report for Congress*. Washington, DC, May 20, 1988.

Leonard, Jonathan S. "Labor Supply Incentives and Disincentives for the Disabled."

Working Paper 1744. Cambridge, MA: National Bureau of Economic Research, October 1985.

Leimer, Dean R., and Selig D. Lesnoy. "Social Security and Private Savings: New Time-Series Evidence." *Journal of Political Economy*, vol. 90 (June 1982), 606–29.

Manser, Marilyn E. "Historical and Political Issues in Social Security Financing." In Felicity Skidmore, ed. *Social Security Financing*. Cambridge, MA: MIT Press, 1982, pp. 21–44.

Modigliani, Franco, and Richard Brumberg. "Utility Analysis and Consumption: An Interpretation of Cross-Section Data." In Kurihara, K. K., ed. *Postkeynesian Economics*. New Brunswick: Rutgers University Press, 1954, pp. 388–436.

Munnell, Alicia H. "The Impact of Public and Private Pension Schemes on Saving and Capital Formation." *Conjugating Public and Private: The Case of Pensions, Studies and Research No. 24.* Geneva: International Social Security Association, 1987, pp. 219–36.

Myers, Robert J. *Social Security*, third edition. Homewood, IL: Richard D. Irwin, Inc., 1985.

Myers, Robert J., and Bruce D. Schobel. "A Money's Worth Analysis of Social Security Retirement Benefits." *Society of Actuaries, Transactions*, vol. 35, 1983, pp. 533–61.

Parsons, Donald O. "The Decline in Male Labor Force Participation." *Journal of Political Economy*, vol. 88 (February 1980), 117–34.

Pechman, Joseph A., Henry J. Aaron, and Michael K. Taussig. *Social Security: Perspectives for Reform.* Washington, DC: The Brookings Institution, 1968.

Ross, Christine M., Sheldon Danziger, and Eugene Smolensky. [1987a]. "Interpreting Changes in the Economic Status of the Elderly, 1949–1979." *Contemporary Policy Issues*, vol. 5 (April 1987), 98–112.

———. [1987b]. "The Level and Trend of Poverty in the United States, 1939–1979." *Demography*, vol. 24 (November 1987), 587–600.

Ruggles, Nancy D., and Richard Ruggles. "The Anatomy of Earnings Behavior." In F. Thomas Juster, ed. *The Distribution of Economic Well-Being*. Cambridge, MA: Ballinger, 1974.

U.S. Congress. House of Representatives, Committee on Ways and Means. *Retirement Income for an Aging Population.* Washington, DC: Committee Print, 100th Congress, 1st Session, WMCP 100–22, 1987.

———. *Background Material and Data on Programs within the Jurisdiction of the Committee on Ways and Means,* 1988 edition. Washington, DC: Committee Print, 100th Congress, 2nd Session, WMCP 100–29, 1988.

U.S. Congress. House of Representatives, Committee on Ways and Means, Subcommittee on Social Security. *Report on Earnings Sharing Implementation Study,* Washington, DC: Committee Print, 99th Congress, 1st Session, WMCP 99–4, 1985.

U.S. Department of Commerce, Bureau of the Census. *Money Income of Families and Persons in the United States: 1975.* Washington, DC: U.S. Government Printing Office, 1977.

———. *Money Income of Households, Families, and Persons in the United States: 1985.* Washington, DC: U.S. Government Printing Office, 1987.

———. *Statistical Abstract of the United States, 1977.* Washington, DC: U.S. Government Printing Office, 1987.

U.S. Department of Health and Human Services, Social Security Administration. *Social Security Bulletin, Annual Statistical Supplement, 1987.* Washington, DC: U.S. Government Printing Office, 1987.

———. *Income of the Population 55 or Older, 1986.* Washington, DC: U.S. Government Printing Office, 1988.

8

The Impact of Government Tax and Expenditure Programs on the Distribution of Income in the United States

Patricia Ruggles

The government of the United States, like most national governments, undertakes many activities that affect both the size and the distribution of the nation's income. Some of these activities are the result of policies that are explicitly designed to affect personal incomes—for example, welfare programs that are intended to alleviate poverty, or tax policies that impose higher rates on those with higher incomes. Other policies affect incomes more or less unintentionally, as a by-product of other goals. Examples of this type might include government purchases of goods and services (e.g., weapons systems) that increase the incomes of earners in specific industries or localities, or tax and regulatory policies that affect the returns to certain types of investment.

In addition to the direct and indirect income effects outlined above, government policies also affect incomes if they result in changes in the performance of the economy as a whole. A period of high unemployment is likely to result in high poverty rates and generally greater income inequality, for example, while continuing high deficits may result in high real interest rates, which may in turn increase the relative return to capital, at least in the short run. Over the longer run, if spending for current consumption crowds out investment for the future, government policies may even affect the distribution of income across generations.

Income distribution in the United States is also affected by the actions of the various state and local jurisdictions that run their own tax and expenditure programs in addition to those of the federal government. All but a handful of states now have their own income tax systems, for example, and most also impose sales and other taxes. Local jurisdictions typically have some sort of property tax, and may have other tax programs as well. On the expenditure side, states and localities contribute to cash transfer programs such as welfare and general assistance, and also contribute to many programs providing in-kind benefits such as hospitals and other medical care, education, and public housing.

This chapter discusses the tax and spending policies of the federal government and of state and local jurisdictions as they affect families at different income levels. As the discussion above outlines, however, it is by no means a simple matter to trace through and distinguish between all the various impacts that different government programs and agencies may have on the economic well-being of American families. Before turning to a discussion of specific tax and expenditure programs and their impacts, therefore, the next section of this chapter considers the major conceptual problems involved in allocating the costs and benefits associated with taxes and expenditure programs in general. The following sections examine the redistributive role of government programs, looking first at the tax system and then at public expenditures. The final section summarizes the findings of the chapter as a whole, considering particularly the role of the government in alleviating poverty in the United States.

Calculating the Distributive Impacts of Government Policies

Although virtually all developed countries have an array of programs designed to affect the incomes of their populations in a variety of ways, it is by no means easy to define what is meant by a seemingly simple question like, "What impact does the government have on family incomes?" Before we can even begin to answer such a question, there are several major issues that must be resolved.

Four such issues are discussed in this section. First is the question of whether direct impacts alone should be considered, or whether at least some indirect effects should be included as well. The second set of questions concerns valuation issues and the treatment of goods whose benefits are not directly allocable to individuals. Third, it is necessary to distinguish between the output effects and the factor effects of taxes and public expenditures. And finally, the impacts of alternative choices of outcome variables on perceived distributional impacts must be assessed. These issues are addressed in turn below.

Direct versus Indirect Impacts of Government

The first step in considering the distributional impacts of government is to decide whether one is primarily interested in direct effects—specific changes in family income that are directly attributable to a specific tax or payment from the government—or whether one also wishes to try and account for indirect impacts. For example, should we consider the beneficiaries of the Social Security program to be only those people, mostly elderly and disabled, who actually receive benefits? Or, on the other hand, should we take into account the benefits to their children, who otherwise might have to support their elderly parents? If, as seems likely, the Social Security program causes people to retire earlier than they otherwise would have, should we consider the resulting increase in jobs for younger workers to be among its benefits? On the tax side, if an increase in corporate taxes reduces the return to capital, should we count only this immediate impact, or should we consider the possibility that lower returns will result in lower levels of investment and, over time, lower productivity increases, eventually reducing returns to labor as well?

At the most global level, this question becomes a debate about how to account for the overall macroeconomic impacts of government actions as a whole. Is it meaningful to allocate the costs and benefits of specific programs on a piecemeal basis, or do we need to take into account the longer range effects of economic policies regarding variables such as the deficit, interest rates, and the level of unemployment? Arguably, these variables have more real impact on both the level and the distribution of national income than do the specific programs that affect family incomes directly, but it is not at all clear how these impacts should be measured, let alone allocated across the income distribution.

Even if we opt to study only the direct impacts of tax and benefit programs, it can be quite difficult to determine who actually pays a given tax or, in some cases, receives a given benefit. For example, although landlords are technically responsible for the payment of local property taxes, if virtually all landlords immediately increase rents by a corresponding amount when property taxes are raised, it may be reasonable to consider the direct impact of a property tax increase as falling principally on renters rather than on landlords. Similarly, it is not entirely clear to whom corporate income taxes should be allocated. To the extent that the tax reduces corporate profits, presumably it is borne by the owners of capital, to whom the profits in question would otherwise accrue. If capital moves between possible investments seeking the highest return, the decline in returns will spread across all owners of capital, not just owners of corporate capital. Further, if savings and hence capital inputs decline as a result of the tax, some of the burden may effectively be borne by labor, through declines in productivity. In fact, even if there is no decline in savings some of the burden may fall on labor in the United States if the tax causes some capital that would otherwise be invested here to move overseas.[1] Although there is probably less general agreement about the appropriate incidence assumptions for allocating the burdens of the corporate income tax than for any other tax, similar questions of incidence can be raised in other cases as well.[2]

Valuation of Goods other than Cash Payments to Individuals

A second problem, closely related to the issue of direct versus indirect effects, is the question of how to treat the large proportion of government expenditures that do not result in direct payments to individuals, but rather aim to provide more general public goods such as national defense. On the one hand, it is not at all clear how one should even value these goods, let alone allocate their benefits across individuals. To the extent that these goods are indeed public goods, their value may be substantially greater, in sum, than their cost of production. By their nature, however, public goods like national defense are likely to be both nonrival (one person's consumption does not reduce another's) and nonexclusive (once the good is produced, there is no way to provide it to some consumers without providing it to all). As a result, the only possible mode of production for such goods is a collective one, and there is no way to compare these goods, in terms of value, to private market goods, or even to publicly produced goods that have some market analog. It is therefore very difficult to assign a total value to these goods, and it is in practical terms impossible to figure out what their value to specific individuals might be.

On the other hand, these "unallocable" public goods account for a very large proportion of our total government spending. As is discussed in more detail in the section on public expenditure impacts, about half of the federal budget falls into the "unallocable" category, along with about one-fourth of state and local expenditures. If the benefits of these expenditures are in fact distributed very differently from those of the allocable public expenditures, excluding them in calculating the distributional impacts of public expenditures may provide a very misleading result.

The approach to this problem adopted by most writers who have attempted to distribute total expenditures has been to allocate these unallocables under several different assumptions about the distribution of their benefits, to see how much difference alternative allocations in fact make.[3] This approach allows allocations to be made across individuals, but some decision about the issue of total valuation must still be made. One approach to the valuation problem, adopted by Ruggles and O'Higgins (1981), for example, is to allocate only the expenditures incurred on behalf of specific types of individuals or households, rather than trying to calculate the value of the benefits received from the household's point of view. In assessing these estimates, therefore, it is important to keep in mind that the amounts allocated may not correspond with the value of good to the recipient, but only with the government's cost of providing the good to individuals of the recipient's type. Nevertheless, even this limited allocation may be useful for some purposes—for example, assessing relative expenditure levels across households of different types. Such an allocation cannot, however, be assessed directly as if all the amounts distributed were the equivalent of cash income, since of course in many cases the value to the recipient of the public expenditures in question will be very different from the value of an equivalent amount of cash.

Even if a decision is made to exclude all but direct benefits to individuals from the allocation of government expenditures, some difficult issues of valuation may remain. Cash transfers such as Social Security or welfare benefits are easy to value, of course, but some benefit programs for individuals provide their benefits in kind rather than in cash. For example, many individuals are covered under the Medicare and Medicaid health programs, which provide payments for medical services consumed by the elderly or disabled or by the poor, respectively. Since the amount of the benefit actually received by a person depends mostly on how sick that person has been, adding the cash value of services received directly to income could be very misleading—the very sick would by definition appear to have high income, even if they had no cash income. While on the one hand medical care may actually be worth much more—even an infinite amount—to the very sick, on the other hand it is not clear how meaningful it is, in terms of the assessment of distributional impacts, to allocate large sums to people who, in terms of cash income, may not have enough to pay the rent or to eat properly. Indeed, an allocation system that results in people appearing better off if they are much sicker than their otherwise identical neighbors would run counter to our intuitive understanding of measures of economic welfare.

Allocating benefits on the basis of their expected value to the group of eligibles as a whole—in other words, on the basis of their insurance value—has greater intuitive appeal, in that the allocation is in some sense based on the availability of health care should it be needed, rather than on the direness of a particular individual's actual health problems. Even this solution is less than perfect, however, in that some individuals—for example, the very old—may still be eligible for very large expected health benefits. These benefits may or may not be worth as much to the recipient as the government's cost of providing them. In the absence of a well-functioning private market for these goods, it is difficult to guess, even on average, what the value of these goods is. But even if the actual dollar value of these benefits to recipients could be calculated, the resulting estimates would not be perfect for all types of distributional analysis. For example, it is not appropriate to add such a measure directly to income if one's goal is to assess income adequacy, since health benefits, even if highly valued, are not fungible—they cannot be traded for food or housing or other goods that may also be necessary to sustain life.

Output versus Factor Effects in Assessing the Impacts of Public Tax and Expenditure Policies

In general, when we think of the impacts of an expenditure or tax policy, we think of its effects on the people who actually receive the goods or benefits produced, or provide the revenues collected. Thus for example the benefits of our national defense program are thought of as accruing to those who are protected under it, while the burdens of a cigarette tax are considered to fall principally on smokers.

An alternative way to look at this question, however, is to consider the factor impacts of government policies—that is, their impacts on those who produce the goods and services affected by the policy. In the national defense example, we could consider not the benefits to those gaining protection, but rather the impacts on those who work in the defense industry. Similarly, with regard to a cigarette tax we could measure not the impact on smokers, but rather the effects on tobacco companies, which may suffer a reduction in the demand for their products. Clearly, taxes will typically create at least some distortions in markets for the goods being taxed, and government purchases of goods and services are often large enough relative to private demand to dominate the relevant markets completely. In some sense, however, these impacts relate more closely to issues such as the broader economic impacts of government action as a whole than they do to a relatively narrow consideration of the distribution of costs and benefits resulting from the government tax and expenditure system. For the latter type of analysis, a more consistent approach that focuses exclusively on the intended direct outcomes of government policies, rather than on their factor impacts, is probably to be preferred.

Choosing the Right Outcome Variables

In addition to all these issues relating to the appropriate tax and expenditure totals to be allocated, there is a further set of issues related to the outcome variables used to measure distributional impacts. Three major groups of issues must be resolved: choosing an income base over which to allocate taxes and benefits; deciding upon the appropriate unit of analysis (e.g., households, families, or persons); and choosing among a broad range of possible measures of total distribution, inequality and adequacy.

Issues relating to the income base generally revolve around the inclusion or exclusion of taxes and expenditures in computing that base.[4] Tax impacts are typically considered across the distribution of before-tax cash incomes, although other bases for allocation are certainly possible, and may be preferable for some analyses (e.g., where tax and transfer impacts are being considered simultaneously). Determining the appropriate income type across which to allocate expenditure benefits is more complex, since many of the benefits in question are in some sense part of basic household income. One possibility is to use pretax, pretransfer income as the basis for allocation, but this can be misleading, since many would argue that the existence of the transfer programs reduces incentives for people to find other sources of income. As a result, their pretransfer incomes are actually much lower than their total income would have been if the programs did not exist. If so, distributional analyses based on the comparison of pre- and post-transfer incomes may exaggerate redistributional impacts of such transfer programs.

In either the tax or expenditure case it is important to maintain similar income definitions in comparing distributive impacts across programs. Simply entering programs sequentially and observing the resulting distributional changes can be quite misleading, since many measures of inequality turn out to be quite sensitive to the order in which programs are entered (since each new program does after all change the underlying distribution of income). Similarly, in computing the impacts of government benefits that are provided in kind, such as medical care, it is inconsistent to exclude privately provided benefits of the same type—for example, employer-provided health insurance—from the income base. Finally, in comparing distributional impacts across time both the specific beginning and end years chosen and the choice of a deflator with which to adjust incomes can be important in determining relative impacts, and should therefore be carefully considered.

In addition to issues involving the income base, issues relating to the unit of measurement are also important in determining perceived distributional outcomes. For example, the elderly appear to be a larger proportion of the poor when a family-based income measure is used than when incomes or poverty rates are counted over persons, since non-elderly families in poverty typically include more people than poor families with elderly members. Some transfer programs such as the Aid to Families with Dependent Children (AFDC) program (the basic cash welfare program for single parent families) have their own definition of an assistance unit, which may be embedded in a larger household. In this case, assistance unit incomes will typically be considerably lower (and more equally distributed) than household incomes, both because the assistance units are smaller and because only they, and not the larger household, are subject to the income tests used to qualify people for AFDC.

Some of these issues, particularly those relating to differences in family size, can be at least partially resolved through the use of equivalence scales that adjust incomes relative to needs. As discussed elsewhere in this volume by Jenkins, Hagenaars, and Smeeding, however, constructing an appropriate equivalence scale also involves a host of conceptual and practical problems. And of course, alternative equivalence scales may have widely differing implications for distributional measures, depending on the relative incomes of those in different demographic groups within the population. In practice, many analysts considering U.S. income distribution issues use the ratios of family needs that are implicit in the U.S. poverty thresholds, which vary by family size (and also by age of household head for one and two person households).

Finally, in addition to all the other decisions discussed above, it is necessary to choose a measure or set of measures to be used to assess the distributional impacts of government programs. The range of possibilities here is very large, and the issues involved in choosing between them are very similar to those that arise in any other type of distributional analysis. Possible measures include not only summary measures of inequality such as those discussed in the chapter by Stephen Jenkins, but also simpler percentage distributions across income categories (or equivalent income categories), or measures focusing primarily on income adequacy, such as the variety of poverty measures discussed in the chapter by Aldi Hagenaars.

Here, as in many of the other choices discussed above, the appropriate measure depends upon the purpose for which the estimates are being prepared. If the overall focus of the analysis is on the impacts of government programs on the inequality of the income distribution as a whole, then some type of summary measure (e.g., a Gini coefficient) is indeed appropriate. If on the other hand one is particularly concerned about some part of the distribution—tax benefits going to the rich, for example, or transfers received by the poor—then a set of measures focusing explicitly on those groups may be more useful. Examination of program impacts across deciles of the income distribution, for example, may be quite helpful for policy analyses where the focus is on the relative incomes of those being helped or hurt, even though this type of analysis does not provide a neat summary of the impacts of programs on total inequality. Similarly, much of the analysis of transfer programs, in particular, has focused on their impacts on the share of income going to the bottom quintile of the income distribution.[5] Finally, if one's major concern is not with the overall distribution but rather with program impacts on income adequacy, then some type of poverty measure (or poverty gap measure) will be most appropriate as an outcome indicator.

Estimates of the Distributional Impacts of Tax Policies

Perhaps because the conceptual problems discussed above are so daunting, and the empirical problems involved are also very large, relatively few attempts have recently been made to estimate the total distributional impacts of federal tax and expenditure programs (although several studies have considered parts of the problem). On the whole, there is probably both more agreement on methods and better data available for the tax side of the equation. Most recent authors in this area have used essentially the same methods and assumptions as those laid out in Joseph Pechman and Benjamin Okner's path-breaking 1974 study, *Who Bears the Tax Burden?* which used household-level microdata to examine the distribution of tax payments under various incidence assumptions and across households of various types. Pechman has recently updated this work (Pechman 1985). An even more recent study of this type has been undertaken by Richard Kasten and Frank Sammartino of the Congressional Budget Office, who have focused particularly on changes in the distribution of federal tax burdens over time (Congressional Budget Office 1987).[6]

The questions concerning the incidence of the corporation income tax noted earlier probably constitute the major conceptual stumbling block in allocating tax burdens across households, although problems related to the availability and quality of data also typically force analysts into some compromises. Nevertheless, as Reynolds and Smolensky (1977) point out, tax revenues constitute a large proportion of total income, and distributions that neglect to consider tax impacts may be quite misleading. In fiscal year 1986 federal tax revenue equaled more than 22 percent of national income, and federal, state and local revenues together totaled more than 37 percent. Payments of this magnitude could clearly create substantial differences in before- and after-tax income distributions.

Before turning to a discussion of the distributional implications of tax policies, it is helpful to consider the types and relative sizes of tax programs at use in the United States today. Tables 8.1 and 8.2 outline the major sources of tax revenues for the federal government and for state and local governments respectively. At the federal level, individual income taxes and social insurance contributions (payroll taxes) are the two largest sources of revenue. Together they account for over 81 percent of the total. Corporate income taxes account for another 10 percent, while all other sources together come to less than 9 percent.

Taxes on personal income are much less important at the state and local level, where individual income taxes account for less than 12 percent of revenues. Sales and property taxes are the two major sources of tax revenue at this level, accounting for 21 percent and 17 percent of revenues respectively. Only 3 percent of state and local revenues come from corporate income taxes. It should also be noted that almost 18 percent of state and local revenues are not raised at the state and local level at all, but rather come from federal government transfers.

Both because better data are available for federal taxes and because the two largest sources of federal revenues, income and payroll taxes, are so closely related to personal income, better and more recent estimates of the impacts of taxes on the distribution of income are available at the federal level than at the state level. Table 8.3, which is taken from Kasten and Sammartino's 1987 study, shows the estimated distribution both of federal tax payments by type and of before- and after-tax incomes.[7] As can be seen there, federal tax payments are mildly redistributive in total, increasing the share of the bottom fifth of the income distribution by about one-half of a percent (from 3.1 to 3.6 percent of total income), and increasing the share of the bottom half by about 1.6 percent (from 18.2 percent to 19.8 percent). This increase comes almost entirely from the top 10 percent of the income distribution, whose share falls from 35.7 percent to 33.9 percent of total income. Over half this total decline comes from changes in the share of the top 1 percent of income recipients.

Not surprisingly, given the underlying distribution of income, the proportion of total tax payments coming from each decile rises across the income distribution for all types of tax, but only the individual income tax and the corporate income tax raise a higher proportion of revenue from the top 10 percent than is accounted for by their share of total before-tax income.[8] Social insurance taxes rise slightly faster than income over most of the top half of the income distribution, but fall relative to income in the top decile, because most earners in this decile reach the cap on social security payments before the end of the year, and therefore do not have payroll taxes deducted from part of their earnings. Excise taxes (taxes on tobacco, liquor, gasoline, etc.), which as noted earlier are a relatively small part of total federal revenues, fall disproportionately on those in the lower half of the income distribution.

Estimating the impacts of the various types of state and local taxes on the distribution of income is substantially more difficult, largely because appropriate data are lacking. The last study to attempt a comprehensive estimate of the

Table 8.1

Sources of Revenue for the Federal Government, Fiscal Year 1987

Source	Receipts (in billions of dollars)	Receipts as a percentage of total receipts
Total receipts[a]	854.1	100.0
Individual income taxes	392.6	46.0
Corporation income taxes	83.9	9.8
Social insurance taxes and contributions	303.3	35.5
Excise taxes	32.5	3.8
Other[b]	41.9	4.9

Source: Economic Report of the President, 1988, Table B–77.

[a] Includes both on-budget and off-budget receipts.

[b] Includes estate and gift taxes, customs duties, federal reserve system earnings, and a small amount from other miscellaneous sources.

Table 8.2

Sources of State and Local Revenues, Fiscal Year 1985–86[a]

Source	Receipts (in billions of dollars)	Receipts as a percentage of total state and local revenues
Total receipts[b]	641.4	100.0
Property taxes	111.7	17.4
Sales taxes	135.0	21.0
Individual income taxes	74.4	11.6
Corporation net income taxes	20.0	3.1
Revenue from federal government	113.1	17.6
Other[c]	187.3	29.2

Source: Economic Report of the President, 1988, Table B–83.

[a] Different state and local governments have different fiscal year definitions. These data are for the local jurisdiction's fiscal year ending between July 1, 1985 and June 30, 1986.

[b] Excludes revenues of publicly owned enterprises (e.g., liquor stores) and insurance trusts. Transfers between state and local governments are also excluded.

[c] Includes other taxes and charges and miscellaneous revenue.

Table 8.3

Distribution of Family Income and of Federal Tax Payments by Population Decile, 1988 (in percent)[a]

	Family income		Federal taxes paid				
Decile[b]	Before tax	After tax	Individual income	Social insur- ance	Excises	Corporate income	All taxes
First[c]	0.9	1.0	−0.1	0.5	4.5	0.3	0.4
Second	2.2	2.6	−0.1	1.5	5.5	0.9	0.8
Third	3.6	4.0	0.6	3.5	6.7	1.7	2.1
Fourth	5.0	5.4	2.0	5.4	7.9	2.9	3.6
Fifth	6.5	6.8	3.7	7.3	8.4	3.8	5.3
Sixth	8.1	8.4	5.7	9.7	9.4	4.9	7.3
Seventh	10.0	10.2	8.0	12.1	10.7	6.3	9.5
Eighth	12.5	12.5	10.9	15.7	12.1	7.2	12.3
Ninth	16.1	16.0	16.1	19.6	14.3	9.9	16.7
Tenth	35.7	33.9	53.2	24.5	18.6	61.7	41.9
Top 5 percent	25.1	23.5	41.0	12.7	10.3	53.0	30.4
Top 1 percent	12.5	11.5	23.8	2.5	3.5	35.4	16.2
All Deciles[d]	100.0	100.0	100.0	100.0	100.0	100.0	100.0

Source: The Changing Distribution of Federal Taxes: 1975–1990, Congressional Budget Office, Table B–1. 1988 projections prepared using CBO tax simulation models.
[a] Corporate income tax allocated to capital income.
[b] Ranked by size of family income.
[c] Excludes families with zero or negative incomes.
[d] Includes families with zero or negative incomes not shown separately.

distribution of local tax impacts, as far as we are aware, was the Ruggles and O'Higgins study of 1981, which used data from the 1970 decennial census.[9] Clearly, there have been some changes since then both in the underlying distributions of income within and across jurisdictions and in state and local tax programs. In 1970, for example, property taxes accounted for about 26 percent of state and local revenues, while sales taxes accounted for about 23 percent. Federal transfers were slightly lower than they are now—under 17 percent—as were individual income taxes, at about 8 percent of total revenues. Corporate income taxes were similar, at about 3 percent.

In spite of these differences, however, the distributions seen in 1970 may be close enough to those of today to provide at least some illustration of general trends in state and local tax burdens. Ruggles and O'Higgins found that, overall, the lowest decile of the income distribution paid almost 3 percent of total state and local taxes, and the bottom fifth paid about 7 percent. Overall, the bottom half paid almost 29 percent of these taxes, while the top 10 percent paid about 21 percent. Although the total distribution of income has become slightly more unequal since 1970, these findings imply that on the whole state and local taxes fall much more heavily on the bottom half of the distribution than do federal taxes. As a result, a distribution of total after-tax incomes based on state and local taxes as well as federal taxes would be slightly more unequal than the after-tax distribution shown in Table 8.3, although given the size of these taxes relative to total income their inclusion would not result in dramatic changes in the income distribution as a whole.

Estimates of the Distributional Impacts of Expenditure Policies

The previous section concludes that, on the whole, tax policies probably make the distribution of income slightly more equal across the population in general, although their impacts are certainly not dramatic. It is harder to arrive at a neat summary of the impacts of expenditure programs. As discussed in the first section of the paper, a major problem in allocating expenditure benefits is that many government expenditures do not directly affect personal incomes, and are in that sense "unallocable." Further, a large proportion even of those programs that provide benefits to individuals provide benefits in kind—e.g., subsidies or direct services—rather than in cash, and these benefits can also be hard to value in a meaningful way. Finally, the "counter-factual" problem identified by Behrens and Smolensky (1973)—the fact that it is impossible to estimate with confidence what incomes would have been in the absence of government policies—applies even more directly to expenditure programs than to taxes.[10]

A first step in tackling these problems is a closer examination of the composition of government expenditures. Tables 8.4 and 8.5 show outlays by function for the federal government and for state and local governments respectively. National defense is the single largest budget category in the federal budget, accounting for about 28 percent of expenditures in fiscal year 1987. Programs that do provide direct benefits to individuals account for roughly half the total budget, with Social Security, at almost 21 percent of the budget, by far the largest. Income security—for the most part, social insurance and means-tested programs, many of which serve the low-income population—and health programs account for the bulk of the remaining benefit programs, with smaller amounts being spent on education, employment, social services, and veterans' programs.

State and local expenditures as a whole are less than 60 percent of federal expenditures for the comparable year.[11] The largest category of state and local expenditures, accounting for more than a third of the total, is education, which includes both local schools and state systems of higher education. Public welfare expenditures and expenditures on health and hospitals are also important components of state and local budgets. Together these three categories account for about 57 percent of spending at this level.

It is more difficult to separate the impacts of spending on benefits by level of

Table 8.4

Federal Outlays by Function, Fiscal Year 1987

Function	Total outlays (in billions of dollars)	Percentage of total federal outlays
Total outlays[a]	1,004.6	100.0
National defense	282.0	28.1
Agriculture	27.4	2.7
Transportation	26.2	2.6
Education, training, employment, and social services	29.7	3.0
Medicare	75.1	7.5
Other health	40.0	4.0
Income security	123.3	12.3
Social security	207.4	20.6
Veterans	26.8	2.7
Other programs[b]	64.7	6.4
Net interest	138.6	13.8
Undistributed offsetting receipts	−36.5	−3.6

Source: Economic Report of the President, 1988, Table B–83.
[a] Includes both on-budget and off-budget outlays.
[b] Includes international affairs, science, energy, natural resources, commerce and housing credits, community and regional development, justice, and general government expenditures.

government than it is for tax impacts, because many benefit programs are funded jointly by the federal government and local jurisdictions. For example, expenditures on welfare for single parent families and on medical care for the poor are both paid for through a system of federal matching grants, under which the federal government pays a predetermined share of each state or locality's expenditures on these programs. The major welfare program for the low-income elderly and disabled, the Supplemental Security Income (SSI) program, is funded at a basic level by the federal government, but over half of the states supplement federal benefits under this program. This means that, on the one hand, more of the state and local share of these benefits is likely to be reported in our data on benefit recipiency and household income, but on the other hand, without detailed information on the beneficiary's jurisdiction of residence it would be very difficult to estimate in any given case what share of the benefit was actually paid for by each type of government. As a result, most analyses of benefit program impacts focus on impacts across all levels of government.[12]

Although, as the summary above has indicated, expenditures on programs other than benefits to individuals account for a large share of total expenditures at all levels of government, most of the discussion of expenditure impacts in this

Table 8.5

State and Local Outlays by Function, Fiscal Year 1984–85[a]

Function	Total outlays (in billions of dollars)	Percentage of total state and local outlays
Total[b]	552.1	100.0
Education	192.7	34.9
Highways	45.0	8.2
Public welfare	69.6	12.6
Health and hospitals	49.7	9.0
Police, fire, and sanitation	47.3	8.6
All other programs[c]	115.4	20.9
Net interest on general debt	32.4	5.9

Source: U.S. Bureau of the Census, Statistical Abstract of the United States, 1988, Table 437.
[a] Data for local jurisdiction fiscal year ending between July 1, 1984 and June 30, 1985.
[b] Direct general expenditures only. Excludes outlays of publicly owned enterprises and insurance trusts. Also excludes transfers between state and local governments.
[c] Includes expenditures on housing and urban renewal, natural resources, parks and recreation, financial and general administration, and other expenditures not elsewhere classified.

section is confined to the analysis of transfer program impacts. As discussed in the first section, various authors have tried to estimate the impacts of total expenditures, although the most recent such estimates that we know of are those of Reynolds and Smolensky, and Ruggles and O'Higgins, both of which are based on 1970 income and expenditure data.[13] Attempting to duplicate these earlier results for some more recent time period was beyond the scope of this analysis. It is worth noting, however, that because this category accounted for over a third of all government expenditures in 1970, Ruggles and O'Higgins found that including it in the distribution base resulted in substantially less apparent redistribution than if benefit programs alone were considered. This result held under several different sets of assumptions concerning the distribution of benefits from unallocable expenditures. It occurs largely because direct benefit programs go so heavily to those in the bottom half of the income distribution that even a population-based distribution of unallocables will cause the totals to appear less redistributive than do the benefit programs alone.

This point is illustrated by the results shown in Table 8.6, which gives the distribution of total cash transfer payments by income decile for three different years. Although those in the very bottom decile actually received less than one-tenth of all transfers, the next three deciles all received a more than proportional share of these expenditures in every year examined. Further, even those at the very top of the income distribution—the top 5 percent and the top 1 percent of all families—still receive substantial amounts of income from government transfer programs.

Table 8.6

Distribution of Transfer Income by Population Decile, 1977, 1984, and 1988
(in percentages)[a]

Decile[b]	1977	1984	1988
First[c]	9.5	7.4	7.9
Second	17.2	15.3	15.5
Third	15.2	13.3	13.1
Fourth	11.3	12.2	11.8
Fifth	10.0	11.0	10.7
Sixth	9.4	9.6	9.6
Seventh	7.5	8.9	8.7
Eighth	6.3	7.8	7.9
Ninth	6.2	6.6	6.7
Tenth	6.9	7.3	7.5
Top 5 percent	3.7	4.0	4.0
Top 1 percent	0.8	0.8	0.8
All Deciles[d]	100.0	100.0	100.0

Source: The Changing Distribution of Federal Taxes: 1975–1990, Congressional Budget Office, Table A–2. 1988 projections prepared using CBO tax simulation models.
[a] Corporate income tax allocated to capital income.
[b] Ranked by size of family income.
[c] Excludes families with zero or negative incomes.
[d] Includes families with zero or negative incomes not shown separately.

Table 8.6 also illustrates the changes in transfer distributions that have oc-curred in the last decade. The most striking change has been the decline in the share of all transfers going to those at the bottom of the income distribution. The share of those in the bottom decile declined from 9.5 percent in 1977 to 7.4 percent in 1984, and the share of the bottom fifth declined from 26.7 percent to 22.7 percent. More recently these shares have risen slightly, but at projected 1988 levels of 7.9 percent and 23.4 percent for the bottom tenth and the bottom fifth respectively they are still well below the 1977 levels. Some of this change probably results from declines in expenditures on means-tested transfer pro-grams. In addition to the cutbacks in these programs during the Reagan years, which were relatively minor, real benefit levels have declined substantially since the mid-1970s, particularly in AFDC.

A more important source of this shift, however, is probably the relative growth of the Social Security program over this time. The Social Security pro-gram is the largest source of government transfers, serving over 38 million people in 1987. In 1986 the Social Security program as a whole accounted for about 36 percent of social welfare expenditures at all levels of government.

Between 1977 and 1986 (the most recent year for which detailed data are available) average Social Security benefits for retired workers and their families approximately doubled, for a real increase (after inflation) of about 12 percent. In contrast, AFDC payments—received by about 11 million people—grew by about 45 percent on average over this period, for an inflation-adjusted decline of about 20 percent. At the same time, the number of people receiving Social Security increased by about 11 percent, while the size of the AFDC caseload actually declined slightly. Because virtually all AFDC recipients are in the bottom fifth of the distribution, but a much smaller proportion of Social Security recipients are in this group (especially after the program increases of the last decade), these shifts alone account for much of the change in the share of transfers received by those in this income group.

Although cash transfers are the easiest type of expenditure to allocate across income groups—after all, few valuation problems arise in dealing with cash—they are by no means the only type of benefit to individuals that is provided by the government. Indeed, the major source of growth in benefit programs since the early 1970s has been in the in-kind programs, especially food and medical programs. Because these programs make up a large and increasing share of government expenditures on benefits, any analysis of distributional impacts that neglected them would be potentially quite misleading.

Table 8.7 addresses the issue of relative tax and transfer program impacts across the income distribution by showing the overall distribution of income relative to the mean under several definitions of income (including different amounts of taxes and benefits).[14] These estimates are subject to several of the caveats discussed in the first section. Probably most important, the category "cash income before transfers" should not be taken as an actual estimate of what people's incomes would have been if the transfer programs did not exist; rather, it simply represents their total cash incomes as reported in the Current Population Survey (CPS) minus their reported cash transfer receipts. Second, it should be borne in mind that transfers are somewhat underreported in the CPS (as in all sample surveys), so their actual impacts may be larger than would be estimated based on these data. Third, the valuation of in-kind benefits such as food, housing, and medical care does indeed present a problem; Table 8.7 uses estimates of the equivalent cash value to recipients of these goods, which have been developed by the census bureau. Estimating these values is quite difficult, however, particularly for goods such as medical care where most of the population receives some type of subsidy for consumption, and even the census bureau describes the data behind these estimates as "weak."[15]

In spite of these caveats, the distributions shown in Table 8.7 tell an interesting story. For families and unrelated individuals as a whole the distribution of pretransfer incomes is indeed quite unequal, with families at the twentieth percentile (based on incomes adjusted for family size) receiving incomes equal

Table 8.7

1987 Family Incomes as Percentage of the Median for Family Type, by Selected Income Sources

Income percentile[a]	Cash income before transfers	All cash income[b]	After-tax cash income[c]	After-tax income including food and housing benefits[d]	After-tax income including all in-kind benefits[e]
All families and unrelated individuals					
20%	27.0	44.3	47.5	48.6	50.4
40	76.1	80.7	82.0	82.0	82.7
50	100.0	100.0	100.0	100.0	100.0
60	126.0	121.2	119.4	119.8	119.7
80	195.8	182.6	173.4	173.4	171.5
Married couples with children					
20%	53.4	55.7	58.0	58.2	58.5
40	85.5	86.0	86.3	86.4	86.7
50	100.0	100.0	100.0	100.0	100.0
60	115.6	115.7	114.7	114.6	115.0
80	161.4	160.6	156.0	155.4	155.8
Single parent families with children					
20%	0.0	41.7	42.0	55.7	58.6
40	51.6	73.9	75.0	82.8	85.2
50	100.0	100.0	100.0	100.0	100.0
60	150.5	136.5	133.0	126.2	122.7
80	283.9	236.5	215.2	199.2	190.6

Families with a head of household aged 65 or over	20%	18.7	57.6	58.2	58.5	60.1
	40	69.6	84.8	85.1	85.1	85.3
	50	100.0	100.0	100.0	100.0	100.0
	60	136.3	118.6	114.9	114.9	113.2
	80	253.2	174.0	163.0	163.0	157.2
Unrelated individuals aged 65 or over	20%	0.0	61.6	61.6	63.9	64.2
	40	37.5	84.8	84.8	84.6	83.9
	50	100.0	100.0	100.0	100.0	100.0
	60	187.5	122.6	121.3	118.3	116.1
	80	492.5	197.6	192.7	187.0	177.7

Source: Computed from the Current Population Survey, U.S. Bureau of the Census (March 1988).

[a] Population percentiles ranked by size of *equivalent* family income (adjusted using U.S. poverty thresholds).

[b] Includes market income plus all government-provided cash transfers. Not adjusted for transfer payment underreporting in the CPS.

[c] Cash income minus federal income and payroll taxes. No adjustment has been made for state and local taxes.

[d] After-tax cash income plus the recipient cash value of government-provided food and housing subsidies. Imputed rent from owner-occupied housing *not* included.

[e] Previous column plus the recipient cash value of government-provided medical benefits.

to only a little over a fourth of the median income.[16] Families at the eightieth percentile, on the other hand, receive almost twice the median in pretransfer income. The addition of cash transfers does substantially narrow the gap between the bottom and the middle of the distribution, bringing incomes at the twentieth percentile up to about 44 percent of the median, and reducing the relative incomes of those in the top fifth of the distribution slightly. Subtracting federal taxes from income narrows the gap still further, both by reducing relative incomes at the eightieth percentile and by increasing relative incomes at the twentieth, although in percentage terms both changes are relatively small (in the range of 5 to 7 percent of total income). The addition of food and housing benefits has no impact outside the bottom fifth of the distribution, but does raise relative incomes at the twentieth percentile by approximately one percentage point (or about 2 percent of income at this level). Finally, the addition of other in-kind benefits, principally medical care, also has a slight equalizing impact, especially at the twentieth percentile, where it raises income relative to the mean by about 2 percentage points, or about 4 percent.[17]

In total, then, the net redistributive impact of government transfer programs and the federal tax system in combination is quite large at the twentieth percentile, where relative incomes almost double, but is fairly small in relative terms across the rest of the distribution. The breakdowns by family type shown in the rest of Table 8.7 help to explain that finding. In particular, they show that the two groups which are the targets of the largest federal cash transfer programs, single-parent families and the elderly, have very low pretransfer incomes at the twentieth percentile even relative to the median for all families of the same type. For both single-parent families and unrelated elderly individuals pretransfer income at the twentieth percentile is actually zero, while for families with elderly heads it is about 19 percent of the median for elderly families.

In other words, among those groups who are eligible for cash transfer programs pretransfer incomes are very unequally distributed indeed, and a substantial minority actually have no pretransfer income. Married couple families with children, on the other hand, who are typically not eligible for substantial amounts of transfers, have pretransfer incomes at the twentieth percentile that are over half the median for this family type as a whole. Of course, it is very difficult to determine the extent to which this situation arises because the existence of cash transfers reduces work effort and the incentive to find other income sources among at least some of those eligible for these programs—or because these groups are being appropriately targeted for transfers because many of their members are in fact unable to generate any substantial amount of income on their own.

Predictably, the impacts of cash transfers on relative incomes at the low end of the scale are very large for single parents and the elderly, and quite small for married couple families. Taxes have relatively small effects across all of these subgroups, although they represent the greatest reduction in relative income for better-off single-parent families, a slightly surprising finding. The only group that is greatly affected by the addition of food and housing benefits is low-income single parent families, whose income relative to the median for their group rises by almost a third as a result of these benefits. Low-income elderly, on the other hand, who are also typically eligible for these programs, receive very little increase in relative income with their addition. Finally, the addition of medical care has only a very small impact on the within-group distributions, especially for married couples and for the elderly. In the first case this probably results from the fact that almost no families in this group receive medical benefits; in the second case, virtually all members of the group, regardless of income, are eligible (and probably receive similar amounts).

Increases or decreases in inequality across income categories are not the whole story with regard to benefit programs, however, which are after all typically designed to aid groups who are perceived as being in some way disadvantaged, at least as workers. As Table 8.8 indicates, there are very substantial differences in median incomes across family types, not only before transfers but even after the transfer system has been applied. Because medians are shown across income groups adjusted for family size, actual income amounts are not very meaningful, and so the entries in Table 8.8 show median income as a proportion of the poverty threshold, which also varies by family size. As a guide to the general size of these incomes, the poverty threshold for a family of three (the median family size) was $9,056 in 1987.

The findings shown in Table 8.8 help to explain why single-parent families and elderly individuals, at least, should be targeted by benefit programs. For both of these groups median incomes before transfers are below the poverty line—implying a very high poverty rate overall. Even after transfers these two groups remain substantially less well off, at the median, than the rest of the population. The median cash income for the population as a whole is over three times the poverty threshold; for single parents it is about 115 percent of the poverty level, and for elderly individuals it is about 164 percent. The addition of in-kind benefits and the subtraction of taxes reduces the gap somewhat, but after all taxes and benefits these groups still have lower median incomes than the population as a whole. In the case of single-parent families, in fact, the post-tax, post-transfer median is only about 45 percent of the median for all families, even after adjustments for differences in family size.

Table 8.8 also illustrates the substantial skew toward the elderly in the U.S. transfer system. Both elderly individuals and elderly families have before-transfer equivalent incomes that are substantially below the median, but both make substantial gains as a result of the transfer system, and elderly families are actually the highest-income subgroup, on median, after taxes and transfers.[18] These findings illustrate the impacts of the differences in transfer programs for the elderly and for other groups, especially families with children.

Table 8.8

Median 1987 Family Incomes as Proportion of the Poverty Line by Family Type and Income Source

Family type	Cash income before transfers	All cash income[a]	After-tax cash income[b]	After-tax income including food and housing benefits[c]	After-tax income including all in-kind benefits[d]
All families and unrelated individuals	2.85	3.16	2.78	2.78	2.84
Married couples with children	3.39	3.43	2.93	2.94	2.94
Single parents with children	0.93	1.15	1.12	1.22	1.28
Families with a head of household aged 65 or over	1.71	3.23	3.16	3.16	3.48
Unrelated individuals aged 65 or over	0.40	1.64	1.64	1.69	1.93

Source: Computed from the Current Population Survey, U.S. Bureau of the Census (March 1988).

[a] Includes market income plus all government-provided cash transfers. Not adjusted for transfer payment underreporting in the CPS.

[b] Cash income minus federal income and payroll taxes. No adjustment has been made for state and local taxes.

[c] After-tax cash income plus the recipient cash value of government-provided food and housing subsidies. Imputed rent from owner-occupied housing *not* included.

[d] Previous column plus the recipient cash value of government-provided medical benefits.

Summary and Conclusions

In summary, although it is difficult if not impossible to determine the distributional impact of government policies as a whole, it is possible to say something much more limited about the direct impacts of policies explicitly designed to affect incomes. On the whole, the direct tax and transfer system in the United States appears to be mildly redistributive, raising the relative incomes of those at the bottom of the distribution and lowering at least slightly the relative incomes of those at the top. Within the system, the tax component appears to have its largest impacts at the top of the distribution, while the largest transfer impacts appear in the bottom half of the distribution (although not necessarily in the bottom decile). Federal taxes are somewhat more equalizing than state and local taxes, which probably offset some of the redistributive impacts seen for federal taxes alone. On the expenditure side, it is particularly difficult to estimate the distributive impacts of expenditures other than direct benefits, but there is some evidence that under most allocation assumptions inclusion of these expenditures would also dampen the redistributive effects seen for benefit programs alone.

In total, then, the net redistributive impacts of government action, at least in the very short run, are probably quite small. In some sense, however, redistributive impacts or net reductions in inequality are the wrong criteria to use in assessing government programs—after all, redistribution per se is not an explicit policy goal of any public program. Instead, the redistribution that does take place tends to result, on the tax side, from a belief that those with a greater ability to pay should bear proportionately larger shares of the tax burden, and on the expenditure side, from a belief that the government should ensure at least some minimal level of support for those who cannot support themselves. We have to some extent already considered the first set of issues in our discussion of tax burdens by income category. To address the second set, however, it is necessary to consider not the total redistributive impacts of tax and benefit programs, but more narrowly, their impacts on income adequacy.

There are of course a number of different measures that could be used to assess the impacts of government actions on the overall adequacy of family incomes. Table 8.9 presents some information on two relatively simple measures, the poverty rate and the poverty gap. The poverty rate is simply the percentage of the population with incomes below the official poverty thresholds, while the poverty gap is the total shortfall in their incomes relative to the poverty line. In addition to all of the caveats about the dangers of pre- and postprogram comparisons cited in the expenditure discussion above, which also apply here, it is important to note that the poverty gap in particular is simply a measure of how much the incomes of the *current* poor fall below official poverty measures. The poverty gap does not tell us how much we would need in new benefit programs to eliminate poverty altogether, both

Table 8.9

Antipoverty Effectiveness of Tax and Transfer Programs, 1986

Income definition	Millions of persons in poverty	Poverty rate (in percent)	Poverty gap (in billions of 1985 dollars)
1. Cash income before transfers	49.7	20.8	116.4
2. 1 plus social insurance other than Social Security	47.5	19.9	110.1
3. 2 plus Social Security	34.5	14.5	65.0
4. 3 plus means-tested cash transfers	32.4	13.6	48.3
5. 4 plus food and housing benefits[a]	29.0	12.2	38.2
6. 5 less federal taxes[b]	31.2	13.1	39.7

Source: Committee on Ways and Means, U.S. House of Representatives, "Background Material and Data on Programs within the Jurisdiction of the Committee on Ways and Means," 1988 Edition, March 24, 1988, Table 7, p. 722.
[a] Valued as in Tables 8.7 and 8.8.
[b] Income and payroll taxes only.

because it would be impossible to target such programs so as to bring all current poor exactly to the poverty line, and because increases in spending of that magnitude would have substantial additional fiscal and budgetary effects. Nevertheless, it is a useful measure of the relative depth of the poverty problem under various income concepts.[19]

Overall, Table 8.9 demonstrates that even though government programs may result in only marginal changes in the income distribution as a whole, they certainly appear to improve the adequacy of the incomes received by those at the very bottom. Although, as discussed extensively elsewhere, cash incomes before transfers undoubtedly understate somewhat the potential nontransfer incomes of actual transfer recipients, both poverty rates and the poverty gap under this income concept are very large. After taxes and benefits, however, the poverty rate is only about two-thirds what it was based on pre-transfer income, and the poverty gap is just over one-third as large.

Table 8.9 also shows that, even though the Social Security program is not explicitly targeted on the poor, it has a very substantial poverty-reducing impact—much larger than that of any other set of programs. On the one hand, of course, expenditures on Social Security are much larger than expenditures for other programs, so it is not too surprising that it has a larger effect. On the other hand, most Social Security beneficiaries are either elderly or disabled, and typically they do not work—consequently, many do have very low pre-transfer incomes indeed.

Means-tested programs have a smaller impact on the overall poverty rate—

typically, their benefit levels are too low to actually bring people's incomes over the poverty line—but they do substantially reduce the poverty gap. Because they are added into the equation after—and often, on top of—cash benefits, food and housing benefits have a larger impact on the poverty rate, but their impact on the poverty gap is smaller, in accordance with the generally smaller size of these programs as a whole. Finally, the addition of income and payroll taxes moves a surprisingly large number of people back below the poverty line, but the impact on the actual poverty gap is very small.[20]

In sum, then, although these programs have only a relatively small impact on the total distribution of income, their effects on the adequacy of the incomes received by the very poorest members of society are probably much larger. Although a large number of people—and especially, of children—are still poor even after all transfers, these programs clearly reduce the income shortfall that such people suffer. In this fairly limited but significant context, therefore, government income support programs do serve a useful and important redistributive function.

Notes

1. These and other theories of corporate tax incidence have been discussed extensively in the literature—see for example Ballentine (1980), Feldstein (1983), and Harberger (1983).

2. For a discussion of payroll tax incidence, for example, see Vroman (1986), and for a review of issues relating to the property tax, see Aaron (1975).

3. See for example Gillespie (1965), Reynolds and Smolensky (1977), and Ruggles and O'Higgins (1981).

4. A second factor of importance in computing income is of course the accounting period over which it is measured. This issue is not discussed in detail here, since in practical terms data on taxes and expenditures are rarely available for any but an annual accounting period. For a discussion of the impacts of transfers on income redistribution over the life cycle, however, see the article by Paul Cullinan in this volume.

5. See Danziger, Haveman, and Plotnick (1981) for a discussion of the use of this and other measures by various authors.

6. Other major studies in this area include Musgrave, Case, and Leonard (1974); Reynolds and Smolensky (1977); and Browning and Johnson (1979).

7. Kasten and Sammartino compute distributions under alternative assumptions concerning the incidence of the corporate income tax; only estimates under the assumption that it is borne by capital are shown here. For more details on alternative estimates see Congressional Budget Office (1987).

8. This effect would be reduced for the corporate income tax if it were assumed to fall principally on labor rather than capital; under that assumption the top decile would pay about 32 percent of the tax.

9. Reynolds and Smolensky (1977) also distribute state and local taxes across income categories (although not income deciles) for 1970 (and two earlier years). Their findings are broadly similar to those of Ruggles and O'Higgins discussed here.

10. For a more detailed discussion of this problem see also Reynolds and Smolensky (1977) and Danziger, Haveman, and Plotnick (1981).

11. State and local expenditures are shown for fiscal years 1984–85 because later years are not yet available in comparable detail.

12. In fact, programs that are shared between the federal and local levels or that provide cash benefits are considerably more likely to be included than are purely local programs providing in-kind benefits, since data on such benefits are less likely to be collected in national surveys. Additionally, control totals for total local spending for a given purpose are relatively difficult to develop, since information must be collected across a large number of jurisdictions. As a result, locally provided in-kind benefits such as education, and public goods such as police, fire, and sanitation services that can in fact be allocated across local jurisdictions, are nevertheless typically excluded from total benefit distributions.

13. Reynolds and Smolensky also examine data for earlier years.

14. This table of course violates one of the principles laid down in the first section, namely, the rule that program impacts should be compared using similar baseline income concepts. There may be slightly more justification for this type of analysis when the categories involved represent income types that are received in sequence, as in this case. For example, market income is taken into account in determining benefit levels for some cash transfers, taxes are imposed on cash incomes, and in-kind benefits, especially food and housing, are typically allocated on the basis of some measure of disposable income. On the other hand, it is clearly true that the specific distributional impacts estimated for each major category might be quite different if the estimates were done in a different order.

15. See U.S. Bureau of the Census (1988) for more details on the derivation of these estimates (as well as for estimates of the extent of underreporting of transfers in the CPS). In addition, a substantial literature exists on the valuation of in-kind benefits, and in fact the census bureau held a special conference on this topic in 1986. See U.S. Bureau of the Census (1986) for the papers presented at that conference and for further references on this topic.

16. The distributions of family incomes shown in Tables 8.7 and 8.8 are based on equivalent family income, which has been adjusted for family size using the needs standards inherent in the U.S. system of poverty thresholds.

17. One other category of in-kind benefits that are at least theoretically allocable is expenditures on education. The census bureau does not include these benefits in its allocations, however, and therefore does not calculate any valuation for them. Although a complete allocation of individually-assignable benefits should probably include them, we have not been able to do so here. (Clearly, if they were assigned, their major benefits would go to families with children, and would be concentrated in the middle brackets of the income distribution.)

18. The official U.S. poverty line for the elderly in one or two person households is about 10 percent lower than comparable poverty lines for the nonelderly. If actual needs vary less than this for the two groups, which seems fairly likely, equivalence scales based on poverty thresholds may overstate the relative incomes of the elderly.

19. Table 8.9 also suffers from the same problem of differential baselines for comparing program impacts that affects Tables 8.7 and 8.8, and which is discussed in more detail in note 14. Further, since unfortunately programs have been added together in a different order in this table than in the two earlier ones, caution should be used in comparing specific impacts by program type across these tables.

20. Medical and other in-kind benefits are not shown in this table because, as discussed earlier, they are not sufficiently fungible to add much to income adequacy. Food and housing benefits are allocated because they are typically low enough relative to the amounts families would have had to spend on these goods anyway in order to stay alive that they do not significantly distort consumption. It may be unrealistic to assume that any expenditures on medical care would occur in cases where income is so low that even food and shelter needs are not being met, however.

References

Aaron, Henry J. *Who Pays the Property Tax? A New View*. Studies of Government Finance. Washington, DC: The Brookings Institution, 1975.

Ballentine, J. Gregory. *Equity, Efficiency, and the U.S. Corporation Income Tax*. Washington, DC: American Enterprise Institute for Public Policy Research, 1980, pp. 32–50.

Behrens, Jean, and Eugene Smolensky. "Alternative Definitions of Income Redistribution." *Public Finance* 28 (1973), 3–4:315–32.

Browning, Edgar K., and William R. Johnson. "Taxes, Transfers and Income Inequality." In Gary M. Walton, ed., *Regulatory Change in an Atmosphere of Crisis: Current-day Implications of the Roosevelt Years*. New York: Academic Press, 1979, pp. 129–152.

Committee on Ways and Means, U.S. House of Representatives. "Background Material and Data on Programs within the Jurisdiction of the Committee on Ways and Means." 1988 Edition, March 24, 1988.

Congressional Budget Office. *The Changing Distribution of Federal Taxes: 1975–1990*. October 1987.

Danziger, Sheldon, Robert Haveman, and Robert Plotnick. "How Income Transfer Programs Affect Work, Savings, and the Income Distribution: A Critical Review." *Journal of Economic Literature*, vol. 19 (September 1981), 975–1028.

Feldstein, Martin. *Capital Taxation*. Cambridge: Harvard University Press, 1983.

Gillespie, W. I. "The Effect of Public Expenditures on the Distribution of Income." In R. A. Musgrave, ed. *Essays in Fiscal Federalism*. Washington, DC: Brookings Institution, 1965.

Harberger, Arnold C. "The State of the Corporate Income Tax: Who Pays It? Should It Be Repealed?" In Charles E. Walker and Mark A. Bloomfield, eds. *New Directions in Federal Tax Policy for the 1980s*. Cambridge, MA: Ballinger, 1983.

Musgrave, R. A., K. E. Case, and H. Leonard. "The Distribution of Fiscal Burdens and Benefits." *Public Finance Quarterly*, vol. 20 (July 1974), pp. 259–311.

Pechman, Joseph A. *Who Paid the Taxes, 1966–85?* Washington, DC: The Brookings Institution, 1985.

Pechman, Joseph A. and B. A. Okner. *Who Bears the Tax Burden?* Washington, DC: The Brookings Institution, 1974.

Reynolds, Morgan, and Eugene Smolensky. *Public Expenditures, Taxes, and the Distribution of Income: The United States, 1950, 1961, 1970*. New York: Academic Press, 1977.

Ruggles, Patricia, and Michael O'Higgins. "The Distribution of Public Expenditure among Households in the United States." *Review of Income and Wealth*, Series 27 (June 1981), 2:137–64.

U.S. Bureau of the Census. *Conference on the Measurement of Non-Cash Benefits: Proceedings*. August 1986.

U.S. Bureau of the Census. *Statistical Abstract of the United States: 1988*, 108th edition. Washington, DC: U.S. Government Printing Office, 1987.

U.S. Bureau of the Census. Technical Paper 58, *Estimates of Poverty Including the Value of Noncash Benefits: 1987*. Washington, DC: U.S. Government Printing Office, 1988.

U.S. Congress. *Economic Report of the President*. Washington, DC: U.S. Government Printing Office, 1988.

Vroman, Wayne. "An Interindustry Analysis of Employer Payroll Tax Incidence." Report to the U.S. Department of Health and Human Services, Washington, DC, June 1986.

Conclusion

Lars Osberg

In this book, we have concentrated on the conceptual and practical issues involved in the measurement of economic inequality and poverty. We have not directly discussed economic "inequity." Since there is plenty of complexity involved in answering the limited question, "How much economic inequality is there?" this book has not attempted to answer the more difficult question, "How much *unjustifiable* economic inequality is there?"

In particular, we have not attempted to apportion the aggregate amount of economic inequality into the percentage which is due to inequality in the opportunities open to individuals and the fraction which is due to differences in the choices made by individuals. We know intuitively that some of the inequality of economic result which we observe in the world arises from the choices which individuals have made but that some arises because the choices which individuals make are subject to very different constraints—and evidence on the inequality of economic result alone cannot reveal the importance of each factor.

To take an example which has been especially important in the 1980s, empirical evidence from the United States, the United Kingdom, and Canada can reveal that greater economic inequality is associated with higher unemployment rates (Dooley 1987; Blank and Blinder 1986; Nolan 1987) and such an association is easily explicable because the experience of unemployment is highly concentrated within the labor force. Those individuals who spend part or all of the year out of paid employment will clearly have lower annual earnings; hence higher unemployment implies more poverty, as well as greater inequality of individual earnings and family incomes.

However, the correlation between economic inequality and unemployment cannot reveal, by itself, the relative importance of unequal opportunities. Economic analysts who view unemployment as a labor/leisure choice, or as the product of intertemporal utility maximization, or as the result of a decision to turn down available jobs and search for higher wages, will view greater unemployment as the result of individual choice, and will not see any need to redress the greater economic inequality which arises from those choices. However, those who view unemployment as largely involuntary, the result of a lack of available jobs, will view the correlation between greater economic inequality and higher unemployment as a reflection of greater inequalities in the opportunity of individuals to obtain paid employment.[1]

In order, therefore, to assess how much of observed economic inequality is inequitable, we need some evidence on the processes which generate command over economic resources, *as well as* evidence on the outcomes which those processes generate. In addition, we need some explicit ethical criteria before we can say whether some inequalities are justifiable while others are unjustifiable. Some would argue that our criterion should be "equality of opportunity" and that inequalities which arise from individual choices are necessarily equitable. But this criterion is not as clear as it may appear, since it can be argued that one should distinguish between individual choice and *informed* individual choice and that many of the disabled workers whom Ruggles identified in chapter 6 as permanently poor had no reasonable opportunity to assess the risks to which they were subjected. Others would argue, too, that one cannot divorce the equity of a process from the outcomes which that process generates, and that a minimal requirement of our criterion of equity should be the guarantee of basic economic and social rights to all the members of a democratic community.

The criterion of equity therefore raises a whole host of ethical issues, to place alongside the issues of measurement and conceptualization of inequality which we have identified in this volume. Moreover, even those who agree on how much of inequality is inequity can sometimes disagree on what to do about it. Although in chapter 8 Patricia Ruggles discusses how one might measure the impact of government on economic inequality, this volume has not discussed the advantages or disadvantages of particular policies which might affect the degree of economic inequality. To do so adequately would require a volume in itself, and the political importance, in a democracy, of careful analysis of the policies to reduce inequality was vividly put by Tawney many years ago (1964, p. 150, 1931 original):

> Given five fat sheep and 95 thin, how to induce the 95 to resign to the five the richest pasture and shadiest corners? By convincing them, obviously, that, if they do not, they will die of rot, be eaten by wolves, and be deprived in the meantime of such pasture as they have. Nor indeed, has it hitherto been difficult to convince them, for there is nothing which frightens thin sheep like the fear of being thinner. Measures, so the argument runs, which have as their object the diminution of inequality, have as their effect the depletion of capital and the discouragement of enterprise. Their ultimate victims are not those on whom taxation is levied, but those for whose benefit it is imposed. The latter lose as workers what they gain as citizens, and pay for illusory improvements

in their social conditions in the hard cash of lower wages and increased unemployment. Thus the wealth of the few is the indispensible safeguard for the modest comforts of the many, who, if they understood their own interests, would not harass the rich with surtaxes and death duties, but would cherish and protect them.

Having identified what this book of readings did not try to do, one should also discuss what it did try to accomplish. Our purpose in bringing together this book of readings was to summarize, as best we could, current knowledge on the extent of economic inequality and poverty. Our hope is that by discussing the way the world is we can lay a better groundwork for discussions of the way the world ought to be, and how to proceed from the former to the latter.

However, in writing this conclusion, I am very aware that books on economic inequality can sometimes seem to produce either educated confusion or learned despair. Educated confusion can arise since the measurement and analysis of economic inequality and poverty raise many difficult conceptual issues. It is all too easy to end up overwhelmed by these difficulties, knowing many objections but few answers. But although there are difficult ambiguities in the ideas of "inequality," "poverty," "wealth," or "income," this does not mean that all measures of these concepts are equally bad. Given one's values about what sort of inequality or poverty matters, the important thing is to distinguish between better and worse measures of inequality and poverty, knowing that measurement is, in general, imperfect.

Similarly, learned despair is an inappropriate response. Learned despair can arise if one begins to think of the study of economic inequality as something akin to the study of the Himalayan mountains—i.e., the study of an enormous, important, difficult-to-measure phenomenon which is beyond human control. In this volume, however, we have compared the inequality and poverty which we observe within nations and we have noted the very significant differences which exist between nations. Although complex conceptual issues are inescapable parts of the analysis and measurement of inequality and poverty and although the aggregate degree of economic inequality within and between nations may change only slowly, we still know that the degree of economic inequality is not constant, either between or within nations. We know also that some identifiable factors (e.g., the rate of unemployment) do affect the degree of inequality and that identifiable policies affect the degree of inequality. Hence, in the final anlaysis, economic inequality is a matter of choice—a social choice as to what type of society we want to live in.

Note

1. In order not to leave my own position ambiguous, I believe that there is strong econometric evidence to support the importance of underemployment constraints to the observed supply of labor and to inequality in earnings—see Osberg and Phipps (1989).

References

Blank, R. M., and A. S. Blinder (1986). "Macroeconomics, Income Distribution and Poverty." In S. H. Danziger and D. H. Weinberg, eds. *Fighting Poverty: What Works and What Doesn't.* Cambridge: Harvard University Press, pp. 180–208.

Dooley, M. D. (1987). "Within Cohort Earnings and Inequality Among Canadian Men, 1971–1982." *Relations Industrielles,* vol. 42, no. 3:594–611.

Osberg, L., and S. Phipps (1989). "Quantity Constraints in the Analysis of Labour Supply." Mimeo, Dalhousie University.

Nolan, B. (1987). *Income Distribution and the Macroeconomy.* Cambridge: Cambridge University Press.

Tawney, R. H. (1964). *Equality.* 5th edition with foreword by R. M. Titmuss, George Allen, and Urwin Gordon. (First published 1931.)

Index

Aaron, H. J., 205, 217n.4, 243n.2
Abel-Smith, B., 137
Absolute poverty line, 136, 146
Additive decomposability, 32–34
Adjusted disposable family income
    (ADPI), 41–42
Adults, 7, 57n.2
AFDC. See Aid to Families with
    Dependent Children
Africa, 78
Age, 120–25
Ahluwalia, M., 89n.22
Aid to Families with Dependent Children
    (AFDC), 226
AIME. See Average indexed monthly
    earnings
Allegrezza, S., 55, 57n.3
Allocation, 223–24
Amin, S., 61
Ando, A., 121
Annual poverty measures, 166–68
Annuities, 98, 197
Anonymity, 19
Asia, 75–78
Assets, 6, 189n.6, 195
Assistance unit, 226
Atkinson, A. B., 35, 39, 42, 58n.7, 61, 99,
    110, 146
Atkinson inequality indices, 26–29
    cross-national comparisons and, 42
    United States and, 153, 154n.6
Augmented wealth, 95–96
Auletta, K., 161
Australia, 46
Average indexed monthly earnings
    (AIME), 200
Avery, R. B., 99
Avrin, M., 207

Ballentine, J. G., 243n.1

Bane, M. J., 157, 176, 177, 178, 179, 180,
    181, 182, 186, 187, 190nn.10, 12,
    13, 14
Banfield, E., 160
Barro, R., 204
Baseline income, 244nn.14, 19
Basic needs, 139–42
Becker, G. S., 135
Beckerman, W., 39
Behrens, J., 231
Benefit distribution, 200–201, 207–11
Bernheim, B. D., 121, 195
Berry, A., 60, 64, 86n.1, 87nn.8, 12, 13,
    15, 88n.18, 89nn.21, 30, 31
Blackorby, C., 36
Blacks, 185
Blank, R. M., 246
Blinder, A. S., 246
Boskin, M. J., 207, 208, 217n.4
Bourguignon, F., 36, 60, 90n.33
Bronfenbrenner, M., 43
Browning, E. K., 243n.6
Brumberg, R., 120, 194
Buhmann, B., 39n, 43, 57n.5, 58n.8, 145
Burkhauser, R. V., 207
Business cycle, 57n.1

Canada, 46
Capability to function, 140
Capital receipts, 6
Capital stock, 203–5
Capital wealth, 96
Cartwright, W. S., 130n.12
Case, K. E., 243n.6
Cash transfers, 235, 238
Census income, 145
Center for Population, Poverty and Policy
    Studies (CEPS), 55
CES. See Committee on Economic
    Security

Champernowne, D. G., 39
Children, 50, 52–53, 164, 165, 180
China, 68–69, 70, 75–78
Coder, J., 39*n.*, 57
Coe, R. D., 176, 184, 185, 187
Coefficient of variation, 14
Cohort approach, 177
Colasanto, D., 139, 145
Commission of the European Economic
    Community 1981, 39
Committee on Economic Security (CES),
    197–98
Comprehensive income, 145
Cone, K., 207
Consumption, 139–42
    life-cycle theory of, 194–95
    world distribution of, 67, 74–78,
        89*nn.24, 26*
Counter-factual problem, 231
Couples, 47,
Corcoran, M., 187
Corporate taxes, 222, 227
Cowell, F. A., 35, 36
CPS. *See* Current Population Survey
Credit, 189*n.6*
Creedy, J., 35
Cross-national comparisons, 39–59
    Luxembourg Income Study in, 40–41,
        54–57
    overall inequality in, 44–46
    perspectives in, 41–44
    relative living levels in, 46–53
Cullinan, P. R., 154*n.3*, 193, 243*n.4*
Culture of poverty, 158, 160–61
Current Population Survey (CPS), 176, 235

Dalrymple, R., 40
Dalton, H., 35
Dalton index, 153
Danziger, S., 35, 39, 40, 42, 58*n.6*, 145,
    206, 212, 243*nn.5, 10*
Dasgupta, P., 35
De Vos, K., 134, 140, 146, 154*n.5*
Deaton, A. S., 35
Decision making under uncertainty, 25–26
Decomposability Axiom, 149
Decomposition analysis, 32–34, 79–82
Demographics, 55, 147, 164
    global inequality and, 79–81, 86,
        89–90*n.33*
    Social Security and, 203

Deprivation, 136–37, 151
DI. *See* Disability Insurance
Direct impact, 221–22
Disability, 184
Disability Insurance (DI), 206–7
Disorder, 16–17
Disposable family income (DPI), 41
Donaldson, D., 36
Dooley, M. D., 246
Douglas, M., 140
DPI. *See* Disposable family income
Duncan, G. J., 134, 157, 176, 177, 180,
    184, 185, 187

Earnings capacity, 136, 145
Earnings-sharing, 209
Economy, 198, 203–7
Education, 211–12, 244*n.17*
Elasticity, 65, 83–86, 86–87*n.4*
Elderly, 53, 194, 214–15
    poverty of, 50, 164, 165, 244*n.18*
    near, 51
    persistent, 179, 182–84
Elliehausen, G. E., 99
Ellwood, D. T., 157, 176, 180, 181, 182,
    186, 187, 190*nn.10, 12, 13, 14*
Emmanuel, A., 61
Employment, 170
Entropy, 16–17
Equity, 247
Equivalent income, 7, 8, 42, 138, 226
Estate data, 99, 104, 105–6, 108
Exchange rate, 65
Exchange value, 97
Expenditure policies, 231–40

Factor effects, 224–25
Family, 41
    income of, 7, 244*n.16*
    size of, 41–42, 44–46
        government programs and, 226
        poverty and, 145
    wealth of, 97–98
Federal expenditures, 231
Federal taxes, 228
Fei, J. C. H., 36
Feldstein, M., 98, 205, 243*n.1*
Female-headed households, 185, 189*n.3*
Fields, G. S., 36
Finnie, R. E., 97
Fisher, F. M., 35

Focus Axiom, 149, 151
Food cost, 141
Food ratio, 142, 145
Food share, 8
Foster, J. E., 3*n*, 35, 36, 146, 148
France, 118–20
Frank, A. G., 61
Friedland, R. B., 130*n.12*
Friedman, J., 124
Fuchs, V., 137, 189*n.2*
Full income, 135
Full wealth, 135
Functioning capability, 140
Fungible wealth, 114

Gallman, R. E., 131*n.16*
Gallup, G., 139
Garfinkel, I., 136, 143, 145
Gastwirth, J. L., 36
Generalized Entropy family (GE family), 29–34
Generalized Lorenz Curve, 25
Generational equity, 51
Getty, Paul, 11
Gibson, M. J., 53
Gillespie, W. I., 243*n.3*
Gini coefficient, 15–16, 18, 42
Global inequality, 60–91. *See also* Cross-national comparisons
    changes in, 70–78
    data for, 65–70, 87–88*n.17*
    decomposition analysis of, 79–82
    household wealth and, 125–28
    methodology for, 64–65, 86*n.2*
GNP. *See* Gross National Product
Goedhart, T., 139
Goldsmith, R. W., 111
Government programs, 220–49
    expenditure policies and, 231–40
    impact calculation and, 221–27
    tax policies and, 227–31
Graebner, W., 196
Graphs, 9–13
Great Depression, 196–97
Greenwood, D., 53, 97, 100, 108, 116
Gross National Product (GNP), 70–78, 203

Hagenaars, A. J. M., 134, 139, 140, 141, 142, 146, 148, 151, 153, 154*n.4*, 226
Hammermesh, D. S., 124

Harberger, A. C., 243*n.1*
Harrington, M., 39, 160, 184
Harrison, A. J., 99
Hauser, R., 39
Haveman, R., 97, 136, 143, 145, 206, 243*nn. 5, 10*
HDW. *See* Household disposable wealth
Heston, A., 88*n.17*
Hill, M. S., 157, 176, 180, 184, 185, 187
Histogram, 9
Home ownership, 105
Household, 7, 135, 153–54*n.1*
Household disposable wealth (HDW), 94, 95
Household income, 55
Household production, 214
Household wealth, 92–133
    cross-sectional comparisons, of, 117–28
    age in, 120–25
    different sources in, 117–20
    international, 125–28
    defined, 94–95
    methodology in, 93–101
    time trends in, 101–17
        Sweden and, 106–7
        United Kingdom and, 101–6
        United States and, 107–17
Human capital, 95
Hunger line, 152
Hurd, M. D., 195

Immigration, 152
Income, 5
    elasticities of, 86
    government programs and, 220–49. *See also* Government programs
    household, 55
    life-cycle theory and, 194
    poverty and, 50–51, 135–39, 172
    Social Security and, 211–16
    world distribution of, 64–65
Income capitalization techniques, 100
Income Evaluation Theory, 143
Income poverty line, 145
Income Survey and Development Program (ISDP), 115–16, 124
Income units, 7, 8–9
Indirect impact, 221–22
Individual, 57–58*n.6*

Inequality measurement, 3–38
    Atkinson family in, 26–29. *See also*
        Atkinson inequality indices
    common measures in, 13–19
    Generalized Entropy family in, 29–34
    government programs and, 226–27
    graphs in, 9–13
    preliminaries of, 4–9
    rankings in, 19–26
    readings in, 35–36
    steps in, 34–36
Inflation, 199
Information theory, 16
Intergenerational transfers, 205, 207–8
Intergenerational transmission of poverty,
    187
International price vector, 66, 67
Interpolation, 34
Irvine, I. J., 35
ISDP. *See* Income Survey and
    Development Program
Isherwood, B., 140
Israel, 44–46

Jenkins, S. P., 3, 36, 134*n*, 138, 149, 151,
    226
Johannson, S., 39
Johnson, W. R., 243*n.6*

Kapteyn, A., 139, 145
Kasten, R., 227, 243*n.7*
Kennickell, A. B., 99
Kessler, D., 118, 125, 129, 130*n.6*
Kilpatrick, R. W., 139
King, M., 129*n.1*
Kolm, S. C., 35
Kravis, I., 65, 66, 86*n.5*, 88*n.4*
Kuga, K., 36

Labor force, 169–70, 185, 205–7
Lamas, E. J., 116
Lambert, P. J., 35
Lampman, R., 99, 108–10, 111, 130*n.9*,
    131*n.16*, 189
Lansley, S., 137
Lapierre, D., 140
LC. *See* Lorenz Curve
LCM. *See* Life cycle model
Leimer, D. R., 205
Leonard, H., 243*n.6*
Leonard, J. S., 218*n.6*

Lesnoy, S. D., 205
Levy, F., 50, 157, 161, 172, 173, 176, 177,
    181, 190*n.11*
Lewis, O., 160, 161, 184, 187, 188
Leyden poverty line, 139, 143, 145, 146
Life cycle model (LCM), 120
Life cycle theory of consumption (LTC),
    194–95
Life cycle wealth, 96
Lifetime income, 7
Lindert, P. H., 108
Liquid wealth, 97
LIS. *See* Luxembourg Income Study
Local expenditures, 231, 244*n.12*
Local taxes, 228–30
Logarithmic variance, 15
Lorenz Curve (LC), 11–13
    cross-national comparisons and, 42, 46
    social welfare and, 20–23
LTC. *See* Life cycle theory of consumption
Luxembourg Income Study (LIS), 40–41,
    54–57

McNeil, J. M., 116
Macroeconomics, 222
Manser, M. E., 217*n.2*
Marley, M., 99, 108, 111, 112, 117, 129
Marriage, 208–9, 215–16
Marris, R., 87*n.5*
Marshall, A., 140
Maslow, A. H., 140
Masson, A., 118, 125, 129, 130*n.6*
Mean-independence, 19
Mean logarithm deviation (MLD), 61,
    83–86
Measurement, 3–38. *See also* Inequality
    measurement
Medical care, 244*n.20*
Mehta, F., 36
Middle class, 43, 52–53
Miller, S. M., 138
Minarik, J. J., 190*n.10*
Mincy, R., 158
Mirer, T. W., 136
MLD. *See* Mean logarithm deviation
Modigliani, F., 120, 121, 194
Monotonicity Axiom, 149
Monthly poverty, 189*n.5*
Moon, M. L., 136
Morawetz, D., 61
Morgan, J. N., 35, 161, 172, 173

Morrison, C., 60
Muellbauer, J., 35
Murray, C., 161, 187
Musgrave, R. A., 35, 243n.6
Myers, R. J., 207

National data, 64
Near-cash benefits, 57n.3
Near-poverty, 43, 51–52
Negative income, 34
Neighborhood, 158
Net value, 95–96
Netherlands, 46
New Consumer Economics, 135
Nolan, B., 246
Noncash income, 136
Normal retirement age (NRA), 200
Norway, 46
Nouvertne, U., 39
NRA. See Normal retirement age
Nygård, F., 35

OASI. See Old Age and Survivors
    Insurance
O'Higgins, M., 40, 223, 230, 233,
    243nn.3, 9
Okner, B. A., 227
Okum, A. M., 36
Old Age and Survivors Insurance
    (OASI), 193–219. See also Social
    Security
Orshansky, M., 141, 142, 188n.1
Osberg, L., 39n, 134n, 246, 248n.1
Outcome variables, 225–27
Output effects, 224–25
Overall inequality, 44–46, 51–52

Paglin, M., 35
Palmer, J., 43, 51
Panel Study of Income Dynamics (PSID),
    161, 173
Parsons, D. O., 207
Paternalism, 197
Payroll tax, 201–2, 217n.3
Pearson Commission Report, 61
Pechman, J. A., 35, 205, 227
Pen, J., 35
Pen's Parade, 9–11
Pension wealth, 95, 98, 104–5. See also
    Retirement wealth
Per capita income, 7

Perkins, 87n.14
Persistent poverty, 172–85
    characteristics of, 181–85
    size of, 172–81
Phipps, S., 248n. 1
Piachaud, D., 142
Plotnick, R., 206, 243nn.5, 10
Pollack, R. A., 35
Pommerehne, W., 40
Poor Britain (Mack & Lansley), 142
Poor Richard's Almanac (Franklin),
    194
Population, 55, 86, 147, 164. See also
    Demographics
Population Homogeneity, 19, 30
Population Homogeneity Axiom, 149
Poverty, 134–56
    aggregation of, 146–53
    cross-national, 47–52
    defined, 43
    duration of, 157–89
        1967–85, 162–72
        persistently poor and, 172–85. See
            also Persistent poverty
        underclass and, 160–62, 185–88
    elderly and, 50, 164, 165, 244n.18
    government programs and, 241–43
    identification of, 134–46
        consumption in, 139–42
        income in, 135–39
        relevance in, 145–46
        welfare in, 142–45
    Social Security and, 214
Poverty gap, 147–48
Poverty index, 153
Poverty line, 8, 135, 153
Preston, S., 51
Principle of Transfers, 17–18, 19, 21, 24
Probability distributions, 25
Projector, D., 99
PSID. See Panel Study of Income
    Dynamics
Public goods, 222–24
Purchasing power parities, 65

Race, 215–16
Radner, D. B., 97, 130n.12
Rainwater, L., 39n., 40, 57, 137, 139, 176,
    184
Range, 13
Rank ordering (RO), 44

Readings in inequality measurement, 35–36
Recession, 46, 165–66
Rein, M., 40, 43, 50, 51, 52, 137, 141
Relative deprivation, 136–37, 151
Relative economic status, 42–44
Relative living levels, 46–53
Relative poverty, 136–38, 140
Retirement wealth, 98, 111–12, 114, 130*n.11*
Reynolds, M., 227, 233, 243*nn.3, 6, 9, 10,* 244*n.13*
Ricketts, E. R., 158
Risk aversion, 25–26
RO. *See* Rank ordering
Roby, P., 138
Roome, G., 40
Roosevelt, F. D., 193, 197
Ross, C. M., 212
Rowntree, B. S., 39, 141
Ruggles, N. D., 111, 116, 212
Ruggles, P., 40, 157, 189*nn.6, 7,* 220, 223, 230, 233, 243*nn.3, 9,* 247
Ruggles, R., 111, 116, 212
Runciman, W. G., 137, 152

Sammartino, F., 227, 243*n.7*
Sample censoring, 177
Sampling errors, 35
Sandström, A., 35
Saving, 194, 203–5
Sawhill, I. V., 158, 187
Sawyer, M., 39
Schmaus, G., 40, 55, 57*n.3*
Schobel, B. D., 207
Schwartz, J., 40
Schwartz, M., 130*n.9*
Second order stochastic dominance, 25–26
Sen, A. K., 35, 42, 88*n.19,* 137, 140, 144, 146, 147–48, 152, 154*n.5*
SFCC. *See* Survey of Financial Characteristics of Consumers
Shorrocks, A. F., 35, 36, 99, 101–6, 110, 121, 130*n.8,* 146
Single parent families, 47, 238–39
SIPP. *See* Survey of Income and Program Participation
Smeeding, R., 39*n*
Smeeding, T. M., 39, 43, 50, 51, 52, 55, 57, 57*n.3,* 136, 145, 226
Smith, A., 137

Smith, J. D., 99, 108, 110, 111
Smolensky, E., 40, 212, 227, 231, 233, 243*nn.3, 6, 9, 10,* 244*n.13*
Social insurance, 50–51
Social participation, 142
Social Security, 193–219
    benefit distribution and, 207–11
    defined, 217*n.1*
    economic effects of, 203–7
    growth of, 234–35
    income distribution and, 211–16
    life-cycle theory and, 194–95
    reasons for, 195–203
    wealth from, 95, 108. *See also* Retirement wealth
Social welfare, 24
Social welfare function (SWF), 20–23
Socialist countries, 69, 75
Soltow, L., 130*n.16*
South Asia, 75–78
Spånt, R., 100, 106–7
Spells of poverty, 178–79, 180, 190*n.14*
Spouses, 208–9
SSI. *See* Supplemental Security Income
Starrett, D., 36
State expenditures, 231
State taxes, 228–30
Stephenson, G., 40
Stewart, C., 100
Stochastic dominance, 25–26
Strong Principle of Transfers, 29
Subannual poverty measures, 166–68
Subgroup Monotonicity Axiom, 149
Subjective poverty line, 138–39, 144
Summers, R., 88*n.17*
Supplemental Security Income (SSI), 232
Survey of Consumer Finances (SCF), 112, 124
Survey data, 99, 112–17
Survey of Financial Characteristics of Consumers (SFCC), 112, 121
Survey of Income and Program Participation (SIPP), 166, 167
Survivor benefits, 198
Sweden, 46, 106–7
SWF. *See* Social welfare function
Symmetry, 19
Symmetry Axiom, 149
Synthetic data, 100

Taussig, M. K., 35, 40, 42, 58*n.6,* 205

Tawney, R. H., 247
Tax return data, Swedish, 106
Taxes, 227–31
  corporate, 222, 227
  Social Security, 201–2
Theil, H., 36
Theil coefficient, 83–86
Theil entropy index, 16–17, 18
Theil inequality index, 42
Theorems, 20, 22, 23, 24, 25, 33
Thon, D., 153
Thurow, L. C., 142
Time period, 6–7, 41
Time trends, 101–17
  Sweden in, 106–7
  United Kingdom in, 101–6
  United States in, 107–17
Torrey, B., 43, 50, 51, 52
Townsend, P., 39, 137, 140, 141, 154n.5
Transfer Axiom, 149, 150, 152
Transfer income, 233–40
  elderly and, 214
  poverty and, 50–51
Transfer sensitivity, 17, 18, 19, 22, 24, 26
Transfer Sensitivity Axiom, 149, 150
Trust funds, 202
Two-parent families, 52

Unallocable public goods, 223
Uncertainty, 25–26
Underclass, 185–88, 189n.8
  defined, 160–62
  poverty duration and, 169–72
Unemployment, 165, 169–70, 246–47
United Kingdom, 101–6
United States, 44
  household wealth in, 107–17
  poverty line in, 145
United States House Ways and Means
    Committee 1988, 51

Unmarried adults, 57n.2
Utility, 136

Van der Gaag, J., 139, 145
Van Praag, B. M. S., 145
Variables, 4–6
Variance, 14
Variance of the logs, 15
Vaughan, D. R., 97, 130n.12
Vroman, W., 243n.2

Wales, T. J., 35
Warlick, J., 207
Watts, H. W., 142, 143, 189n.1
Wealth, 92–133. See also Household
    wealth
  life-cycle theory and, 195
  pensions and, 98
Weighted benefit formula, 208
Weighting of income units. 8–9
Weinberg, D., 39
Weiss, G., 99
Welfare, 142–45, 151, 207–8
Well-being, 69
Well-to-do, 43, 44, 52–53
Who Bears the Tax Burden? (Pechman &
    Okner), 227
Williams, R., 166, 167, 189n.5
Williamson, J. G., 108
Wilson, W. J., 158
Wolfe, B. L., 97
Wolff, E. N., 53, 92, 94, 96, 97, 98, 99,
    100, 108, 111, 112, 116, 117, 121,
    124, 129, 130n.4
Women, 111, 209
World Bank Atlas, World Development
    Report, 88n.17
World inequality, 60–91
World Tables 1976, 87n.17
World Tables 1980, 87–88n.17

Contributors

Albert Berry

Professor of Economics
University of Toronto
Toronto, Canada

François Bourguignon

Professor of Economics
D.E.L.T.A., France

Paul R. Cullinan

Principal Analyst
Congressional Budget Office
Washington, D.C.

Aldi J. M. Hagenaars

Professor of Economics
Erasmus University
Rotterdam, The Netherlands

Stephen Jenkins

Lecturer, School of Social Sciences
University of Bath
Bath, England

Christian Morrisson

O.E.C.D. Development Center
Paris, France

Lars Osberg

Professor of Economics
Dalhousie University
Halifax, Canada

Patricia Ruggles

Senior Research Associate
The Urban Institute
Washington, D.C.

Timothy M. Smeeding

Professor of Economics and Public Administration
Syracuse University
Syracuse, New York

Edward N. Wolff

Professor of Economics
New York University
New York, New York